任务型跨文化交际

孙静波 贾 颖 杨润芬 张雪丹 编著

知识产权出版社
全国百佳图书出版单位

图书在版编目（CIP）数据

任务型跨文化交际/孙静波等编著．—北京：知识产权出版社，2018.6
ISBN 978-7-5130-5453-9

Ⅰ.①任… Ⅱ.①孙… Ⅲ.①文化交流—高等学校—教材 Ⅳ.①G115

中国版本图书馆 CIP 数据核字（2018）第 040312 号

内容提要

本书包括十个单元，每个单元由两部分构成，每一部分包含两篇阅读文章和各种相关任务活动。活动分为任务前、任务中、任务后三个部分。阅读文章的主题包括跨文化交际的基本知识，语言交际，非语言交际，日常跨文化差异、价值观跨文化差异，特定语境中的跨文化差异、文化障碍和文化冲击，跨文化交际中的文化身份，以及如何成为有效的跨文化交际者等前沿敏感的跨文化问题。任务设计则力求通过丰富的内容、多样的活动，增加学生跨文化交际的情感体验和语言应用能力，从而实现学生跨文化交际的能力的形成和提高。全书每个单元的任务都设有特定的目标，其他部分均围绕该目标来设计；所有任务活动部分均要求学生以小组为单位来完成，不同年龄、不同英语水平的学生可以发挥各自的优势，一起完成活动的准备和展示，在共同提高应用能力的同时还能培养团队合作精神和协作能力。

本书遵循任务型语言教学的理念，融合跨文化主题，交际功能和语言应用于一体，直接通过课堂教学让学生用英语完成各种真实的跨文化交际任务，将课堂教学的目标真实化、任务化，从而达到语言综合应用能力培养和跨文化交际能力培养的双重目标。

本书可作为大学英语 1~3 年级非英语专业学生学习。通过本书的学习，非英语专业学生可以达到《大学英语课程教学要求》中所提到的"在今后学习、工作和社会交往中能用英语有效地进行交际""提高综合文化素养，以适应我国社会发展和国际交流的需要"等教学要求。

同时，本书还可供其他英语学习者、国际商务从业人员、中外旅游者、文化研究者或文化爱好者使用。

责任编辑：国晓健　　　　　　　　**责任校对：潘凤越**
封面设计：臧　磊　　　　　　　　**责任印制：刘译文**

任务型跨文化交际

孙静波　贾　颖　杨润芬　张雪丹　编著

出版发行：	知识产权出版社有限责任公司	网　　址：	http://www.ipph.cn
社　　址：	北京市海淀区气象路 50 号院	邮　　编：	100081
责编电话：	010-82000860 转 8385	责编邮箱：	guoxiaojian@cnipr.com
发行电话：	010-82000860 转 8101/8102	发行传真：	010-82000893/82005070/82000270
印　　刷：	北京虎彩文化传播有限公司	经　　销：	各大网上书店、新华书店及相关专业书店
开　　本：	787mm×1092mm　1/16	印　　张：	21.5
版　　次：	2018 年 6 月第 1 版	印　　次：	2018 年 6 月第 1 次印刷
字　　数：	371 千字	定　　价：	68.00 元
ISBN 978-7-5130-5453-9			

出版权专有　侵权必究
如有印装质量问题，本社负责调换。

前　言

教育部于2007年颁发的《大学英语课程教学要求》指出："大学英语的教学目标是培养学生英语综合应用能力，特别是听说能力，使他们在今后工作和社会交往中能用英语有效地进行口头和书面的信息交流，同时增强其自主学习能力、提高综合文化素养，以适应我国经济发展和国际交流的需要。"大学生的英语水平及英语运用能力是他们参与社会竞争、迎接未来挑战的必备条件之一。同时《大学英语课程教学要求》还在大学英语的课程设置部分特别提出："大学英语课程不仅是一门语言基础知识课程，也是拓宽知识，了解世界文化的素质教育课程。因此，设计大学英语课程时也应充分考虑对学生的文化素质培养和国际文化知识的传授。要尽可能地利用语言载体，让学生了解科学技术、西方社会文化等知识。"2014年，教育部颁布的《高等教育专题规划》中关于深化本科教育教学部分也特别强调要培育学生的国际视野和尊重多元文化的博大胸怀。由此可见，教育部门对本科人才的跨文化交际能力培养关注度大为提高，同时跨文化交际能力也是衡量现代高等教育人才培养质量的重要标准。

在全球化的趋势愈加明显，中国作为世界大国日益崛起的趋势下，本科教育培养的人才不论精通任何专业知识，如果要具备真正的国际竞争力，那么其跨文化交际的能力是不可或缺的素质之一。随着中国经济建设的发展和改革开放的深化，社会越来越需要具有扎实的专业功底并能直接用英语与外国专家、投资者、管理人员等进行交流沟通的大学毕业生。这种"专业知识＋跨文化交际能力"型的人才在社会上的需求量必将快速增长。因此，在大学英语公共基础课的教学中，注重非英语专业本科生跨文化交际能力的培养是具有重要现实意义的。

本书主要针对非英语专业本科生大学英语的拓展课程发展改革而设计，可以作为大学英语实验班或后续拓展课程以及通识类选修课程的材料。本书主要围绕跨文化交际的重要理论进行了选材，目的是让学生对跨文化交际的学习有一定的高度。同时，为了满足学生的学习兴趣并提升其理解能力，本书还选取了大量的案例和影视作品作为学生对跨文化学习的真实环境的补充，希望能通过真实的情景使学生对跨文化交际有直观和感性的认识，使跨文化交际的学习更为全面和客观，从而实现增强跨文化交际意识，提高跨文化交际能力，有效开展跨文化交际活动的目标。

本书具有三个显著的特色：

（1）有效结合大学英语语言技能与跨文化交际知识的学习。每个章节设有两个部分，每个部分设有两篇跨文化交际内容的文章，一篇侧重理论，一篇侧重实际应用。同时两篇文章还以不同的语言学习形式呈现，一篇是精读形式，一篇是泛读形式。这样，就实现了跨文化理论知识与语言学习的自然结合，使学生的语言学习更有实际意义。

（2）突出强化跨文化交际学习的实践情景和实践意义。跨文化学习最有效的方式是要有与不同文化接触的真实体验，然而目前国内很多院校极度缺乏多元文化的环境。因此本书通过提供具体案例和关于跨文化交际的影视作品展开分析讨论。这样不仅能大大改善跨文化学习的环境，还能通过更具体的例子和情景，更直观的画面和语言对不同国家的文化现象、风俗习惯以及思维模式等与文化息息相关的各个方面都有更直接的认识，进而增加学生对目的语言文化的深层理解。

（3）基于任务驱动式的教学设计激发学生学习兴趣。本书的每个章节都设有任务前、任务中、任务后三个环节，让学生的学习从问题和任务开始，从任务前的面对任务不知所措，到任务中集中学习相关知识，再到任务后用相关知识解决实际问题，促使学生成为学习的主体，激发其学习兴趣和主动性。

本书是北京物资学院大学英语教学改革中的阶段性研究成果。感谢北京物资学院和外语学院的支持。

本书第一章至第十章分别由孙静波、贾颖、杨润芬、张雪丹编写。

本书难免存在错误疏漏之处，敬请广大读者批评指正。

编者

2017 年 8 月 31 日

Introduction

    Globalization and economical development in China contribute to an increasing development of English learning in all levels of educational sectors. The changes in education directly affect students and instructors in their learning and teaching experiences. Global awareness, interest for world affairs, and studying a second language are crucial to equip students with proper skills needed in the global workforce. Therefore, one of the main goals of English teaching in college English teaching is to arouse the students' intercultural communication awareness and equip them with intercultural communication competence and skills. An intercultural communication orientation in the curriculum involves new strategies, methods, materials and teaching plans that prepare teachers to get the students engaged in college English learning. The curriculum of intercultural communication was introduced into college English teaching only a few years ago. Many textbooks prefer to focus on the theories of intercultural communication, which turns out to be a bit incompatible with the aim of language learning for college English learners. Therefore, this book attempts to facilitate the students' learning of intercultural communication by using a practical task-based method.

    According to Hymes and Halliday's theory, the ultimate goal of language teaching is to cultivate the learner's ability to communicate with the target language, which encompasses not only the ability of listening, speaking, reading and writing, but also the flexibility of employing these abilities into the practical language communication. In order to cultivate effective communicator with accurate, fluent and appropriate language competence, the best method is to provide the students with authentic application opportunities and create real situations for language practice besides the exploding of teaching contents and the inputting of intercultural communication knowledge. In reality, there is a great lack of authentic communication environment in Chinese colleges. Therefore, task-based method can be employed in intercultural communication in order to make up the disadvantage of learning environment. Task-based method refers to actualizing language teaching and socializing classroom teaching. In other words, task-based method is to guide the learners to achieve a real task through communication activities. This method can help the students learn through doing and using. In this book, the whole learning process is divided into three stages of pre-task, while-task and after-task. Pre-task aims to stimulate learners' interest and thinking of some intercultural problems by providing some real examples. While-task is designed to provide the learners with necessary communication theories and knowledge by reading materials. After-task focuses on the expanding of real intercultural communication experiences by watching movies and other simulated intercultural tasks.

Another feature of this book is to employ a variety of movie materials to create more authentic intercultural experiences for the students. Movies are a great medium to use not only to practice English, but also to facilitate intercultural learning. Today, English is a global language spoken by people from many countries and cultural backgrounds. Since culture greatly impacts communication, it is helpful for teachers to introduce lessons and activities that reveal how different dialects, forms of address, customs, taboos, and other cultural elements influence interaction among different groups. Numerous movies contain excellent examples of inter-cultural communication and are highly useful resources for teachers and learners. There are some other additional reasons to incorporate movies in class and encourage their students to watch movies in English. Firstly, movies combine pleasure and learning by telling a story in a way that captures and holds the viewer's interest. Secondly, movies simultaneously address different senses and cognitive channels. For example, spoken language is supported by visual elements that make it easier for students to understand the dialogues and the plot. Students are exposed to the way people actually speak. Moreover, movies involve the viewers appeal to their feelings, and help them empathize with the protagonists. Also, movies usually come with subtitles in English, which facilitates understanding and improves reading skills. In this book, different movies which particularly represent different inter-cultural communication issues are carefully selected for different cultural themes. Movies also cover all kinds of bi-cultural and multi-cultural phenomenon. They will well enrich and expand classroom discussions so as to broaden students' vision, stimulate their further reflection and learning, and enhance their inter-cultural communication awareness.

In conclusion, the purpose of this book is to provide conceptual tools needed to understand culture, communication, how culture influence communication and the process of communication between people from different cultures, and cultivate students' intercultural communication awareness and competence as well as language skills by using task-based method added by case study and movie supplement.

Contents

Chapter 1 Culture and Cultural Diversity ································ 1
  Section I Culture ··· 1
    I Pre-tasks ··· 1
      Task 1 Poem reading ··· 1
      Task 2 The metaphor of culture ································ 3
    II While-tasks ·· 4
      Task 1 Reading comprehension ································ 10
      Task 2 Case study ·· 11
    III After-tasks ··· 14
      Task 1 Movie and culture discussion *The Babel* ············ 15
      Task 2 Extended reading ······································· 16
  Section II Culture Diversity ·· 21
    I Pre-tasks ·· 21
      Task 1 Which is the real Mulan? ····························· 21
      Task 2 Which is the real self? ································ 22
    II While-tasks ··· 22
      Task 1 Reading comprehension ································ 27
      Task 2 Case study ·· 29
    III After-tasks ··· 30
      Task 1 Movie and culture discussion *Modern Family* ······ 30
      Task 2 Extended reading ······································· 32

Chapter 2 Intercultural Communication ········ 36

Section I Communication ········ 36

I Pre-tasks ········ 36

Task 1 Proverb sharing ········ 36

Task 2 Conversation analysis ········ 37

II While-tasks ········ 38

Task 1 Reading comprehension ········ 43

Task 2 Case study ········ 45

III After-tasks ········ 46

Task 1 Movie and culture discussion *The God Must Be Crazy* ········ 46

Task 2 Extended reading ········ 48

Section II Intercultural Communication ········ 51

I Pre-tasks ········ 51

Task 1 Yes or No ········ 51

Task 2 Who is the quickest counter? ········ 52

II While-tasks ········ 52

Task 1 Reading comprehension ········ 58

Task 2 Case study ········ 60

III After-tasks ········ 61

Task 1 Movie and culture discussion *Shanghai Calling* ········ 61

Task 2 Extended reading ········ 63

Chapter 3 Verbal Intercultural Communication ········ 68

Section I What is communication ········ 68

I Pre-tasks ········ 68

Task 1 Talk or communication ········ 68

Task 2 Picture analysis ········ 69

II While-tasks ········ 69

Task 1 Reading comprehension ········ 73

Task 2 Case study ········ 75

III After-tasks ········ 76

Task 1　Movie and culture discussion *The Joy Luck Club* ············· 76
　　　Task 2　Extended reading ··· 78
　Section II　Verbal Communication ·· 80
　　I　Pre-tasks ·· 80
　　　Task 1　Talking with your friends ·· 80
　　　Task 2　Analyzing everyday communication ································ 81
　　II　While-tasks ·· 81
　　　Task 1　Reading comprehension ·· 86
　　　Task 2　Case study ··· 88
　　III　After-tasks ·· 89
　　　Task 1　Movie and culture discussion *The Pursuit of Happiness* ········· 89
　　　Task 2　Extended reading ··· 91

Chapter 4　Non-verbal Intercultural Communication ························· 96
　Section I　What Is Non-verbal Communication? ································ 96
　　I　Pre-tasks ·· 96
　　　Task 1　Game playing ·· 96
　　　Task 2　What is happening here? ··· 96
　　II　While tasks ·· 97
　　　Task 1　Reading comprehension ·· 102
　　　Task 2　Case study ··· 104
　　II　After-tasks ·· 105
　　　Task 1　Movie and culture discussion Charlie Chaplin swept the
　　　　　　　world with his silent films ··· 105
　　　Task 2　Extended reading ··· 107
　Section II　What Are the Universal Gestures? ································ 110
　　I　Pre-tasks ·· 110
　　　Task 1　Talking without saying ··· 110
　　　Task 2　Handshakes around the world ······································ 111
　　II　While-tasks ·· 112
　　　Task 1　Reading comprehension ·· 116

Task 2　Case study ········· 118
　Ⅲ　After-tasks ········· 119
　　Task 1　Movie and culture discussion *Lie to Me* ········· 119
　　Task 2　Extended reading ········· 122

Chapter 5　Daily Life Differences in Intercultural Communication ········· 125
　Section Ⅰ　How Do People Communicate in Daily Life? ········· 125
　　Ⅰ　Pre-tasks ········· 125
　　　Task 1　Cultural puzzles ········· 125
　　　Task 2　Interview ········· 126
　　Ⅱ　While-tasks ········· 126
　　　Task 1　Reading comprehension ········· 132
　　　Task 2　Case study ········· 133
　　Ⅲ　After-tasks ········· 135
　　　Task 1　Movie and culture discussion *Crash* ········· 135
　　　Task 2　Extended reading ········· 137
　Section Ⅱ　Cross-culture in Daily Life ········· 141
　　Ⅰ　Pre-tasks ········· 141
　　　Task 1　Situation analysis ········· 141
　　　Task 2　Dialogue analysis ········· 141
　　Ⅱ　While-tasks ········· 142
　　　Task 1　Reading comprehension ········· 145
　　　Task 2　Case study ········· 146
　　Ⅲ　After-tasks ········· 147
　　　Task 1　Movie and culture discussion *Pushing Hands* ········· 147
　　　Task 2　Extended reading ········· 149

Chapter 6　Value Differences in Intercultural Communication ········· 153
　Section Ⅰ　What Is Value? ········· 153
　　Ⅰ　Pre-tasks ········· 153
　　　Task 1　Who is the real hero? ········· 153

        Task 2   Mobility ……………………………………………………… 154
    II   While-tasks ………………………………………………………………… 154
        Task 1   Reading comprehension ……………………………………… 162
        Task 2   Case study …………………………………………………… 163
    III After-tasks ………………………………………………………………… 165
        Task 1   Movie and culture discussion *Flipped* ……………………… 165
        Task 2   Extended reading …………………………………………… 167
  Section II   Belief and Culture ……………………………………………… 169
    I   Pre-tasks ………………………………………………………………… 169
        Task 1   Moral kidnapping …………………………………………… 169
        Task 2   Filiality ……………………………………………………… 169
    II   While-tasks ……………………………………………………………… 169
        Task 1   Reading comprehension ……………………………………… 175
        Task 2   Case study …………………………………………………… 176
    III After-tasks ……………………………………………………………… 178
        Task 1   Movie and culture discussion   *Everybody's Fine*
                  Vs. *My Father and I* ………………………………………… 178
        Task 2   Extended reading …………………………………………… 180

Chapter 7   Contextual Differences in Intercultural Communication …… 184
  Section I   Culture and Context ……………………………………………… 184
    I   Pre-tasks ………………………………………………………………… 184
        Task 1   Different greetings …………………………………………… 184
        Task 2   Of studies …………………………………………………… 185
    II   While-tasks ……………………………………………………………… 186
        Task 1   Reading comprehension ……………………………………… 193
        Task 2   Case study …………………………………………………… 195
    III After-tasks ……………………………………………………………… 197
        Task 1   Movie and culture discussion   *Aliens in America* …………… 197
        Task 2   Extended reading …………………………………………… 198
  Section II   Business Context ………………………………………………… 202

  I Pre-tasks ································ 202
   Task 1 Alternatives ························ 202
   Task 2 A reception dinner ···················· 202
  II While-tasks ···························· 203
   Task 1 Reading comprehension ················ 209
   Task 2 Case study ························· 211
  III After-tasks ····························· 215
   Task 1 Movie and culture discussion *Outsourced* ········· 215
   Task 2 Extended reading ····················· 216

Chapter 8 Culture Barrier and Culture Shock ················ 220

 Section I Culture Barrier ······························ 220
  I Pre-tasks ······························ 220
   Task 1 Matching game ······················ 220
   Task 2 Game playing ······················· 221
  II While -tasks ···························· 221
   Task 1 Reading comprehension ················ 226
   Task 2 Case study ························· 227
  III After-tasks ····························· 229
   Task 1 Movie and culture discussion *Lost in Translation* ······ 229
   Task 2 Extended reading ···················· 230
 Section II Culture Shock ······························ 234
  I Pre-tasks ······························ 234
   Task 1 The same world, different map? ············ 234
   Task 2 Elsa's diary ······················· 234
  II While-tasks ····························· 235
   Task 1 Reading comprehension ················ 239
   Task 2 Case study ························· 241
  III After-tasks ····························· 243
   Task 1 Movie and culture discussion *Fresh off the Boat* ······ 243
   Task 2 Extended reading ···················· 245

Chapter 9 Cultural Identity in Intercultural Communication 250

Section I Cultural Identity 250

I Pre-tasks 250

Task 1 Cultural markers 250

Task 2 Who is more beautiful? 251

II While-tasks 251

Task 1 Reading comprehension 257

Task 2 Case study 258

III After-tasks 259

Task 1 Movie and culture discussion Exploring Emigration: Cultural Identity 259

Task 2 Extended reading 260

Section II Intercultural Communication 265

I Pre-tasks 265

Task 1 Impacts of Brexit 265

Task 2 Trump's Great Wall 265

II While-tasks 265

Task 1 Reading comprehension 271

Task 2 Case study 272

III After-tasks 275

Task 1 Movie and culture discussion *My Big Fat Greek Wedding* 2 (2016) 275

Task 2 Extended reading 278

Chapter 10 Being an Effective Intercultural Communicator 281

Section I Effective Intercultural Communication 281

I Pre-tasks 281

Task 1 Quote discussion 281

Task 2 Differences and connections 282

II While-tasks 282

Task 1　Reading comprehension ……………………………………… 288
Task 2　Case study ………………………………………………… 290
　Ⅲ　After-tasks ……………………………………………………… 291
Task 1　Movie and cultural discussion *A United Kingdom* …………… 291
Task 2　Extended reading …………………………………………… 292
Section Ⅱ　Intercultural Competence ………………………………… 297
　Ⅰ　Pre-tasks ………………………………………………………… 297
Task 1　Intercultural marriages ……………………………………… 297
Task 2　Road and belt ……………………………………………… 297
　Ⅱ　While-tasks ……………………………………………………… 298
Task 1　Reading comprehension ……………………………………… 303
Task 2　Case study ………………………………………………… 305
　Ⅲ　After-tasks ……………………………………………………… 307
Task 1　Movie and cultural discussion　*The Karate Kid* …………… 307
Task 2　Extended reading …………………………………………… 309

References ……………………………………………………………… 313
Keys …………………………………………………………………… 317

Chapter 1

Culture and Cultural Diversity

Section I Culture

I am pleased to see that we are different. May we together become greater than the sum of both of us.

—Confucius

Culture is one of the two or three most complicated words in the English language.

—Raymond Williams

There never were, in the world, two opinions alike, no more than two hairs, or two grains, the most universal quality is diversity.

—Montaigne

All cultures are simultaneously very similar and very different.

—Harry Triandis

I Pre-tasks

Task 1 Poem reading

    We and They
Father, Mother, and Me
Sister and Auntie say
All the people like us are We,
And everyone else is They.
And They live over the sea,

While We live over the way,
But—would you believe it?—They look upon We
As only a sort of They!

We eat pork and beef
With cow-horn-handled knives.
They who gobble Their rice offer a leaf,
Are horrified out of Their lives;
And They who live up a tree,
And feast on grubs and clay,
(Isn't it scandalous?) look upon We
As a simply disgusting They!

We shoot birds with a gun.
They stick lions with spears.
Their full-dress is un-.
We dress up to Our ears.
They like Their friends for tea.
We like Our friends to stay;
And, after all that, They look upon We
As an utterly ignorant They!

We eat kitcheny food.
We have doors that latch.
They drink milk or blood,
Under an open thatch.
We have Doctors to fee.
They have Wizards to pay.
And (impudent heathen!) They look upon We
As a quite impossible They!

Chapter 1 Culture and Cultural Diversity

All good people agree,

And all good people say,

All nice people, like Us, are We

And every one else is They:

But if you cross over the sea,

Instead of over the way,

You may end by (think of it!) looking on We

As only a sort of They!

(Rudyard Kipling. Definitive Edition. Garden City. NY: Doubleday, 1940)

Questions:

1. What is the main idea of this poem?
2. What do the words "We" and "They" refer to?
3. What creates the differences between "We" and "They"?

Task 2 The metaphor of culture

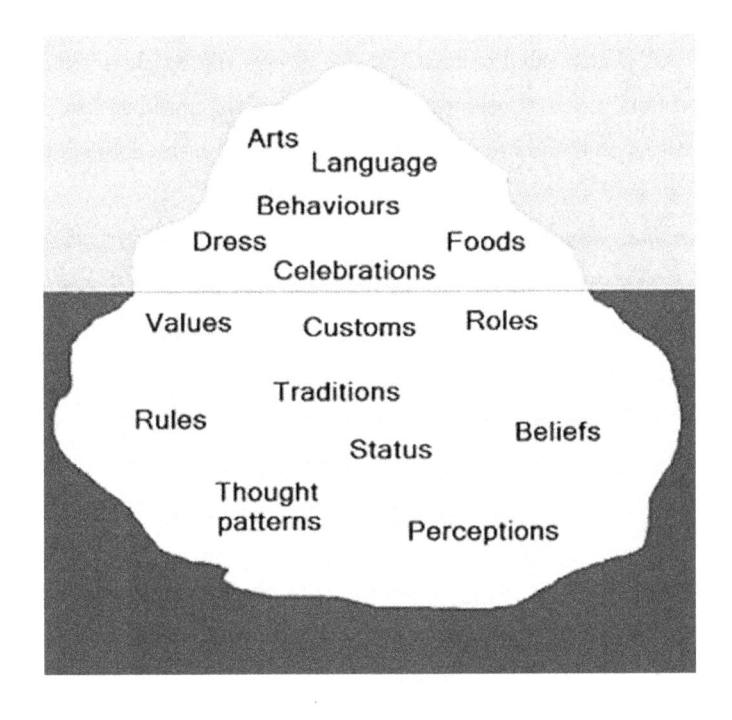

```
                Arts
                    Language
                Behaviours
         Dress            Foods
                Celebrations
        ─────────────────────────
         Values    Customs    Roles
                 Traditions
          Rules                Beliefs
                    Status
              Thought
              patterns    Perceptions
```

Questions:

1. What is the metaphor of culture according to this picuture?
2. What have you learned from this picture of culture iceburg?
3. What are the concrete examples of visible and invisible cultures?
4. What will be your metaphor of culture?

II While-tasks

What is Culture?

Culture is an integral part of every society. It is a learned pattern of behavior and ways in which a person lives his or her life. Culture is essential for the existence of a society, because it binds people together. In the explicit sense of the term, culture constitutes music, food, arts and literature of a society. However, these are only the products of culture followed by the society and cannot be defined as culture.

The word "culture" is one of the most favored vocabulary of man and has been labeled to almost every aspect of human society. There is Chinese culture and American culture, Asian culture and European culture, ancient culture and modern culture, tea culture and clothing culture, material culture and nonmaterial culture, everyday culture and sophisticated culture, etc. Cultures could be classified into different types if viewed from different perspectives. "Culture" is considered to be a complex term, and a variety of anthropologists and researchers have defined it in various ways. Some of these definitions have been listed below.

Culture is those deep, common, unstated experiences which members of a given culture share, which they communicate without knowing, and which from the backdrop against which all other events are judged.

—*Edward T. Hall*

Culture is that complex whole which includes knowledge, belief, art, morals, law, customs and any other capabilities and habits acquired by individuals as members of society.

—*Edward Tylor*

Culture embraces all the manifestations of social habits of a community, the reactions of the individual as affected by the habits of the group in which he lives, and the product of human activities as determined by these habits.

—*Franz Boas*

Chapter 1　Culture and Cultural Diversity

Culture is what makes you a stranger when you're away from home.

—Philip Bock

Culture is a well-organized unity divided into two fundamental aspects—a body of artifacts and a system of customs.

—Bronislaw Malinowski

Culture is the collective programming of the mind distinguishing the members of one group or category of people from another.

—Geert Hofstede

Culture is something that a person learns from his family and surroundings, and is not ingrained in him from birth. It does not have any biological connection because even if a person is brought up in a culture different from that in which he was born, he imbibes the culture of the society where he grows up. It is also not a hidden fact that some people feel the need to follow the beliefs and traditions of their own culture, even though they might be not subscribing to certain ideologies within.

Culture is a complex tool which every individual has to learn to survive in a society. It is the means through which people interact with others in the society. It acts in a sub-conscious way and whatever we see and perceive, seems to be normal and natural. Sometimes, other societies and people seem to be a little odd because they have a different culture from ours. We must remember that every society has a distinct culture that forms the backbone of the society. Culture does not remain stagnant, on the other hand it is evolving constantly and is in fact somewhat influenced by the other cultures and societies.

Every society has a different culture, where people share a specific language, traditions, behaviors, perceptions and beliefs. Culture gives them an identity which makes them unique and different from people of other cultures. When people of different cultures migrate and settle in another society, the culture of that society becomes the dominant culture and those of the immigrants from the subculture of the community. Usually, people who settle in other nations imbibe the new culture, while at the same time strive to preserve their own.

Although every society has a specific culture, there are certain elements of culture that are universal. They are known as cultural universals, in which there are certain behavioral traits and patterns that are shared by all cultures around the world. For instance, classifying relations based on blood relations and marriage, differentiating between good and bad, having some form of art, use of jewelry, classifying people according to gender and age, etc., are common in all cultures of the world.

Some people believe that humans are the only living beings who have a culture. But, there is a group of people who believe in the existence of culture even in animals. It is said that animals have certain social rules which they teach their young ones as a medium for survival.

Culture is necessary to establish an order and discipline in the society. It is not only a means of communication between people, but also creates a feeling of belonging and togetherness among people in the society.

Why culture is important?

Culture is that invisible bond, which ties the people of a community together. It refers to the pattern of human activity. The art, literature, language and religion of a community represent the community's culture. Culture manifests itself through the lifestyle of the individuals of a community. The moral values of the people of a community also represent their culture. The importance of culture lies in its close association with the living of the people. The different cultures of the world have brought in diversity in the ways of life of the people inhabiting different parts of the world. You might want to know about the characteristics of culture.

Culture is related to the development of one's attitude. One's culture plays an important role in shaping the principles of the individual's life. The cultural values of an individual have a deep impact on his/her attitude towards life. According to the behaviorist definition of culture, it is the ultimate system of social control where people monitor their own standards and behavior. A community's culture lays the foundation of the living of its people. The cultural values serve as the founding principles of one's life. They shape an individual's thinking and influence his/her mindset.

Why is culture important? It is definitely because it gives an individual a unique identity. The culture of a community gives its people a character of their own. Culture shapes the personality of a community. The language that a community speaks, the art forms it hosts, its staple food, its customs, traditions and festivities comprise the community's culture. The importance of culture cannot be stressed enough as it is an integral part of living. For those of you interested in exploring the different cultures of the world, here is your guide to world culture and heritage.

What are the characteristics of culture

In order to better understand culture, it is useful to closely examine its characteristics. Learning about the characteristics of culture will help to understand culture's advantages and shortcomings.

Culture is learned behavior

Patterns of culture are not inherent with any individual. They are not genetically passed down from previous generations; rather, they are acquired through the process of learning or interacting with the individual's environment. The process of cultural acquisition is called enculturation. The learning environment includes the family, neighborhood, schools, social groups, physical surroundings, etc. If the environment is different, the culture that each individual learns or acquires will be different too.

Culture is usually acquired unconsciously

It should be noted that the learning of culture is usually done unconsciously. Our relationship with culture is like that between birds and the sky, fish and water or people and air. Only when we are deprived of our own culture or put into a completely new culture can we realize the importance of culture to us. Without culture we cannot survive. Since culture is often learned unconsciously, we often fail to account for our behavior. In intercultural studies, we should make deliberate effort to understand how culture influences our own behavior as well as that of other people.

Culture is shared among its members

The learned cultural patterns are not the property of any individuals but shared by the members of the same group or society. When we say A and B come from the same culture, we assume A and B share the same patterns of living: the same set of symbols used for communication, the same rules of speaking, the same idea about what we can be eaten as food and what cannot, the same belief about nature and man, and so on. Though individuals may have different preferences over one way of conduct or another, they must share one and the same system out of which their personal choice is made. Within the same system, individuals can easily understand one other and adjust themselves to their surroundings. If we intend to understand people from other cultures, and communicate effectively with them, we must try to understand their ways of living.

Culture is persistent and enduring

Culture is not created and developed overnight. It is the deposit of human knowledge and collection of both material and non-material wealth created by man over the long process of human civilization. This nature of culture gives continuity to the development of a culture and provides reinforcement to its members in their lifetime learning of the culture.

Culture manifests itself both implicitly and explicitly

Some aspects of culture are easily observable and some are not. The ways of dressing, talking and working are readily noticeable, but the ideas and motivations underlying these superficial behaviors are generally unrecognized. The study of culture and its people should involve not only the learning of the explicit rules but also those implicit beliefs, values attitudes that relate to them.

Culture is adaptive and changeable

Though culture is persistent and enduring, it is not static. Any great inventions and process of mankind will bring about changes in people's ideas, way of life, mode of behavior, etc. and these changes often take place on the superficial levels of a culture, while the deep structures, i. e. ideological perceptions, values and value orientations, world views and beliefs, are likely to stay or change slowly. Therefore, the study of culture should take a dynamic perspective. We must not assume that any trait of culture is forever fixed. The belief that culture is adaptive and changeable also makes it possible for us to learn about new cultures and adapt ourselves to them.

Culture is relational

Any culture is an integrated entity. All the components of culture are interrelated. The change of one aspect of culture will certainly bring about changes in other aspects as well. The study of culture and people should also take a relational approach. In other words, we should study one aspect of culture in relation to other aspects. Only in this way can we gain a true understanding of a culture and its people. (1783 words)

(Adapted from Annette Bruno, "Leading the Way")

Chapter 1　Culture and Cultural Diversity

Word list：

1. perspective [pəˈspektɪv]
    n. 透镜，望远镜；观点，看法；远景，景色；洞察力
    adj. （按照）透视画法的；透视的
2. sophisticated [səˈfɪstɪkeɪtɪd]
    adj. 复杂的；精致的；富有经验的；深奥微妙的
    v. 使变得世故；使迷惑；(sophisticate 的过去分词形式) 篡改
3. anthropologist [ˌænθrəˈpɒlədʒɪst]
    n. 人类学家
4. manifestation [ˌmænɪfeˈsteɪʃ(ə)n]
    n. 表示，显示；示威
5. distinguishing [dɪsˈtɪŋgwɪʃɪŋ]
    adj. 有区别的；
    v. (distinguish 的现在分词) 辨别，区别；使出众；（凭任何感觉器官）识别出；看清
6. imbibe [ɪmˈbaɪb]
    vt. 吸收；吸取；喝；吸气
7. subscribe [səbˈskraɪb]
    vt. & vi. 认购；认捐，捐赠；签署，题词，署名；订阅，订购
8. subconscious [ˌsʌbˈkɒnʃəs]
    adj. 潜意识的；下意识的
9. stagnant [ˈstægnənt]
    adj. 污浊的；不流动的，停滞的；不景气的；迟钝的，呆笨的
10. perception [pəˈsepʃn]
    n. 知觉；观念；（力）觉察；（农作物的）收获
11. invisible [ɪnˈvɪzəbl]
    adj. 看不见的；不易为视线所见的，隐匿的；（指银行、旅游等服务）无形的；不引人注目的
    n. 看不见的人
12. mindset [ˈmaɪndset]
    n. 观念模式，思维倾向；心态
13. enculturation [enˌkʌltʃəˈreɪʃən]
    n. 对某种文化的适应

Task 1 Reading comprehension

Exercise One: Work with your partners, decide whether the following statements are true (T) or false (F) according to what you have learned in the passage.

1. _____ Culture is essential in people's live and people are usually born with certain cultural characteristics.
2. _____ Culture can be classified into different types if viewed from different perspectives and therefore it is easy to be defined from different views.
3. _____ According to Edward T. Hall, culture is shared by all members in a group or community.
4. _____ According to Philip Bock, cultural factors will differentiate people from a place to another place.
5. _____ Culture usually has biological connection with the society where a person grows up.
6. _____ Culture is a complex whole which includes knowledge, belief, art, morals, law, customs and other capabilities and habits. Therefore, it is stable and unchangeable in a long-term.
7. _____ Every society has a specific culture and there are no similarities in any different cultures.
8. _____ Culture manifests itself through the lifestyle of the individuals of a community. Therefore, it is obvious to be observed in people's life.
9. _____ A community's culture lays the foundation of the living of its people. The cultural values serve as the founding principles of one's life. Hence people's attitude is always influenced by the culture that they live with.
10. _____ Learning about the characteristics of culture is necessary and important for oneself to live in his own society.

Exercise Two: Fill in the blanks with the words given below and change the form when necessary.

enduring	unconsciously	subscribing	integral	effectively
stagnant	constitute	enculturation	surrounding	perspective

1. Culture is essential for the existence of a society for it binds people together and is an _____ part of every society.

2. In the explicit sense of the term, culture _____ the music, food, arts and literature of a society.

3. Cultures could be classified into different types if viewed from different _____. A variety of anthropologists and researchers have defined it in various ways.

4. Culture is something that a person learns from his family and _____, and is not ingrained in him from birth.

5. It is also not a hidden fact that some people feel the need to follow the beliefs and traditions of their own culture, even though they might be not _____ to certain ideologies within.

6. Culture does not remain _____, on the other hand, it is evolving constantly and is in fact somewhat influenced by the other cultures and societies.

7. The process of cultural acquisition is called _____. The learning environment includes the family, neighborhood, schools, social groups, physical surroundings etc.

8. Since culture is often learned _____, we often fail to account for our behavior.

9. If we intend to understand people from other cultures, and communicate _____ with them, we must try to understand their ways of living.

10. Culture is not created and developed overnight. It is persistent and _____.

Task 2 Case study

Case 1

Environments significantly influence one's cognition, effect, and behavior. One feels the impact of the different culture especially when one comes into a foreign country. Shen-Lan, who is from Taiwan, was satisfied for her first twenty-five years of life because she was surrounded by the people who have loved her and whom she has loved. Her friends used to ask her why she looked very happy all time. Even though her parents limited her behaviors or activities because of social bias, she accepted those controls because she understood her parents really loved her. Also, her parents did everything for her, such as taking care of her, cooking for her and making decisions for her. She complied with what her parents expected. She had never left home before she came to America. When she came to America, culture shock obviously influenced her self-concept, self-esteem, and self-presentation.

In Chinese culture, she was taught to be interdependent. She had to care not only about herself but also about the people who were around her, for example, parents, siblings, and friends, even neighbors. However, in American society, she noticed that everyone was very independent, and minded his/her own business, and nobody cared about one another. Because she did not want to get hurt, she knew that she had to make some changes.

Questions for discussion:

1. In this case, what are the problems that Shen-Lan's facing with in another country?

2. From a cultural perspective, what characteristics can be observed in this case?

3. If you were Shen-Lan, how would you deal with this difficult situation?

Case 2

Three weeks ago, on the evening of January 31st, the Chinese Culture Association (CCA) hosted China Night, celebrating the Chinese New Year in lunar calendar with more than 200 students from MHC and the Five Colleges. Among them, the most noticeable was the large group of Chinese students: more than half of MHC's Chinese students body showed up, according to CCA's statistics. Some were performing on the stage in traditional dances, skit, and fashion show etc. ; the others were savoring the cultural feast of authentic Chinese food; all smiled with overflowed joyfulness and pride. Hosting China Night on the eve of Chinese New Year, a day of family reunion, the CCA endeavored to bond Chinese students together and present a homelike celebration for the homesick.

CCA was always the heart of Chinese students, not only on the China Night, but also in daily life. Chinese students hang out with CCA on movie nights, fall outings, and other various activities. In fall, my first-year friends and I went to the Meet & Greeting hosted by CCA, sharing fun personal stories and MHC experience intimately with other CCA members. Many went to the board members election. Fei Wang, the secretary of CCA expressed the voice of many Chinese students in CCA, "I naturally find a sense of self-aligning or reliance here, and thus hoped to be active and contribute to the largest extend to MHC's Chinese community as a board member in CCA. " The Chinese bond not only existed in this small campus, but also was represented to the broader Chinese community. In 2013, a disasters shocked Chinese all around the world: the Ms. 7. 0 earthquake in Ya'an, a city in China, caused 196 people dead, 24 missing, at least 11,826 injured with more than 968 seriously injured. Chinese citizens both inside the country and abroad shared the huge pain, and all offered as much help as possible. CCA immediately called its members to voluntarily donate their personal belongings to sell on campus, attracting lots of students and raised considerable amount of money. "At the moment when I donate the money we raised, I felt I represented the Chinese body in MHC, which, though small, can have a voice, and make a real contribution to China," said Boyuan Ni, one of the co-chairs of CCA.

However, despite of the tight bond among Chinese students, a sense of loneliness still haunted them for hardly being understood. Longing for being accepted and embraced by the US, CCA had strived to jump out of the cultural exclusiveness and promote Chinese culture to the general student body. Also Boyuan and the CCA were all suffering frustrations when running CCA. The primary one was the ideological dilemma: how make sense of Chinese authentic culture to foreigners? CCA's primary standard for the cultural nights was the "authenticity": they neither accept shows that compromised or distorted Chinese culture nor provide American Chinese cuisines. But the feedback by foreign audience was disappointing: people felt confused and exclude in the celebrations. Because of cultural gap, they were not able to understand or share the joy with Chinese students. "The Chinese culture we were presenting was based on many Chinese historical facts, people's values, and foundational philosophies that were natural to Chinese students but foreign to students from other countries. " Boyuan signed. The script for the skit in China Night once confused the scrip writer's American friend because in the story, a poor Chinese mother devoted the money she saved her whole life to send her son study abroad and the son, who didn't succeed in US society, took pains to please his mother even risking to lie. "Why the poor mother would rather put all of her money on her son's college? And why the son always followed his mother's opinion instead of being independent?" Americans would ask. This skit was based on the idea of Xiao, an idea of filial piety raised by Confucius and practiced by all the Chinese people. In China, it was taken for granted that family came the first, then personal pursuit; and children were supposed to obey to their parents. But in US, few could emphasize with this lifelong principle rooted in Chinese's hearts. "We can change the style of shows and the flavor of Chinese cuisine to cater foreign audience, but we can't change the spirits of Chinese culture, which is hard to be comprehend but inevitable." said Boyuan.

What should be on the stage of China Night? What will, instead of only be seen, but truly be understood and even appreciated by students out of China? How can we really build a bridge between Chinese students and the western world? The question is still left to the CCA and every culture carrier to be solved.

Questions for discussion:

1. What are the cultural characteristics that can be particularly manifested by this case?

2. What are the functions of organizing the Chinese Culture Association (CCA) in a different culture?

3. How could the show of China Night on stage be rearranged in order to build a bridge between Chinese students and the western world according to this case?

III After-tasks

Introduction to the movie *The Babel*

Chapter 1 Culture and Cultural Diversity

Task 1 Movie and culture discussion *The Babel*

The biblical story of Babel takes up a handful of verses in the 11th chapter of Genesis, and it illustrates, among other things, the terrible consequences of unchecked ambition. As punishment for trying to build a tower that would reach the heavens, the human race was scattered over the face of the earth in a state of confusion—divided, dislocated and unable to communicate. More or less as we find ourselves today.

It tells four distinct stories, disclosing bit by bit the chronology and causality that link them and making much of the linguistic, cultural and geographical distances among the characters. The movie travels—often by means of jarringly abrupt cuts and shifts of tone—from the barren mountains of Morocco, where the dominant sound is howling wind, to fluorescent Tokyo, where the natural world has been almost entirely supplanted by a technological environment, to the anxious border between the United States and Mexico. Each place has its own aural and visual palette. The languages used by the astonishingly diverse cast include Spanish, Berber, Japanese, sign language and English. The misunderstandings multiply accordingly, though they tend to be most acute between husbands and wives or parents and children, rather than between strangers.

The most glamorous cast members are Brad Pitt and Cate Blanchett, who play an American couple on a desultory vacation in Morocco, trying to repair the damage done to their marriage by the death of their infant son. Their movie-star charisma is turned down to a low, flickering flame, and the easy sense of entitlement they sometimes betray belongs naturally to their characters, Susan and Richard, who nonetheless receive a brutal reminder that even the privileged are vulnerable toaccident.

The gunmen and their victim are never in the frame together, and the consequences of the incident unfold in parallel crises. Susan and Richard wind up in a small town, waiting for an ambulance, facing the panic and impatience of their fellow holiday makers and relying on the kindness of strangers. Abdullah and his sons and neighbors, for their part, must deal with the harsh attentions of the Moroccan police, who are trying to defuse what threatens to become an international incident.

Of all the characters in *The Babel* she seems most surprising and least tethered to cultural stereotype (in spite of the short-skirted schoolgirl uniform she wears). And her story, unfolding without evident connection to the other three, does not seem quite as bound by the fatalism that is Mr. Arriaga's hallmark—as well as his limitation—as a storyteller.

Questions:
1. Why is the film named *The Babel*?
2. How many people from different nationalities are involved in this film and what are the differences between them?
3. Do you think it is a tragedy and what are the possible causes of it?

Task 2   Extended reading

Learning More about Culture

People Usually Are Not Aware of Their Culture

The way that we interact and do things in our everyday lives seems "natural" to us. We are unaware of our culture because we are so close to it and know it so well. For most people, it is as if their learned behavior was biologically inherited. It is usually only when they come into contact with people from another culture that they become aware that their patterns of behavior are not universal.

The common response in all societies to other cultures is to judge them in terms of the values and customs of their own familiar culture. This is ethnocentrism. Being fond of your own way of life and condescending or even hostile toward other cultures is normal for all people. Alien culture traits are often viewed as being not just different but inferior, less sensible, and even "unnatural". For example, European cultures strongly condemn other societies that practice polygamy and the eating of dogs—behavior that Europeans generally consider to be immoral and offensive. Likewise, many people in conservative Muslim societies, such as Afghanistan and Saudi Arabia, consider European women highly immodest and immoral for going out in public without being chaperoned by a male relative and without their bodies covered from head to toe so as to prevent men from looking a tthem. Ethnocentrism is not characteristic only of complex modern societies. People in small, relatively isolated societies are also ethnocentric in their views about outsiders.

Our ethnocentrism can prevent us from understanding and appreciating another culture. When anthropologists study other societies, they need to suspend their own ethnocentric judgments and adopt a cultural relativity approach. That is, they try to learn about and interpret the various aspects of the culture they are studying in reference to that culture rather than to the anthropologist's own culture. This provides an understanding of how such practices as polygamy can function and even support other cultural traditions. Without taking a cultural relativity approach, it would otherwise be difficult, for example, to comprehend why women among the Masai cattle herding people of Kenya might prefer to be one of several co-wives rather than have a monogamous marriage.

Masai women

Taking a cultural relativity approach is not only useful for anthropologists. It is a very useful tool for diplomats, businessmen, doctors, and anyone else who needs to interact with people from other societies and even other sub-cultures within their own society. However, it can be emotionally difficult and uncomfortable at first to suspend one's own cultural values in these situations.

From an objective perspective, it can be seen that ethnocentrism has both positive and negative values for a society. The negative potential is obvious. Ethnocentrism results in prejudices about people from other cultures and the rejection of their "alien ways". When there is contact with people from other cultures, ethnocentrism can prevent open communication and result in misunderstanding and mistrust. This would be highly counter productive for businessmen trying to negotiate a trade deal or even just neighbors trying to get along with each other. The positive aspect of ethnocentrism has to do with the protection that it can provide for a culture. By causing a rejection of the foods, customs, and perceptions of people in other cultures, it acts as a conservative force in preserving traditions of one's ownculture. It can help maintain the separation and uniqueness of cultures.

We Do Not Know All of Our Own Culture

No one knows everything about his/her own culture. In all societies, there are bodies of specialized cultural knowledge that are gender specific—they are known to men but not women or vice versa. In many societies there are also bodies of knowledge that are limited largely to particular social classes, occupations, religious groups, or other special purpose associations.

Gender based skills, knowledge, and perceptions largely stem from the fact that boys and girls to some extent are treated differently from each other in all societies. While there may be considerable overlap in what they are taught, there are some things that are gender specific. In the Western world, for instance, it is more common to teach boys about the skills of combat and how machines work. Girls are more often exposed to the subtleties of social interaction and the use of clothing and make up to communicate intentions. Not surprisingly, men are more likely to know how to fix their car or computer, while women generally are better at predicting the outcome of social interaction and make finer distinctions in fabric and color terms. You can test your own gender related cultural knowledge with the following pictures of relatively common items from North America:

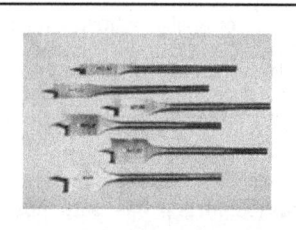 What are the intended functions of these objects?	 How would you describe the cloth pattern of the material used in this woman's skirt?	 Do you think that this woman is wearing make up? If so, what kinds of makeup is she using? Look closely and take your time.

There are many professions in large-scale societies. Each one usually has its own terminology and specialized tools. Lawyers, medical doctors, soldiers, and other specialists use numerous technical terms in their professions. To make it even more obscure for outsiders, these professionals often use abbreviations to refer to their technical terms. For instance, orthopedic surgeons commonly refer to a particular kind of knee operation as ACL surgery. ACL stands for anterior cruciate ligament. Most people outside of the medical fields who have not had this surgery are unlikely to know where this ligament is and what it does, let alone know what the abbreviation means. You can test your knowledge of another common profession in North America with the following picture:

	Who is most likely to use this tool? What is its function?

Culture Gives Us a Range of Permissible Behavior Patterns

Cultures commonly allow a range of ways in which men can be men and women can be women. Culture also tells us how different activities should be conducted, such as how one should act as a husband, wife, parent, child, etc. These rules of permissible behavior are usually flexible to a degree — there are some alternatives rather than hard rules. In North America, for instance, culture tells us how we should dress based on our gender, but it allows us to dress in different ways in different situations in order to communicate varied messages and statuses. The clothing patterns of women in this society can be particularly rich and complex. Their clothing can be intentionally business-like, recreational, as well as sexually attractive, ambiguous, neutral, or even repulsive. North American women are generally more knowledgeable than men about the subtleties of using clothing and other adornment to communicate their intentions. The wide range of permissible ways of being a woman in North America today makes women somewhat unpredictable as individuals when others are trying to understand their intentions but do not fully comprehend the cultural patterns. It is particularly hard for men from other cultures to comprehend the subtle nuances. This at times can result in awkward or even dangerous situations. For instance, the easy friendliness and casual, somewhat revealing dress of young North American women in the summertime is sometimes interpreted by traditional Latin American and Middle Eastern men as a sexual invitation. What messages do the clothes and body language of the women in the pictures below communicate to you? How do you think they might be interpreted by members of the opposite gender and by people in other cultures? Do you think that the age of the observer might play a part in their interpretation?

The range of permissible ways of dressing and acting as a man or woman are often very limited in strictly fundamental Muslim, Jewish, Christian, and Hindu societies. In Afghanistan under the Taliban rule during the late 1990's, men were expected to wear traditional male clothing and were beaten or jailed by morality police for not having a full beard, playing or listening to music, or allowing female family members to go out in public unchaperoned. Women were similarly punished for being in public without wearing a plain loose outer gown that covered their face and entire body including their feet. They were also not allowed to go to school or to work outside of the home. To the surprise of Europeans and North Americans, many of these conservative cultural patterns did not disappear with the end of Taliban control. They are deeply ingrained in the Islamic tradition of Afghanistan and in the more conservative nations of the Middle East.

Conservative Muslim women in the Middle East. They are fully covered for modesty in public and are being escorted by a male relative.
(Note: Women in some predominantly Muslim countries lead lives that are much less constrained by tradition.)

Cultures No Longer Exist in Isolation

It is highly unlikely that there are any societies still existing in total isolation from the outside world. Even small, out of the way tribal societies are now being integrated to some extent into the global economy. That was not the case a few short generations ago. Some of the societies in the Highlands of New Guinea were unaware of anyone beyond their homeland until the arrival of European Australian miners in the 1930's. A few of the Indian tribes in the Upper Amazon Basin of South America remained unaware of the outside world until explorers entered their territories in the 1950's and 1960's. Members of these same New Guinean and Amazonian societies today buy clothes and household items produced by multinational corporations. They are developing a growing knowledge of other cultures through schools, radios, and even televisions and the Internet. As a result of this inevitable process, their languages and indigenous cultural patterns are being rapidly replaced. Virtually all societies are now acquiring cultural traits from the economically dominant societies of the world. The most influential of these dominant societies today are predominantly in North America and Western Europe. However, even these societies are rapidly adopting words, foods, and other cultural traits from all over the world.

Chapter 1 Culture and Cultural Diversity

Australian Aborigine wears European style clothes.

The emergence of what is essentially a shared global culture is not likely to result in the current major cultures disappearing in the immediate future the same way many of the small indigenous ones have. Language differences and ethnocentrism will very likely prevent that from happening. There are powerful conflicting trends in the world today. At the same time that many people are actively embracing globalism, others are reviving tribalism. The break-up of the former empire of the Soviet Union into largely ethnic based nations is an example of the latter. Likewise, some of the nations in Africa whose boundaries were arbitrarily created by Europeans during the colonial era are now experiencing periodic tribal wars that may result in the creation of more ethnically based countries.

(Adapted from Dennis O'Neil, Characteristics of Culture)

Critical thinking questions:

1. What are the reasons for people's unawareness of their own culture? Can you give an example to explain this phenomenon?

2. Some people assume that culture is inherited in a society, so a man should know all about his own culture. Do you agree or disagree with this statement? Try to provide convincing explanations.

3. Some people is concerned about the disappearance of many small indigenous cultures due to the emergence of globalization. What is your possible explanations?

Section II Culture Diversity

I Pre-tasks

Task 1 Which is the real Mulan?

Look at the following pictures and talk about the ideal image of Mulan in your mind. What are the possible reasons for the different portray of the same character?

Task 2 Which is the real self?

Look at the following figures and talk about the self concept with your neighbours. Try to find the one that suits you and explain why.

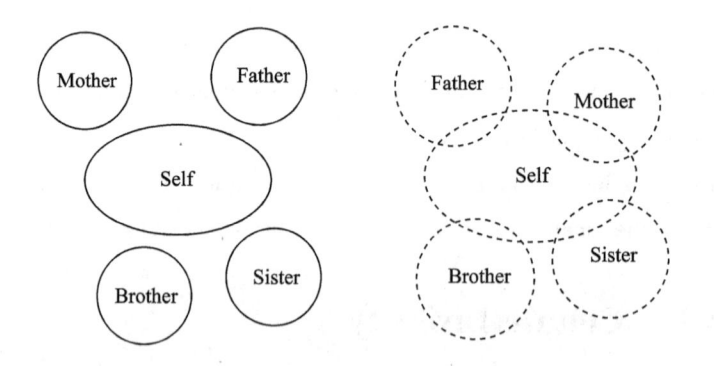

II While-tasks

Different Lands and Different Families

Family structure is the core of any culture. A major function of the family is to socialize new members of a culture. As children are raised in a family setting, they learn to become members of the family as well as members of the larger culture. The family provides the model for all other relationships in society. Through the observations and modeling of the behavior of other family members, children learn about the family and society including the values of the culture. Family structure and their inherent relationships and obligations are a major source of cultural difference.

The family is the center of most traditional Asians' lives. Many people worry about their families' welfare, reputation, and honor. Asian families are often extended, including several generations related by blood or marriage living in the same home. An Asian person's misdeeds are not blamed just on the individual but also on the family-including the dead ancestors.

Traditional Chinese, among many other Asians, respect their elders and feel a deep sense of duty toward them. Children repay their parents' sacrifices by being successful and supporting them in old age. This is accepted as a natural part of life in China. In contrast, taking care of aged parents is often viewed as tremendous burden in the United States, where aging and family support are not honored highly.

Filipinos, the most Americanized of Asians, are still extremely family-oriented. They are dedicated to helping their children and will sacrifice greatly for their children to get an education. In turn, the children are devoted to their parents, who often live nearby. Grown children who go away and leave the country for economic reasons typically send large parts of their salary home to their parents and the rest of the family.

The Vietnamese family consists of people currently alive as well as the spirits of the dead and of the as-yet unborn. Any decisions or actions are done from family considerations, not individual desires. People's behavior is judged on whether it brings shame or pride to the family. Vietnamese children are trained to rely on their families, to honor elderly people, and to fear foreigners. Many Vietnamese think that their actions in this life will influence their status in the next life.

Fathers in traditional Japanese families are typically strict and distant. Japanese college students in one study said they would tell their fathers just about as much as they would tell a total stranger. The emotional and communication barrier between children and fathers in Japan appears very strong after children have reached a certain age.

In South Africa, the basic unit of South African society is the family, which includes the nuclear family and the extended family or tribe. In traditional African society, the tribe is the most important community as it is the equivalent of a nation. The tribe provides both emotional and financial security in much the same way the nuclear family does to white or colored South Africans. The colored and more traditional African cultures consider their extended family to be almost as important as their nuclear family, while the English-speaking white community places more emphasis on the nuclear family. The nuclear family is the ultimate basis of the tribe. The tribal and family units are being disrupted by changes in the economic reorganization of the country. As more people move into the urban areas, they attempt to maintain familial ties, including providing financial support to family members who have remained in the village.

Among Israeli Jews, the great majority of families, of both European and Afro-Asian origin, combine traditional Jewish family values and norms with modern features. These are medium-size families with an average of three children. Marriage is seen primarily, though not only, as a framework for raising children. The man is expected to be the major breadwinner and the woman to fulfill the duties of wife and mother. Although 70 percent of the women work outside the home, work is secondary to childrearing. Divorce is viewed as a failure, not as an opportunity for growth. At the same time, under the impact of feminism and Israel's egalitarian ideology, the men in these families are increasingly involved in childcare, decisions are made jointly, and resources are divided democratically.

The traditional Arab family is hierarchical, patriarchal and collectivist. Individuals are expected to subordinate their wishes to the needs of their families, and wives' to those of their husbands. The nuclear family nests within the clan, an extensive kinship network formed by the ties of marriage and blood, whose traditional function was to provide its members with cohesion and financial support. Over the latter part of the 20th century, the Arab family has been undergoing a process of modernization, the clan has been whittled down in size and the status and the authority of its elders undermined. Arab men have seen their traditional role as head of the family eroded and their authority over their wives and children diminished. Arab woman have become increasingly educated and able to carry the economic burden. The structure of the Arabic family is three fold. The first and the closest consists of the husband, the wife, their children, their parents who live with them, and servants, if any. The next group, the central fold of the family, consists of a number of close relatives, whether they live together or not, who have special claims upon each other, who move freely inside the family, with whom marriage is forbidden and between whom there is no veil. These are the people who also have prior claim on the wealth and resources of a person, in life as well as in death. The crucial thing in this respect is that they are regarded as Mahram(宗教领袖), those with whom marriage is prohibited. This constitutes the real core of the family, sharing each other's joys, sorrow, hopes and fears. This relationship emerges from consanguinity, affinity and foster-nursing.

The family is a part of the Islamic social order. The society that Islam wants to establish is not a sensate society. It establishes an ideological society, with a high level of moral awareness, strong commitment to the ideal of Khilafah(哈里发) and purposive orientation of all human behavior. Its discipline is not an imposed discipline, but one that flows out of every individual's commitment to the values and ideals of Islam. In this society a high degree of social responsibility prevails. The entire system operates in a way that strengthens and fortifies the family.

Traditional Latin Americans are as family-centered as the traditional Asians. The family is the number one priority, the major frame of reference. Latin Americans believe that family members must help each other. Children in Latin America (of whom there are many, due to high fertility rates) are taught to respect authority and are given many responsibilities at home. The Latin American family emphasizes authority with the males and older people being the most important. The family in most parts of Latin American includes many relatives, who remain in close contact. Family connections are the main way to get things done; dropping names (mentioning the names of important people the family knows) is often necessary to accomplish even simple things.

Although there has been much talk about "family values" in the United States, the family is not a usual frame of reference for decisions in US mainstream culture. Family connections are not so important to most people. Dropping the names of wealthy or famous people the family knows is done in the United States, but it is not viewed positively. More important is a person's own individual "track record" of personal achievement.

Thus, many cultural differences exist in family structures and values. In some cultures, the family is the center of life and the main frame of reference for decisions. In other cultures, the individuals, not the family, is primary. In some cultures, the family's reputation and honor depend on each person's actions; in other cultures, individuals can act without permanently affecting the family life. Some cultures value old people, while other cultures look down on them. (1396 words)

(Adapted from R. L. Oxford R. C. Scarcella, A Few Family Structures and Values Around the Globe)

Word list:

1. inherent [ɪn'hɪərənt]
   adj. 天生；固有的，内在的
2. family-oriented 以家庭为中心的；顾家的，重视家庭的
3. equivalent [ɪ'kwɪvələnt]
   adj. 相等的，相当的，等效的；等价的，等积的；[化学] 当量的
   n. 对等物；[化学] 当量
4. egalitarian [ɪˌgælɪ'teərɪən]
   adj. 平等主义的；主张平等的
   n. 平等主义；平等主义者
5. hierarchical [ˌhaɪə'rɑːkɪkl]
   adj. 分层的；按等级划分的，等级（制度）的
6. patriarchal [ˌpeɪtrɪ'ɑːkl]
   adj. 父权的；父系；家长的；族长的
7. collectivist [kə'lektɪvɪst]
   n. 集体主义者
8. subordinate [sə'bɔːdɪnət]
   adj. 下级的；级别或职位较低的；次要的；附属的
   n. 部属，部下；下级
   vt. 使……居下位，使在次级；使服从；使从属
9. clan [klæn]
   n. 氏族；宗族；庞大的家族；宗派
10. whittle ['wɪtl]
    v. 削弱；切，削（木头）；减少
    n. 屠刀

11. undermine [ˌʌndəˈmaɪn]

   v. 逐渐削弱；使逐步减少效力；从根基处破坏；挖……的墙脚

12. erode [ɪˈrəʊd]

   vt. & vi. 侵蚀，腐蚀

   vi. 逐渐毁坏；削弱，损害

13. sensate [ˈsenseɪt]

   adj. 感知的，知觉的

14. prevail [prɪˈveɪl]

   vi. 流行，盛行；获胜，占优势；说服，劝说

15. consanguinity [ˌkɑnsæŋˈɡwɪnəti]

   n. 同源，血亲，同族；密切关系

16. affinity [əˈfɪnəti]

   n. 密切关系，姻亲关系；（男女之间的）吸引力；吸引人的异性；类同；类似，近似

Task 1 Reading comprehension

Exercise One：Work with your partners, decide whether the following statements are true (T) or false (F) according to what you have learned in the passage.

1. _____ Any family member was born to be a social member of a society.

2. _____ In different countries, all family structures are inherent from tradition, therefore few differences exist in different families.

3. _____ In Asian countries, each family member should be responsible for his only misdeeds. No one will blame him.

4. _____ Among Chinese and many other Asians, aging and family support are not honored highly.

5. _____ Filipinos are very Americanized Asians, so their family values have been greatly depreciated than before.

6. _____ Family values of Vietnamese are very similar to Chinese ones.

7. _____ As an Asian country, Japanese family members have very tight bond with each as many other Asians do.

8. _____ In South Africa, many tribes attach great importance to unclear family as American people do.

9. _____ In Israel families, fathers usually play very important role in childcare.

10. _____ The traditional Arab family is hierarchical, patriarchal and collectivist, but now the men's role as head of the family and their authority over their wives and children are diminishing gradually.

Exercise Two: Fill in the blanks with the words given below and change the form when necessary.

extend   extensive   nuclear   priority   sacrifice   cohesion
family-oriented   frame   diminish   hierarchical   prohibit   commitment

1. In South Africa, the colored and more traditional African cultures consider their _____ family more important, while the English-speaking white community prefer _____ family.

2. In Israel, divorce is usually _____ in every family, because it is regarded as a failure.

3. As the traditional Asians, traditional Latin Americans are usually _____. Every family members must think their family as the first choice.

4. The structure of the Arabic family is three fold. The first fold is _____ by the husband, the wife, their children, their parents who live with them, and servants.

5. In modern society, the size of a family is not very big and an average family does not have very _____ kinship.

6. A man is usually considered as the _____ in an Arabic family. Wives and children both should obey him.

7. In China, the parents will _____ everything they have in order to ensure their children's success.

8. In a family-centered culture, every family member should have very strong _____ to the family affairs.

9. In a traditional Arab family, the function of a marriage is to provide its members with _____ and financial support.

10. In many ancient Asian countries, the structure of society and a family is _____, citizen have to obey the king, and the son have to follow the father, the wife have to serve the husband.

Task 2 Case study

Case 1

Marta worked in an American company. It wasn't the first time that Marta's manager asked her to copy-edit the store flyer. Their company served a large Latino population and Marta was happy that more Latino items were being offered at local supermarkets. As she worked on the flyer featuring the new products, Marta noticed that the items were not being promoted in a way that would appeal to Latinos. She thought of approaching her manager with her observations but she felt that the boss would take them as criticism of the advertising team who had created the copy. So she kept her mouth shut. Later, when Marta mentioned her decision to Jim, an Anglo colleague, he said Marta's boss would probably welcome the suggestions. Marta followed Jim's advice and bravely told her manager her own opinion. It turned out that Jim was right. The manager was very happy to hear her suggestions for improving products and services. Surprisingly, Marta was invited as a special assistant by the advertising team to help with the revision of the product promotion. Instead of arising criticism, Marta was highly evaluated by her manager as well as the company.

Questions for discussion:
1. Why was Marta hesitant to speak up her own opinion at first?
2. Is it a good thing if a company has to deal with divers employees?
3. Would you like to work in a company full of diversities?

Case 2

One night in Kunming, China last December an American visiting scholar, Ms. Steinny was out to dinner with a Chinese professor, a middle-aged woman. The Chinese professor introduced each dish in details or even historical stories to her with a lot of pride. She had just returned from a trip to Washington D. C. and told Ms. Steinny about the hard days in America without Chinese food. She also criticized that the food in China Town was not the traditional and real Chinese food. And then they began contrasting America and China on a number of different fronts: infrastructure, geography, weather, fashion. When Ms. Steinny brought up the differences between Chinese and American cultures, the Chinese professor interjected, "What is American culture? The US is too young a country to have a culture," she began arguing. In her mind, real culture was something that could only exist after thousands of years of civilization. Besides, she argued, American culture is merely a collection of snippets from other cultures. It is not a true culture. This was not the first time Ms. Steinny had heard such criteria for culture from a Chinese friend. Ms. Steinny strongly expressed her disagreement and emphasized that American ideas of culture acknowledge a certain package of shared traits—food, language, music, customs—as a base requirement. American cultures, such as, American English, American philosophies, as well as elements of popular culture including American music, food, literature and film were well accepted or learned by many other countries. So America is a country with diversified cultural elements. Finally, the two scholars could not persuade each other and the dinner ended up in a kind of awkwardness.

Questions for discussion:

1. Do you think America is a country without its own culture?

2. What kind of cultural mistake that the two scholars had made during the dinner time.

3. Why do many people tend to believe that their own culture is better than others'?

III After-tasks

Task 1 Movie and culture discussion *Modern Family*

Modern Family is an American television mockumentary sitcom that premiered on ABC, which follows the lives of Jay Pritchett and his family, all of whom live in suburban Los Angeles. Pritchett's family includes his second wife, her son and his stepson, as well as his two adult children and their spouses and children. The director conceived the series while sharing stories of their own "modern families". *Modern Family* revolves around three different types of families (nuclear, step- and same-sex) living in the Los Angeles area who are interrelated through Jay Pritchett and his children, Claire Dunphy and Mitchell Pritchett. Patriarch Jay is remarried to a much younger woman, Gloria Delgado Pritchett, a passionate Colombian with whom he has an infant son, Fulgencio (Joe) Pritchett, and a son from Gloria's previous marriage, Manny Delgado. Jay's daughter Claire was a homemaker, but has returned to the business world. She now works in her father's closet business. She is married to Phil Dunphy, a realtor and self-professed "cool Dad". They have three children: Haley Dunphy, a stereotypical ditzy teenage girl; Alex Dunphy, a nerdy, smart middle child; and Luke Dunphy, the off-beat only son. Jay's lawyer son Mitchell and his husband Cameron Tucker have an adopted Vietnamese daughter, Lily Tucker-Pritchett. As the name suggests, this family represents a modern-day family and episodes are comically based on situations which many families encounter in real life.

Modern Family is an ensemble comedy that offers a poignant and laughably honest portrayal of contemporary family life. The three families featured include a same-sex couple and their adopted daughter, and a post-midlifer and his much younger Latina second wife and stepson. So different family structures and distinct parenting are pronouncedly presented to the audience. Various themes such as love, education, parenting, responsibility, independence, equality, divorce, death or even prejudice and stereotype are extensively dealt with in different ways, which evidently demonstrate the diversity of American culture and family. The ultimate message conveyed by this series is that tolerance and the lasting connection among family members of all shapes, sizes, and colors should be always valued and treasured.

Questions:
1. Which family would you like to live with if you had a chance and why?
2. What are the causes for their family differences?

3. Are their any similarities among the different families?

Task 2 Extended reading

Teaching Young People about Cultural Diversity

If we look to our species' primate past and to our more recent history of dealing with cultural difference, there is little reason to be optimistic. Our initial response to difference is usually to avoid it. Imagine, if you will, a group of our primate ancestors gathered around their fire, gnawing on the day's catch. Another group of primates comes into view, heading toward the fire. I wonder how often the first group looked up and said (in effect), "Ah, cultural diversity, how wonderful." More likely it was fight or flight, and things have not changed that much since then. We flee to the suburbs or behind walls to avoid cultural difference, and if we are forced to confront it, there is often a fight.

Historically, if we were unsuccessful in avoiding different people, we tried to convert them. Political, economic, and religious missionaries sought out opportunities to impose their own beliefs on others. The thinking seemed to be, "if only people were more like us, then they would be all right to have around." This assumption can still be seen in the notion of the "melting pot" prevalent this century in the United States. It is difficult for many people to believe that any understanding at all is possible unless people have become similar to one another.

Given this history of dealing with difference, it is no wonder that the topic of appreciating it, respecting it—is central to all practical treatments of interculturalcommunication. Yet this emphasis on difference departs from the common approaches to communication and relationships based within a single culture.

Intercultural communication—communication between people of different cultures—cannot allow the easy assumption of similarity. By definition, cultures are different in their languages, behavior patterns, and values. So an attempt to use one's self as a predictor of shared assumptions and responses to messages is unlikely to work. Because cultures embody such variety in patterns of perception and behavior, approaches to communication in cross-cultural situations guard against inappropriate assumptions of similarity and encourage the consideration of difference. In other words, the intercultural communication approach is difference—based and cultural diversity is unavoidable in our life.

Cultural diversity is when differences in race, ethnicity, age, ability, language, nationality, socioeconomic status, gender, religion or sexual orientation are represented within a community. The community can be a country, region, city, neighborhood, company or school. The group is culturally diverse if a wide variety of groups are represented.

There is no denying the fact that young people today are faced with more diversity than we parents were at their age. America is the "melting pot" of the world and that is a good characteristic. It is here in America you can experience the different cultures of the world without leaving this country and for many without leaving their state or city. All of the diversity raises a very good question though, how as parents we teach our children about cultural diversity and tolerance.

In order to teach young people about cultural diversity and tolerance, we as parents need to figure out what our beliefs are about those two topics. How open are we to people from another culture or race. Knowing if we have any biases or prejudices against people that are different. Knowing if we do, admitting that we do and then figuring out why we have those beliefs is the first step. The goal is to teach our children about the different cultures and introduce them to the different way people live and why. We do not want to cloud their judgment and give them biases.

As adults, it can be hard to open ourselves up enough to recognize and deal with our prejudices, but it is something we need to do for our children's sake. You want your children to be open to new experiences and new people. In order for them to be that way, you need to be that way. Read books with your children about other cultures. Many libraries have wonderful selections about different cultures and societies fromaround the world. Talk to your local librarian and check out a few books and read them with your children. Make sure that they are age appropriate and if your child has more questions, the two of you can use the Internet together to get answers.

Where we live, the schools have done a really nice job about bringing out the different cultures that are present among the students in the school. They all do reports about different cultures where they have to do the research, write a report and create something from that culture to share with the class. They also do a "Cultural Awareness" night at school. For this, families are asked to set up a booth in the gym with posters, and maps and traditional clothing and present something about their culture to the people that come through the "fair". Thankfully, many families participate and there is food and music and dances and art and toys from all over the world right there in the gym. That is something that the kids really look forward to and we enjoy doing with them. We participate in the fair, our family has a nice cultural mix. I am from America and my husband is from Pakistan. We were both raised very differently but have come together and created a wonderful harmony that has allowed our children to experience many things that most of their friends haven't. They have friends from different cultures and we all get together and have dinners and celebrate different events together. We decided as parents that we would educate our children about the different religions and spiritualities and when they were ready, they could make the decision about what they believed in. We do not eat pork, we do celebrate the holidays, and we honor diversity and celebrate the fact that we are our own culture. We do this because kids are smarter than many adults give them credit for. When we talk to our children about where we have come from, or about other people that we know and that they are friends with we talk to them intelligently. If we don't have an answer for a certain question we tell them that we do not know and then we find the answer together.

  The best way to teach young people about cultural diversity is to let them see you are accepting and tolerant. Our children emulate us, they act the way they do because of what they see their parents do. If you are open to other people, and make an effort to learn more about the different cultures, your child will eagerly want to do the same. Make an effort to get to know your neighbor. Have dinner with a family that is different than your own. Encourage your child to make friends with other children. Ask them about the other kids on their class. We taught our children that they need to look at each person as a person. We all look different on the outside, different colors of hair, eyes and skin. We all believe differently about a lot of different things. Pointing out those differences and uses those differences as reasons to not talk to someone is never acceptable. We have also told them that it is never okay for another person to something to them that makes them feel bad or hurts them or others. Tolerance means understanding and openness, it does not mean acceptance of cruel behavior. That goes for everyone regardless of their culture.

Young people have to learn that people with different backgrounds have different interpretations of events. They contribute unique perspectives. That allows the group to look at problems from all angles and create innovative results. For diversity brings strength, it must be valued and integrated into company practices and philosophy. This takes time and a commitment to celebrate diversity. It requires the willingness to be open-minded and non-judgmental about the value of differences. Without that commitment, cultural diversity can weaken a group. Differences in interpretation of events can lead to miscommunication. If not addressed, awkwardness and hostilities arise. Prejudices will worsen that effect. People can jump to conclusions and misinterpret behaviors. Therefore, teaching young people about the cultural diversity is beneficial for their future communication in a global world. (1390 words)

(Adapted from Milton Bennett, "Basic Concepts of Intercultural Communication: Paradigms, Principles, and Practices")

Critical thinking questions:

1. Do you think that people in the modernized world have changed their attitudes toward cultural differences compared with our species' primate in the past? Can you find some examples to specify?

2. Why is it necessary for the young people to learn about cultural diversity? What is your point of view?

3. Do you think the role of adults' is influential for the young people to deal with cultural diversity?

4. Could you talk about your experience of dealing with cultural diversity?

Chapter 2

Intercultural Communication

See at a distance and undesirable person;
See close at hand a desirable person;
Come close to the undesirable person;
Move away from the desirable person;
Coming close and moving apart;
How interesting life is.

—Gensho Ogura

Nearing Autumn's close.
My neighbor—
How does he live, I wonder?

—Basho

Section I   Communication

I   Pre-tasks

Task 1   Proverb sharing

Please read the following proverbs in pictures and try to define communication in your own words.

Chapter 2 Intercultural Communication

> Communication is the Fuel that keeps the fire of your relationship burning; without it, your relationship goes cold.
> — William Presley

> Communication is the life line of any relationship. Without it, the relationship will starve itself to death.
> — Elizabeth Bourgeret

> My belief is that communication is the best way to create strong relationships.
> — Jada Pinkett Smith

> Trust is the glue of life. It's the most essential ingredient in effective communication. It's the foundational principle that holds all relationships.
> — Stephen R. Covey

Task 2 Conversation analysis

Read the following conversation between an Arabic and a visiting US businessman. Try to find out the possible problems in this conversation and provide your explanation.

Abu Bakr: Mr. Armstrong! How good to see you.

Armstrong: Nice to see you again, Hussan.

Abu Bakr: Tell me, how have you been?

Armstrong: Very well, thank you, and you?

Abu Bakr: Fine, fine. All ah be praised.

Armstrong: I really appreciate your agreeing to see me about these distribution arrangements. Now could we...

Abu Bakr: My pleasure. So tell me. How is your trip? Did you come direct or did you have a stopover?

Armstrong: No stopover this time. I'm on a tight schedule. That's why I'm so grateful you could see me on such a short notice. So about the...

Abu Bakr: Not at all. How is my good friend, Mr. Wilson?

Armstrong: Wilson? Oh, fine, fine. He's been very busy with this distribution problem also, which is what we need to discuss.

Abu Bakr: You know, you have come at an excellent time. Tomorrow is the Prophet's birthday—blessings and peace be upon Him—and we're having a special feast at home. I'd like you to be our guest.

Armstrong: Thank you very much.

II While-tasks

The Communication Process

Communication is the process through which participants create and share information with one another as they move toward reaching mutual understanding. Communication is involved in every aspect of daily life, from birth to death. It is universal. Because communication is so pervasive, it is easy to take it for granted and even not to notice it. Many people think communication is simply the act of transferring information from one place to another. However, the actual subject of communication becomes a lot more complex. There are various categories of communication and more than one may occur at any time. The different categories of communication include: Spoken or Verbal Communication: face-to-face, telephone, radio or television and other media; Non-Verbal Communication: body language, gestures, how we dress or act—even our scent; Written Communication: letters, e-mails, books, magazines, the Internet or via other media; Visualizations: graphs and charts, maps, logos and other visualizations can communicate messages.

The process of interpersonal communication cannot be regarded as a phenomena which simply "happens", but should be seen as a process which involves participants negotiating their role in this process, whether consciously or unconsciously. Senders and receivers are of course vital in communication. In face-to-face communication the roles of the sender and receiver are not distinct as both parties communicate with each other, even if in very subtle ways such as through eye-contact or lack of eye-contact and general body language. There are many other subtle ways that we communicate, perhaps even unintentionally, with others. For example the tone of our voice can give clues to our mood or emotional state, whilst hand signals or gestures can add to a spoken message. In written communication the sender and receiver are more distinct. Today we can all write and publish our ideas online, which has led to an explosion of information and communication possibilities.

The communication process (figure) is the process that a message or communication is sent by the sender through a communication channel to a receiver, or to multiple receivers. The sender must encode the message (the information being conveyed) into a form that is appropriate to the communication channel, and the receiver(s) then de-

The Communication Process

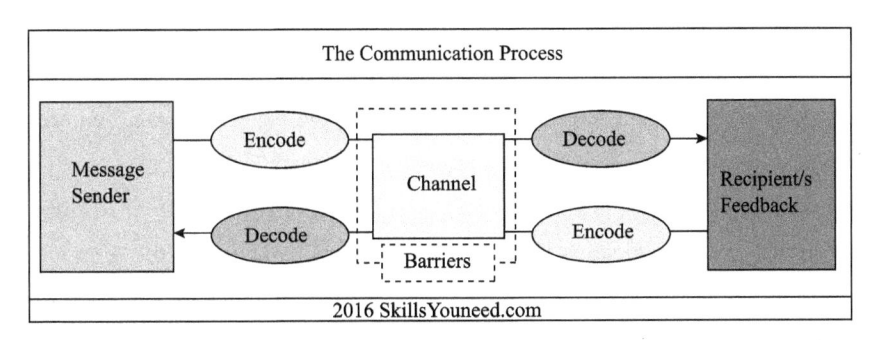

```
Message Sender → Encode → Channel → Decode → Recipient/s Feedback
Recipient/s Feedback → Encode → Channel → Decode → Message Sender
                        Barriers
```

2016 SkillsYouneed.com

codes the message to understand its meaning and significance. Misunderstanding can occur at any stage of the communication process. Effective communication involves minimizing potential misunderstanding and overcoming any barriers to communication at each stage in the communication process. An effective communicator understands their audience, chooses an appropriate communication channel, hones their message to this channel and encodes the message to reduce misunderstanding by the receiver (s). They will also seek out feedback from the receiver(s) as to how the message is understood and attempt to correct any misunderstanding or confusion as soon as possible. Receivers can use techniques such as clarification and reflection as effective ways to ensure that the message sent has been understood correctly. The process of interpersonal communication is irreversible, you can wish you hadn't said something and you can apologize for something you said and later regret, but you can't take it back. We often behave and therefore communicate to others based on previous communication encounters. These encounters may or may not be appropriate points of reference. We stereotype people, often subconsciously, maybe by gender, social standing, religion, race, age and other factors. Stereotypes are generalizations, often exaggerated. Because of these stereotypes, when we communicate with people we can carry with us certain preconceptions of what they are thinking or how they are likely to behave, we may have ideas about the outcome of the conversation. These preconceptions affect how we speak to others, the words we use and the tone of voice. We naturally communicate in a way that we think is most appropriate for the person we are talking to. Unfortunately our preconceptions of others are often incorrect. This can mean that our communication is inappropriate and therefore more likely to be misunderstood. As the goal to all communication has to be understanding it can be said that we have failed to communicate. By communicating in this way, being influenced by preconceived ideas, we feedback further stereotypes to the person we are speaking to, thus exasperating the problem. Start all interpersonal communication with an open mind; listen to what is being said rather than hearing what you expect to hear. You are then less likely to be misunderstood or say things that you regret later.

Communication involves a sender and a receiver (or receivers) conveying information through a communication channel. Communication channel is the term given to the way in which we communicate. There are multiple communication channels available to us today, for example face-to-face conversations, telephone calls, text messages, E-mail, the Internet (including social media such as Facebook and Twitter), radio and TV, written letters, brochures and reports to name just a few. Choosing an appropriate communication channel is vital for effective communication as each communication channel has different strengths and weaknesses. For example, broadcasting news of an upcoming event via a written letter might convey the message clearly to one or two individuals but will not be a time or cost effective way to broadcast the message to a large number of people. On the other hand, conveying complex, technical information is better done via a printed document than via a spoken message since the receiver is able to assimilate the information at their own pace and revisit items that they do not fully understand. Written communication is also useful as a way of recording what has been said, for example taking minutes in a meeting. An important step in communication is to encode messages. All messages must be encoded into a form that can be conveyed by the communication channel chosen for the message. We all do this every day when transferring abstract thoughts into spoken words or a written form. However, other communication channels require different forms of encoding, e. g. text written for a report will not work well if broadcast via a radio programme, and the short, abbreviated text used in text messages would be inappropriate if sent via a letter. Complex data may be best communicated using a graph or chart or other visualization. Effective communicators encode their messages with their intended audience in mind as well as the communication channel. This involves an appropriate use of language, conveying the information simply and clearly, anticipating and eliminating likely causes of confusion and misunderstanding, and knowing the receivers' experience in decoding other similar communications. Successful encoding of messages is a vital skill in effective communication. The other step is to decode messages. Once received, the receiver(s) need to decode the message. Successful decoding is also a vital communication skill. People will decode and understand messages in different ways based upon any barriers to communication which might be presented, their experience and understanding of the context of the message, their psychological state, and the time and place of receipt as well as many other potential factors. Understanding how the message will be decoded, and anticipating as many of the potential sources of misunderstanding as possible, is the art of a successful communicator. Following encoding and decoding is the step of feedback. Receivers of messages are likely to provide feedback on how they have understood the messages through both verbal and non-verbal reactions. Effective communicators pay close attention to this feedback as it's the only way to assess whether the message has been understood as intended, and it allows any confusion to be corrected. Bear in mind that the extent and form of feedback will vary according to the communication channel used. For example, feedback during a face-to-face or telephone conversation will be immediate and direct, whilst feedback to messages conveyed via TV or radio will be indirect and may be delayed, or even conveyed through other media such as the Internet.

To achieve effective communication, some basic principles should be followed. These principles govern the effectiveness of our communications; they may be simple to understand but can take a lifetime to master. First of all, interpersonal communication is not optional. We may, at times, try not to communicate; but not communicating is not an option. In fact the harder we try not to communicate, the more we do. By not communicating we are communicating something: perhaps that we are shy, perhaps that we are angry or sulking, perhaps that we are too busy. Ignoring somebody is communicating with them, we may not tell them we are ignoring them but through non-verbal communication we hope to make that apparent. We communicate far more and far more honestly with non-verbal communication than we do with words. Our body posture and position, eye-contact (or lack of it), the smallest and most subtle of mannerisms are all ways of communicating with others. Furthermore we are constantly being communicated too, we pick up signals from others and interpret them in certain ways and whether or not we understand is based on how skilled we are at interpreting interpersonal communication. (1494 words)

(Adapted from Jane Jackson, "Introducing Language and Intercultural Communication")

Word list：

1. pervasive [pəˈveɪsɪv]
   adj. 普遍的；扩大的；渗透的；弥漫的
   adv. 无处不在地；遍布地
   n. 无处不在；遍布

2. visualization [ˌvɪʒuəlaɪˈzeɪʃn]
   n. 形象（化），形象化；想象；目测

3. explosion [ɪkˈspləʊʒn]
   n. 爆发；爆炸，炸裂；扩张，激增；（感情，尤指愤怒的）突然爆发

4. multiple [ˈmʌltɪpl]
   adj. 多重的；多个的；复杂的；多功能的
   n. <数> 倍数

5. encode [ɪnˈkəʊd]
   vt. （将文字材料）译成密码；编码，编制成计算机语言

6. decode [ˌdiːˈkəʊd]
   vt. 译（码），解（码）；分析及译解电子信号

7. feedback [ˈfiːdbæk]
   n. 反馈；反应；反馈噪音

8. clarification [ˌklærəfɪˈkeɪʃn]
   n. 净化；（液体的）澄清；澄清法；（意义等的）澄清、说明

9. reflection [rɪˈflekʃn]
   n. 反映；（关于某课题的）思考；（声、光、热等的）反射；映像

10. irreversible [ˌɪrɪˈvɜːsəbl]
    adj. 不可逆的；不能翻转的；不能倒置的；［法］不可取消的

11. stereotype [ˈsterɪətaɪp]
    n. 陈规旧习，旧规矩；固定的形式；铅版；铅版制版法，铅板印刷
    vt. 使成陈规；把……浇铸成铅版；使用铅版；使固定

12. generalization [ˌdʒenrəlaɪˈzeɪʃn]
    n. 归纳；一般化；普通化；概论

13. exasperate [ɪɡˈzæspəreɪt]
    vt. 使恼怒；使恶化；使加剧

14. assimilate [ə'sɪməleɪt]

    vi. 同化；吸收，消化

    vt. 透彻理解；使吸收

15. abbreviate [ə'briːvɪeɪt]

    vt. 缩略；使简短；缩简；使用缩写词

    n. 使用缩写词的人；缩短，缩写（词、短语、名字、名称）

16. mannerism ['mænərɪzəm]

    n. 言谈举止；风格主义；习性；（绘画、写作中）过分的独特风格

Task 1 Reading comprehension

Exercise One：Work with your partners, decide whether the following statements are true (T) or false (F) according to what you have learned in the passage.

1. _____ Communication is the process of sending message and then understanding it.
2. _____ Communication is universal and happens anytime and anywhere. In other words, communication is simply the act of transferring information from one place to another.
3. _____ Graphs and charts, maps, logos etc. are categorized as visualizations. They are also a form of communication because they can communicate messages.
4. _____ Face-to-face communication only happens when the senders and receivers exchange messages consciously.
5. _____ Body language including the tone of our voice and hand signals is also an important part in people's actual communication.
6. _____ The communication process is the process that a message or communication is sent form one sender through a communication channel to the other receivers.
7. _____ In an effective communication, the potential misunderstanding and communication barriers can be eliminated completely.
8. _____ The process of interpersonal communication is a one-way process, you can wish you hadn't said something and you can apologize for something you said and later regret, but you can't take it back.

9. _____ Stereotypes are generalizations which can provide people some basic understanding about the people in communication. Knowing what they are thinking or how they are likely to behave, we may have ideas about the outcome of the conversation.

10. _____ Living in this high-tech world, communication can be very simple and convenient. Telephone calls, text messages, E-mail, the Internet, radio and TV are the most effective communication channels for all kinds of communication.

Exercise Two: Fill in the blanks with the words given below and change the form when necessary.

minimize   exaggerate   category   anticipate   distinct
encounter   explosion   clarification   interpersonal   unintentionally

1. Stereotypes are often _____ generalizations, so people's preconception can be misled and the misunderstanding may occur in the real communication.

2. Spoken or Verbal Communication, Non-Verbal Communication, Written Communication, and Visualizations are the main communication _____ according to communication studies.

3. The process of _____ communication should be seen as a process which involves participants negotiating their role in this process, whether consciously or unconsciously. It cannot be simply regarded as a phenomena which simply "happens".

4. The tone of our voice can give clues to our mood or emotional state, whilst hand signals or gestures can add to a spoken message. They are regarded as the subtle ways of communication which often happen _____.

5. In effective communication, the potential misunderstanding and barriers to communication at each stage may not be eliminated, but at least can be _____.

6. People can accumulate communication experience with previous _____, and then take it as reference for future communication.

7. Effective communication involves an appropriate use of language, conveying the information simply and clearly, _____ and eliminating likely causes of confusion and misunderstanding, and knowing the receivers' experience in decoding other similar communications.

8. In face-to-face communication the roles of the sender and receiver are not _____ as both parties communicate with each other, even if in very subtle ways such as through eye-contact or lack of eye-contact and general body language.

9. Today we can all write and publish our ideas online, which has led to an _____ of information and communication possibilities.

10. Using effective ways such as _____ and reflection to ensure that the message sent has been understood correctly is very helpful for receivers.

Task 2 Case study

Case 1

A British boss asked a new, young American employee if he would like to have an early lunch at 11 A. M. each day. The employee answered, "Yeah, that would be great!" But the boss responded with a curt, "With that kind of attitude, you may as well forget about lunch!" The employee was bewildered. What had gone wrong?

Questions for discussion:

1. Why did the boss change his idea suddenly? What was going wrong?

2. Can you try to use the theory of the communication process to explain the problems in their communication?

Case 2

Rika Kumata, a Japanese student, walked into the office of one of the authors at the University of Miami. She sat down on the sofa. The professor said:

"Hi, Rika, do you have your advising folder?"

"Oh, Dr. Steinfatt, this is not about advising. Should I come back another time?"

"No, this is fine. How can I help you?"

"Dr. Steinfatt, I don't know how to explain what happened last night, and thought you might be able to help me. Drew, an American boy, lives down the hall from me in the dorm. He and a friend knocked on my door and said, 'Hi, Rika, we're going over to the Rat. Don't you want to go with us?'"

She paused. "Well, I did not want to go with them because I was studying, but

I don't want to be impolite. So I smiled, nodded and said 'No' and went to the other room to get my keys. But then I heard Drew say, 'Oh, okey, maybe some other time.' When I came back, the door was closed and they had gone. I don't understand. I agreed to go with them, but they left without me."

Questions for discussion:
1. Suppose if you were Dr. Steinfatt, how would you like to answer Rika's question?
2. What kind of communication problems you can observe from this case?

III After-tasks

Task 1   Movie and culture discussion *The God Must Be Crazy*

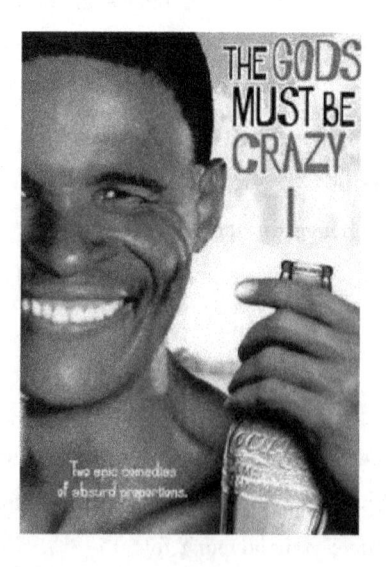

The film is a collision of three separate stories—the journey of a Ju/hoansi bushman to the end of the earth to get rid of a Coca-Cola bottle, the romance between a bumbling scientist and a schoolteacher, and a band of guerrillas on the run.

Xi and his tribe of San/Bushmen relatives are living well off the land in the Kalahari Desert. They are happy because the gods have provided plenty of everything, and no one in the tribe has unfulfilled wants. One day, a glass Coke bottle is thrown out of an aeroplane and falls to earth unbroken. Initially, this strange artifact seems to be another boon from the gods—Xi's people find many uses for it. But unlike anything that they have had before, there is only one bottle to go around. This exposes the tribe to a hither to unknown phenomenon, property, and they soon find themselves experiencing things they never had before: jealousy, envy, anger, hatred, even violence.

Since it has caused the tribe unhappiness on two occasions, Xi decides that the bottle is an evil thing and must be thrown off of the edge of the world. He sets out alone on his quest and encounters Western civilization for the first time. The film presents an interesting interpretation of civilization as viewed through Xi's perceptions.

There are also plot lines about shy biologist Andrew Steyn (Marius Weyers) who is studying the local animals (which, because of his nervousness around women, he was once described as "manure-collecting"); the newly hired village school teacher, a former newspaper reporter named Kate Thompson (Sandra Prinsloo); and some guerrillas led by Sam Boga (Louw Verwey), who are being pursued by government troops after an unsuccessful attempt to massacre the Cabinet of the fictional African country of Burani. Also taking a share of the limelight is Steyn's Land Rover, dubbed the Antichrist (also "son of a mlakka") by his assistant and mechanic, M'pudi, for its unreliability and constant need of repair. Also part of the chaos is a fresh safari tour guide named Jack Hind, who has designs on Thompson and would often steal Steyn's thunder.

Xi happens upon a farm and, being hungry as well as oblivious to the concept of ownership, shoots a goat with a tranquilizer arrow. For this he is arrested and jailed for stealing livestock. M'pudi, who lived with the bushmen for a long time, realizes that Xi will die in the alien environment of a prison cell. He and Steyn manage to hire Xi as a tracker for the 11 weeks of his prison sentence, with the help of M'pudi, who speaks Xi's language. Meanwhile, the guerrillas invade the school where Kate teaches and use her and her pupils as human shields for their escape by foot to the neighboring country. Steyn and Xi manage to immobilize the guerrillas as they are passing by and save Kate and the children. Steyn allows Xi to leave to continue his quest to the edge of the world.

Xi eventually finds himself at the top of a cliff with a solid layer of low-lying clouds obscuring the landscape below. This convinces Xi that he has reached the edge of the world, and he throws the bottle off the cliff. This scene was filmed at a place called God's Window in the then Eastern Transvaal, South Africa (now Mpumalanga). This is at the edge of the escarpment between the Highveld and Lowveld of South Africa. Xi then returns to his band and receives a warm welcome.

This film is presented in a genre of comedy, but can seriously arose viewers' deep thinking. Besides the theme of the coexistence between human beings and nature, a variety of cultural differences between the Aborigines and the Western culture are also successfully exhibited.

Questions:
1. How do you understand this title "The God Must Be Crazy"?
2. What is you impression of Africa after watching this movie?
3. What typical differences can you see from this movie between the Aborigines and the Western culture?

Task 2 Extended reading

Japanese Pickles and Mattresses

All international business activities involve communication. Within the international and global business environment, activities such as exchanging information and ideas, decision making, negotiating, motivating, and leading are all based on the ability of managers from one culture to communicate successfully with managers and employees from other cultures. Achieving effective communication is a challenge to managers worldwide even when the workforce is culturally homogeneous, but when one company includes a variety of languages and cultural backgrounds, effective two-way communication becomes even more difficult.

Perhaps the most difficult skill in cross-cultural communication involves standing back from yourself, or being aware that you do not know everything, that a situation may not make sense, that your guesses may be wrong, and that the ambiguity in the situation may continue. In this sense the ancient Roman dictum "knowledge is power" becomes true. In knowing yourself, you gain power over your perceptions and reactions; you can control your own behavior and your reactions to others' behavior. Cross-cultural awareness complements in-depth self awareness. A lack of self-awareness negates the usefulness of cross cultural awareness.

One of the most poignant examples of the powerful interplay between description, interpretation, evaluation, and empathy involves a Scottish businessman's relationship with a Japanese colleague. The following story recounts the Scottish businessman's experience.

It was my first visit to Japan. As a gastronomic adventurer, and because I believe cuisine is one route which is freely available and highly effective as a first step towards a closer understanding of another country, I was disappointed on my first evening when the Japanese offered me a Western meal. As tactfully as possible I suggested that some time during my stay I would like to try a Japanese menu, if that could be arranged without inconvenience. There was some small reluctance evident on the part of my hosts (Due of course to their thought that I was being very polite asking for Japanese food which I didn't really like, so to be good hosts they had to politely find a way of not having me eat it!). But eventually, by an elegantly progressive route starting with Western food with a slightly Japanese bias through to genuine Japanese food, my hosts were convinced that I really wanted to eat Japanese style and was not "posing".

From then on they became progressively more enthusiastic in suggesting the more exotic Japanese dishes, and I guess I graduated when, after an excellent mealone night (apart from the Japanese pickles) on which I had lavished praise, they said, "Do you like Japanese pickles?" To this, without preamble, I said "No!", to which reply, with great laughter all round, they responded, "Nor do we!" During this gastronomic getting-together week, I had also been trying to persuade them that I really did wish to stay in traditional Japanese hotels rather than the very Westernized ones my hosts had selected because they thought I would prefer my "normal" lifestyle. (I should add that at this time traditional Japanese hotels were still available and often cheaper than, say, the Osaka Hilton.)

Anyway, after the pickles joke it was suddenly announced that Japanese hotels could be arranged. For the remaining two weeks of my stay, as I toured the major cities, on most occasions a traditional Japanese hotel was substituted for the Western one on my original schedule. Many of you will know that a traditional Japanese room has no furniture except a low table and a flower arrangement. The "bed" is a mattress produced just before you retire from a concealed cupboard, accompanied by a cereal-packed pillow. One memorable evening my host and I had finished our meal together in "my" room. I was expecting him to shortly make his "good night" and retire, as he had been doing all week, to his own room. However, he stayed unusually long and was, to me, obviously in some sort of emotional crisis. Finally, he blurted out, with great embarrassment, "Can I sleep with you?!" As they say in the novels, at this point I went very still! My mind was racing through all the sexual taboos and prejudices my own upbringing had instilled, and I can still very clearly recall how I analyzed: "I'm bigger than he is, so I can fight him off, but then he's probably an expert in the martial arts, but on the other hand he's shown no signs of being gay up until now and he is my host and there is a lot of business at risk and there's no such thing as rape, etc. !"

It seemed a hundred years, though it was only a few seconds, before I said, feeling as if I was pulling the trigger in Russian roulette, "Yes, sure." Who said that the Orientals are inscrutable? The look of relief that followed my reply was obvious. Then he looked worried and concerned again, and said, "Are you sure?" I reassured him and he called in the maid, who fetched his mattress from his room and laid it on the floor alongside mine. We both went to bed and slept all night without any physical interaction.

Later I learned that for the traditional Japanese one of the greatest compliments you can be paid is for the host to ask, "Can I sleep with you?" This goes back to the ancient feudal times, when life was cheap, and what the invitation really said was, "I trust you with my life. I do not think that you will kill me while I sleep. You are my true friend." To have said "No" to the invitation would have been an insult— "I don't trust you not to kill me while I sleep" —or, at the very least, my host would have been acutely embarrassed because he had taken the initiative. If I refused because I had failed to perceive the invitation as a compliment, he would have been out of countenance on two grounds: the insult to him in the traditional context and the embarrassment he would have caused me by "forcing" a negative, uncomprehending response from me. As it turned out, the outcome was superb. He and I were now "blood brothers", as it were. His assessment of me as being "ready for Japanization" had been correct and his obligations under ancient Japanese custom had been fulfilled. I had totally misinterpreted his intentions through my own cultural conditioning. It was sheer luck, or luck plus a gut feeling that I'd gotten it wrong, that caused me to make the correct response to his extremely complimentary and committed invitation.

Cross-cultural communication confronts us with limits to our perceptions, our interpretations, and our evaluations. Cross-cultural perspectives tend to render everything relative and slightly uncertain. Entering a foreign culture is tantamount to knowing the words without knowing the music, or knowing the music without knowing the beat. Our natural tendencies lead us back to our prior experience: our default option becomes the familiarity of our own culture, thus precluding our accurate understanding of others' cultures. Strategies to overcome our natural parochial tendencies exist: with care, the default option can be avoided. We can learn to see, understand, and control our own cultural conditioning. In facing foreign cultures, we can emphasize description rather than interpretation or evaluation, and thus minimize self-fulfilling stereotypes and premature closure. We can recognize and use our stereotypes as guides rather than rejecting them as unsophisticated simplifications. Effective cross-cultural communication presupposes the interplay of alternative realities: it rejects the actual or potential domination of one reality over another. (1258 words)

(Adapted from Nancy J. Adler &Allison Gundersen, "International Dimensions of Organizational Behavior")

Critical thinking questions:

1. How to successfully work in an international company with a variety of languages and cultural backgrounds?

2. What are the cultural connotations of Japanese "pickles" and "mattresses" according to the passage?

3. What would be the biggest difficulty for you in a cross-cultural environment?

Section II Intercultural Communication

I Pre-tasks

Task 1 Yes or No

Please read the following 10 sentences with your partners and try to find the similarities in them. What are the advantages of using this kind of reply in conversations? Try to make different conversations by using different sentences with your partners.

1. "Yes! Now tell me which of these five priorities should I drop?"

2. "Yes, sure! But I can only do it next week."

3. "Yes, sure! I'd love to help your team finish the project. But if I stay tonight, I won't be here tomorrow morning to help you run the event."

4. "Yes, sure! I'd love to help you with this. The only thing is that if I do X you'll have to do Y for me."

5. "Yes, sure! I'd love to take on John's responsibilities. It will mean that I have to work weekends for two months to do my job and finish his project. So can we talk about how I'd be compensated for that additional time?"

6. "I'm flattered you thought of me for this. Unfortunately, I'm overcommitted right now, so I'll have to pass."

7. "I'm flattered but I have a previous commitment. However, I'd like to suggest someone who'd be great for this."

8. "Thank you for thinking of me for this opportunity. Unfortunately, I'm so overcommitted that I wouldn't be able to give my best to the project. So, I'll have to pass this time."

9. "Thank you for thinking of me! I would love to do it! Unfortunately right now, I have no time to take it on and do a good job. But I'd be happy to train someone else to do it."

10. "I'd love to do it. Let me check my calendar to make sure I have the time."

Task 2 Who is the quickest counter?

Please read the following sentence and quickly count the number of F's in the sentence. Think about why different people can see different F's?

FINISHED FILES ARE THE RESULT OF YEARS OF SCIENTIFIC STUDY COMBINED WITH THE EXPERIENCE OF YEARS

II While-tasks

Different Cultures and Different Communication Styles

Communicating across cultures is challenging. Each culture has set rules that its members take for granted. Few of us are aware of our own cultural biases because cultural imprinting is begun at a very early age. And while some of one culture's knowledge, rules, beliefs, values, phobias, and anxieties are taught explicitly, most of the information is absorbed subconsciously. The challenge for multinational communication has never been greater. Worldwide business organizations have discovered that intercultural communication is a subject of importance—not just because of increased globalization, but also because their domestic workforce is growing more and more diverse, ethnically and culturally.

We are all individuals, and no two people belonging to the same culture are guaranteed to respond in exactly the same way. However, generalizations are valid to the extent that they provide clues on what you will most likely encounter when dealing with members of a particular culture.

All international communication is influenced by cultural differences. Even the choice of communication medium can have cultural overtones. The determining factor may not be the degree of industrialization, but rather whether the country falls into a high-context or low-context culture. High-context cultures (Mediterranean, Slav, Central European, Latin American, African, Arab, Asian, American-Indian) leave much of the message unspecified, to be understood through context, nonverbal cues, and between-the-lines interpretation of what is actually said. By contrast, low-context cultures (most Germanic and English-speaking countries) expect messages to be explicit and specific.

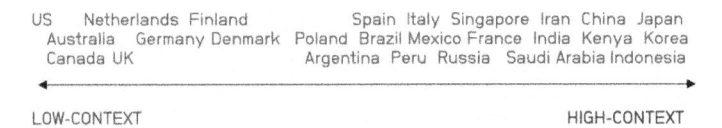

```
US    Netherlands  Finland           Spain Italy Singapore Iran China Japan
  Australia  Germany  Denmark  Poland Brazil Mexico France India Kenya Korea
  Canada UK                       Argentina Peru Russia  Saudi Arabia Indonesia
◄─────────────────────────────────────────────────────────────────────►

LOW-CONTEXT                                                    HIGH-CONTEXT
```

What is illustrated in the figure is how far the cultural context in communication can span. On the left side of low-context, the message is precise and clear. On the other side, high-context communication is nuanced and multi-layered. If the words spoken flow like water, the implicit is the undertow guiding the force, and the explicit is totally visible to the naked eye, like waves. The right side look for additional meaning when speaking to someone with the left, who is speaking at direct face value.

In different cultures, time is perceived differently. Some cultures think of time sequentially, as a linear commodity to "spend", "save", or "waste". Other cultures view time synchronically, as a constant flow to be experienced in the moment, and as a force that cannot be contained or controlled. In sequential cultures (like North America, England, Germany, Sweden, and the Netherlands), business people give full attention to one agenda item after another. In synchronic cultures (including South America, southern Europe and Asia) the flow of time is viewed as a sort of circle, with the past, present, and future all interrelated. This viewpoint influences how organizations in those cultures approach deadlines, strategic thinking, investments, developing talent from within, and the concept of "long-term" planning. Orientation to the past, present, and future is another aspect of time in which cultures differ. Americans believe that the individual can influence the future by personal effort, but since there are too many variables in the distant future, we favor a short-term view. Synchronistic cultures' context is to understand the present and prepare for the future. Any important relationship is a durable bond that goes back and forward in time, and it is often viewed as grossly disloyal not to favor friends and relatives in business dealings.

In intercultural communication practices, reason and emotion both play a role. Which of these dominates depends upon whether we are affective (readily showing emotions) or emotionally neutral in our approach. Members of neutral cultures do not telegraph their feelings, but keep them carefully controlled and subdued. In cultures with high affect, people show their feelings plainly by laughing, smiling, grimacing, scowling, and sometimes crying, shouting, or walking out of the room. This doesn't mean that people in neutral cultures are cold or unfeeling, but in the course of normal business activities, neutral cultures are more careful to monitor the amount of emotion they display. Emotional reactions were found to be least acceptable in Japan, Indonesia, the UK, Norway, and the Netherlands and most accepted in Italy, France, the US, and Singapore. Reason and emotion are part of all human communication. When expressing ourselves, we look to others for confirmation of our ideas and feelings. If our approach is highly emotional, we are seeking a direct emotional response: "I feel the same way." If our approach is highly neutral, we want an indirect response: "I agree with your thoughts on this." It's easy for people from neutral cultures to sympathize with the Dutch manager and his frustration over trying to reason with "that excitable Italian". After all, an idea either works or it doesn't work, and the way to test the validity of an idea is through trial and observation. That just makes sense—doesn't it? Well, not necessarily to the Italian who felt the issue was deeply personal and who viewed any "rational argument" as totally irrelevant!

In intercultural communication, there are also different communication styles which can affect the actual communication. These styles are present in all cultures, and the use of different styles varies depending on the context. Culturally, one particular style might however be considered more appropriate in a given situation.

The first two opposite styles are direct and indirect communication styles. In direct communication style, both parties, the speaker/writer and the listener/reader, expect explicit verbal expression of intentions, wishes, hopes, etc. (e. g. , "I am hungry", "I love you"). In indirect communication style the speaker/writer expresses his/her thoughts implicitly, or using hints or modifiers (e. g. , "perhaps", "maybe"). The listener/reader is expected to monitor the nonverbal communication, to read contextual cues, to relate what has been stated to all information available about the speaker/writer and the situation at hand in order to read the real meaning.

Communication styles have been associated with cultural values: direct style with individualism and indirect style with collectivism. Indirect communication is often used in situations where mutual harmony is considered important for maintaining good relationships. This is the case in collectivistic cultures, where people in general feel more mutual interdependency than in individualistic cultures. Open criticism, for instance, would be inappropriate in public situations, for face-saving reasons. In some Asian cultures, for example, indirectness is also considered to be an elegant style of communication. Training for paying attention to minimal cues and considering the feelings of the other starts in early childhood. Nevertheless, there are communicative situations where communication is very direct. Increasing industrialization, urbanization, and lately, globalization, influence communication behavior, also in Asia. There are considerable differences in directness and indirectness also between the generations. Indirect communication can tell about achieved harmony also in individualistic cultures. To be able to communicate successfully indirectly, mutual rapport and understanding is needed. This is often the case in old established relationships (e. g. , couples or working partners).

In cross-cultural studies where cultural groups are compared, or when people compare themselves to others, Northern Europeans often come out as being very direct and straight forward. However, these kinds of assumptions should been seen in relative terms. Finns, for instance, who consider themselves direct, are, in certain situations, considered by Spanish to be very indirect. We should remember that all features and phenomena can be found in all cultures, and there are no "typical" individuals. The use of directness and indirectness varies, depending on whether the situation is formal or informal, or how close or distant the interlocutors feel to be to each other.

Elaborate and succinct communication style is another conflicting pair. The amount of speech as well as one's expressiveness are criteria for the elaborate and succinct communication styles. Volubility and rich language are characteristic for everyday discussions in the cultures of Middle East, for instance, metaphors, idioms, and proverbs are common. Characteristic for the succinct style are frequent pauses, silence and "low key" verbal expressions that go to the point. Again, there are contextual and individual variations within cultures.

Like directness and indirectness, personal and contextual communication styles also are related in cross-cultural studies to individualism and collectivism. These styles also express cultural differences in power distance (hierarchy). Person-centered communication style is informal and emphasizes the individual and equalitarian relationships. The person-centeredness is reflected, for instance, by the use of the pronoun "I". The contextual style is status and role oriented. Formality and asymmetrical power distance is often emphasized. Personal pronouns are not often used. All information does not need to be explicitly expressed. Yet common background knowledge is assumed, or in essential parts conveyed during the interaction, often indirectly.

Instrumental and affective communication styles can be also related on one hand to individualism and collectivism, on the other hand to low-context and high-context approaches, respectively. Instrumental communication style is goal oriented and sender focused. Affective communication style is process oriented and listener focused. Verbally this means explicitness (instrumental style) and implicitness (affective style). Instrumental style is gradually becoming the style of international business and other professional contexts, particularly in the Western world.

When it comes to communication, what's proper and correct in one culture may be ineffective or even offensive in another. In reality, no culture is right or wrong, better or worse—just different. In today's global business community, there is no single best approach to communicating with one another. The key to cross-cultural success is to develop an understanding of, and a deep respect for, the differences. (1538 words)

(Adapted from Carol Kinsey Goman, "Communication Styles")

Word list:

1. bias [ˈbaɪəs]
    n. 偏见；倾向；偏爱，爱好；斜纹
    vt. 使倾向于；使有偏见；影响；加偏压于
    adj. 斜纹的；斜的，倾斜的；斜裁的
    adv. 偏斜地，倾斜地；对角地

2. imprint [ɪmˈprɪnt]
    n. 痕迹；盖印；特征；版权标记
    v. 盖（印）；刻上（记号）；使铭记

3. phobia [ˈfəʊbɪə]
    n. 恐惧；厌恶

4. valid [ˈvælɪd]
    adj. 有效的；有法律效力的；正当的；健全的

5. overtone [ˈəʊvətəʊn]
    n. 次要的意义；暗示，言外之意

6. undertow [ˈʌndətəʊ]
    n. 回头浪

7. span [spæn]
    n. 跨度，墩距；一段时间
    vt. 缚住或扎牢；跨越时间或空间；以掌测量，以手围绕测量类似测量

8. high-conte
    xt. 高语境文化；高语境

9. low-conte
    xt. 低语境；低语境文化

10. synchronic [sɪŋˈkrɒnɪk]
    adj. 不考虑历史演进的，限于一时的

11. sequential [sɪˈkwenʃl]

    adj. 序贯；时序；按次序的，相继的；构成连续镜头的

12. affective [əˈfektɪv]

    adj. 情感的；表达感情的

13. neutral [ˈnjuːtrəl]

    adj. 中立的；（化学中）中性的；暗淡的；不带电的

    n. （汽车或其他机器的）空挡位置；中立人士；中立国；素净色

14. elaborate [ɪˈlæbərət]

    vi. 详尽说明；变得复杂

    vt. 详细制定；详尽阐述；[生理学] 加工；尽心竭力地做

    adj. 精心制作的；精巧的；复杂的；（结构）复杂的

15. succinct [səkˈsɪŋkt]

    adj. 简明的，简洁的，简练的；<古>束紧的，像是用腰带围绕的

16. equalitarian [ɪˌkwɒlɪˈteərɪən]

    adj. 平等主义的

    n. 平等主义者

17. asymmetrical [ˌeɪsɪˈmetrɪkl]

    adj. 不均匀的，不对称的；非对等的

18. subdue [səbˈdjuː]

    vt. 制伏；征服；克制

Task 1　Reading comprehension

Exercise One：Work with your partners, decide whether the following statements are true (T) or false (F) according to what you have learned in the passage.

1. _____ Cultural imprinting is begun at a very early age, therefore some of one culture's knowledge, rules, beliefs, values, phobias, and anxieties are only taught explicitly in childhood.

2. _____ The increased globalization, and the growing domestic workforce, as well as the ethnical and cultural diversity have made intercultural communication very important worldwide business.

3. _____ Generalizations are valid and helpful, so what you will most likely encounter when dealing with members of a particular new culture can be predicated.

Chapter 2 Intercultural Communication

4. _____ High-context cultures leave much of the message unspecified, to be understood through context, non-verbal cues, and between-the-lines interpretation of what is actually said, so it would be difficult to communicate with Arabs if you don't know their communication style.

5. _____ Low-context cultures expect messages to be explicit and specific, therefore there will be no barrier if you speak with people from Germanic and English-speaking countries.

6. _____ Time is universally shared, so different cultures perceive time in similar ways.

7. _____ Sequential cultures think of time as a linear commodity to "spend", "save", or "waste". Everything has to be done quickly one after another.

8. _____ Japanese believe that the individual can influence the future by personal effort, but since there are too many variables in the distant future, they favor a short-term view.

9. _____ Reason and emotion are very personal qualities. It is impossible to hide or control people's feelings because we need to be honest and frank when communicating with others.

10. _____ Hints like "perhaps", "maybe" are always used in indirect communication in order to express to speaber's or writer's thoughts implicitly.

Exercise Two: Fill in the blanks with the words given below and change the form when necessary.

guarantee   succinct   variable   orientation   assumption
subconscious   dominate   cue   volubility   nuanced

1. In intercultural communication, some culture knowledge is learned and most of the information is absorbed _____.

2. Even in the same culture, different individuals cannot be _____ to respond in exactly the same way.

3. The high-context communication is _____ and multi-layered. If the words spoken flow like water, the implicit is the undertow guiding the force, and the explicit is totally visible to the naked eye, like waves.

4. Time _____ can be tend to the past, present, and future in different cultures which may further affect people's behaviors in intercultural communication.

5. Culture is very complex, because there are a lot of unpredictable _____ related culture.

6. Being emotionally neutral can better _____ people's reason and emotion, and keep their feelings carefully controlled and subdued.

7. In some Asian cultures, training for paying attention to minimal _____ and considering the feelings of the other starts in early childhood, because indirectness is also considered to be an elegant style of communication.

8. Comparatively, Northern Europeans often come out as being very direct and straightforward. However, it is only one of the _____ which may turn out to be not so true if they communicate with the Spanish.

9. If metaphors, idioms, and proverbs are common in people's language, so _____ may be considered as their conversational characteristic.

10. Characteristic for the _____ communication style are frequent pauses, silence and "low key" verbal expressions that go to the point.

Task 2　Case study

Case 1

This case occurred in a group of international and American students. The teacher had asked a question about early dating practices, and the Americans all answered with fairly concise statements that made some explicit connection to the question. When a Nigerian in the group replied, however, he began by describing the path through his village, the tree at the end of the path, the storyteller that performed under the tree, and the beginning of a story the storyteller once told. When, in response to the obvious discomfort of the Americans in the group, the teacher asked the Nigerian what he was doing, he said, "I'm answering the question." The American students protested at that, so the teacher asked, "How are you answering the question?" He replied, "I'm telling you everything you need to know to understand the point." "Good," said one of the Americans. "Then if we're just patient, you will eventually tell us the point." "Oh, no," replied the Nigerian. "Once I tell you everything you need to know to understand the point, you will just know what the point is!"

Questions for discussion:

1. Do you think the Nigerian student was answering the teacher's question?

2. What kind of cultural explanation can you provide for the problem in this communication?

Case 2

Le Clerc, an American business man, was undertaking a business project with a Korean company. Everything went well with the project and almost every article was going to be settled until one day when he crossed paths with the head of human resources. During this minutes-long interaction with the head of human resources, Le Clerc mentioned being appreciative of the opportunity to work together with the Korean company. Though the deal was not yet closed, there was no more direct contact related to the project from the Korean company. Le Clerc kept waiting for 3 days to proceed the following negotiation, but nobody showed up. When Le Clerc called back the Korean company, he was told that Le Clerc's American company had turned down this deal and the Korean company had announced the termination of the project officially. Le Clerc was very puzzled and upset. He had never made any formal decision about the this deal and had no idea of what was wrong.

Questions for discussion:

1. Can you help Le Clerc find out the problem in this business case?

2. What kind of cultural conflicts may lead to the failure of this business cooperation?

III After-tasks

Task 1 Movie and culture discussion *Shanghai Calling*

Imagine a steady stream of immigrants, traveling across a vast ocean to a foreign country, searching for new jobs and better lives. But the immigrants are Americans, and the country they are moving to… is China. *Shanghai Calling* is a romantic comedy about modern-day American immigrants in an unfamiliar land. When an ambitious

New York attorney is sent to Shanghai on assignment, he immediately stumbles into a legal mess that could spell the end of his career. Sam Chao (Daniel Henney) is sent to his law firm's Shanghai office to close an important deal. Things go disastrously wrong and he finds his career in jeopardy. But with help from a beautiful relocation specialist, a well-connected foreign businessman, a clever but unassuming journalist, and a street-smart assistant, Sam might just save his job, discover romance, and learn to appreciate the many wonders Shanghai has to offer.

Sam (Henney) is an attorney being promoted at his New York law firm. But first he has to prove himself by handling a tricky client in Shanghai. Sam, born and bred in the US, is ethnically Chinese so his bosses assume he's the right man for the job. It's a setup that almost parallels the inspired *Local Hero* from 1984. There are probably twenty minutes of culture-clash jokes as Sam makes his way to Shanghai.

Amanda (Eliza Coupe) is a relocation specialist. She is in charge of getting Sam settled and oriented. Sam also meets his law-firm assistants (including Zhu Zhu), his American expatriate client (Alan Ruck), and members of the American expat community including fried-chicken entrepreneur Donald Cafferty (Bill Paxton). Sam's first experience with his client turns out to be a mistake, and he spends the rest of the movie trying to correct it. That allows for the introduction of another friend, a private investigator named Awesome Wang (Geng Le) who can help Sam track down key people for his client's case. The formulaic screenplay also has subplots to do with Donald's run for mayor of America town, with the office romances in Sam's firm, and with Sam's increasingly involved relationship with Amanda and her daughter. Interestingly, Amanda's blond-haired daughter is in the same boat as Sam. She too has the "wrong" skin color and is assumed to be foreign, when in fact she is no other country.

Sam has been dispatched to a city, Shanghai, which is widely regarded as one sitting on the cutting edge of global development. It embraces the crazy quilt of tradition and modernity that is 21st-century which is totally different form the past. *Shanghai Calling* doesn't aspire to fresh insight or profundity. But it's nice to see the American migration narrative get out of the house for some fresh air. And if this irresistibly high-spirited confection performs well worldwide. Snobbery and prejudice will be shed, along with ambition. Love will walk in, along with an improved attitude and refreshed ethnic pride.

Questions:
1. Why was Sam's business mission not very successful at the beginning?
2. How did Sam change his strategies of doing business in Shanghai?
3. How would you like to comment on his communication experiences in Shanghai from a cultural perspective?

Task 2 Extended reading

Cultural Differences in Intercultural Friendships

Intercultural friendships are likely as old as human cultures. Human tribes had neighbors, and world history is rife with migrations to distant lands. We can assume that friendships across cultural lines were formed at least occasionally.

Throughout recorded history, in literature, film, and the performing arts, "odd couples" and "unlikely friendships" have captured the imagination. Whether fictional or biographical, and whether in form of relationships that bridge a divide or as alliances for a common cause, friendships between dissimilar individuals make for interesting narratives. It was not until the 20th century, however, that opportunities for intercultural-friendship formation became common place and scholars in communication studies and other social sciences began to study such relationships.

According to the similarity-attraction effect, people tend to form relationships on the basis of similarity, including similarity in values, interests, age, gender, race, educational level, and religion. The tendency is especially pronounced in cultures with high self-esteem and relational mobility. In cultures, for example Japan, where relationships are generally formed within enduring in groups, similar individual attributes play a lesser role.

Additionally, when we interact with people from our own culture, their behaviors are largely consistent with our expectations and therefore easy to predict. Cultural similarity thus gives attributional confidence. When we meet culturally dissimilar people, however, our expectations (e. g. , of language and nonverbal behavior) may not be fulfilled—a process described in the expectancy violation theory. The extent of the violation depends on the degree of difference between the cultures at hand. While some cultures are relatively similar in aspects, such as communication patterns, value orientations, and customs (e. g. , the United States and Canada), others differ markedly (e. g. , the United States and China). The anxiety and uncertainty frequently accompanying interactions with dissimilar strangers can be alleviated by eliciting and providing self-disclosure. In communication theory, these processes find expression in the uncertainty reduction theory and in the anxiety uncertainty management theory. Additionally, the social penetration theory explains that self-disclosure allows interactants to move from the orientation and exploratory stages of relationship development, when cultural differences are most salient, to the affective and stable stages when relationships have a personalized focus and cultural dissimilarities retreat into the background. Once interactants have formed a friendship, a relational identity also emerges. While cultural difference may be less salient at this stage, it will remain important for the interactants to balance their own cultural identities with this new relational identity.

Of special interest in intercultural-friendship formation are cultural differences that have direct impact on the early stages of social penetration. Foremost, these are differences in communication and friendship patterns. Much of the cross-cultural literature on communication patterns focuses on the difference between collectivism in the East and individualism in the West. In highly collectivistic cultures, the social relationships into which one is born are also the source of one's friendships. As a result, there is less need for the friendship initiation skills that are required in individualistic cultures (including small talk). In addition, communication in the collectivistic cultures of Asia is high context (i. e. , more implicit and less verbal than the low-context communication common in individualistic cultures). East Asians make up the largest contingent of international students in individualistic Anglophone countries worldwide but reportedly have the fewest host-national friends. Some of the difficulty in establishing relationships with host nationals derives from the limited importance of communication initiation skills and verbal expressiveness in their home cultures.

The lower levels of verbal ability in East Asia also affect self-disclosure in friendships. In addition, self-disclosure in East Asia is regulated due to the importance of saving face, for example, found that both rate and amount of self-disclosure in Japan are more modest than in the United States. Friendships in India are enacted through self-suppression (disclosure avoidance). This is in contrast to the United States, where they are enacted through self-expression. (American extensive talk and the direct expression of viewpoints were perceived unfavorably by the Indian respondents in Hastings' study.) In a somewhat related vein, a greater number of taboo topics in conversations of Chinese versus British students. The tendency toward revealing interpersonal exchanges common in the West is avoided in the East. Similarly, nonverbal expressions of intimacy are more subdued in East Asia. Conversational constraints theory suggests that individualists are concerned with clarity, whereas collectivists are concerned with others' feelings and want to minimize imposition.

Cultures also differ in the expression of support. For instance, while Americans use verbal and nonverbal expressions of appreciation evenly, Chinese favor nonverbal expression. Likewise, scholarship comparing love expression between the United States and other cultures has shown that verbal expression of affection, including toward friends, is more common in the United States than elsewhere.

Cultural degrees of expressiveness also find an explanation emotionality versus neutrality orientation. In affective cultures (e.g., Kuwait, Egypt, Spain), people display emotions freely and outwardly; in neutral cultures (e.g., Ethiopia, Japan, Poland), emotion expression is controlled. It should be noted that expressiveness is not only linked to culture but also to gender. The traditional image in the United States, for example, is of females spending time with friends in intimate conversation whereas males prefer activities, such as sports. In some cultures, gender differences mirror this image: East Asian women are less guarded in self-disclosure than men; Kenyan females use more nonverbal immediacy than males; women in Brazil expect more emotional involvement in friendships than men. Some cultures, however, show no gender differences concerning friendship-related communication. For example, there is no difference between women and men in India in overall disclosure, activities, and how they loved their friends.

Focusing largely on the friendship experiences of international students studying abroad, numerous benefits of intercultural-friendship formation have been identified, including stronger language skills, greater life satisfaction, lower levels of stress, and enhanced perceptions of the host country. Despite these benefits, the lack of friendship between sojourners and host nationals is a common finding and a concern for the many educational institutions worldwide that are attempting to internationalize. Therefore, factors that influence intercultural-friendship formation have been focused and, increasingly, on measures for promoting intercultural friendship.

First among the factors affecting the development of intercultural friendships is cultural difference. Cultural similarity provides attributional confidence and reduces uncertainty; that is, interactants can more easily predict and explain behaviors in people who are similar to them. Highly dissimilar cultures often exhibit differences in communication patterns, value dimensions, and friendship styles that can impede relationship development, especially in the orientation and exploratory stages of social penetration, during which cultural complexities are most critical. Another prominent factor is the interactants' motivation to form relationships across cultural lines. In one of the prime arenas for intercultural contact, international student exchange, for example, sojourners seeking cultural knowledge and personal growth generally have more interest in interaction and friendships with host nationals than students who are task oriented and focus on education for better career prospects after returning home. Similarly, host environment factors, such as host receptivity (ranging from welcoming attitudes to discrimination) influence the likelihood with which intercultural friendships are formed. Other factors affecting intercultural-friendship formation include communicative competence, intercultural sensitivity, and aspects of identity and personality (e. g. , cultural versus personal identification, empathy, and open-mindedness). Among measures for promoting intercultural-friendship formation are infrastructures that facilitate proximity and frequency of contact, provide foreign language training, support experience abroad, and offer intercultural education and training to further intercultural competence and the appreciation of difference.

More than ever, people from different cultures meet and have the opportunities to form close relationships. To overcome thresholds along the way requires the motivation, skills, and knowledge of both sojourners and hosts. Being a key catalyst for optimal intergroup contact and prejudice reduction, intercultural friendship holds the promise not only for individual enrichment but as a means to grow international good will and build peace. (1295 words)

(Adapted from Elisabeth Gareis, "Communication and Culture, Interpersonal Communication")

Critical thinking questions:

1. How is intercultural friendship different from intercultural relationship?

2. What could be the most difficult problem in making intercultural friends?

3. How do you understand the function of social penetration in intercultural friendship?

Chapter 3

Verbal Intercultural Communication

"Careful with fire," is good advice, we know; "Careful with words," is ten times doubly so.

—Will Carleton

People with communicative competence should know when, where and what to speak to whom and how.

—D. Hymes

Section I What is communication

I Pre-tasks

Task 1 Talk or communication

Read the following situation and try to answer the following questions: What is the difference in meaning between "talk" and "communicate"? What does the wife mean?

A wife and her husband are sitting in their living room, both of them look very upset. Here are their dialogues:

Husband: "I don't know why you always complain I don't talk to you, I keep on talking with you, what do you really want?"

Wife: "Yes, George. I know you can talk, but I want you to communicate."

Task 2 Picture analysis

Look at the following picture and try to answer the following questions:
A. Is it possible to perceive the world as other people perceive it?
B. Why do people differ in the manner in which they communicate?
C. Can communication patterns be changed?

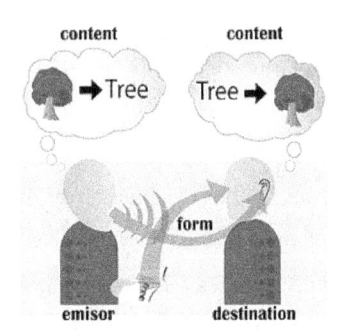

II While-tasks

Communication and Communication Skills

The ability to communicate effectively is important in relationships, education and work. Here are some steps and tips to help you develop good communication skills.

Anyone who wants to improve communication skills needs to understand the basics of communication skills, knowing what communication really is. Creating relationships through careful communication is the process of transferring signals/messages between a sender and a receiver through various methods (written words, nonverbal cues, spoken words). It is also the mechanism we use to establish and modify relationships. Besides, you should have courage to say what you think. Be confident in knowing that you can make worthwhile contributions to conversation. Take time each day to be aware of your opinions and feelings so you can adequately convey them to others. Individuals who are hesitant to speak because they do not feel their input would be worthwhile need not fear. What is important or worthwhile to one person may not be to another and may be more so to someone else.

Developing advanced communication skills begins with simple interactions. Communication skills can be practiced every day in settings that range from the social to the professional. New skills take time to refine, but each time you use your communication skills, you open yourself to opportunities and future partnerships.

Engaging Your Audience

Look at people in the eye. (Make eye contact.) Whether you are speaking or listening, looking into the eyes of the person with whom you are conversing can make the interaction more successful. Eye contact conveys interest and encourages your partner to be interested in you in return.

One technique to help with this is to consciously look into one of the listeners' eyes and then move to the other eyes. Going back and forth between the two makes your eyes appear to sparkle. Another trick is to imagine a letter "T" on the listener's face, with the crossbar being an imaginary line across the eye brows and the vertical line coming down the center of the nose. Keep your eyes scanning that "T" zone.

Use gestures. These include gestures with your hands and face. Make your whole body talk. Use smaller gestures for individuals and small groups. The gestures should get larger as the group that one is addressing increases in size.

Don't send mixed messages. Make your words, gestures, facial expressions and tone match. Disciplining someone while smiling sends a mixed message and is therefore ineffective. If you have to deliver a negative message, make your words, facial expressions, and tone match the message.

Be aware of what your body is saying. (Communicate with Body Language.) Body language can say so much more than a mouthful of words. An open stance with arms relaxed at your sides tells anyone around you that you are approachable and open to hearing what they have to say.

Arms crossed and shoulders hunched, on the other hand, suggest disinterest in conversation or unwillingness to communicate. Often, communication can be stopped before it starts by body language that tells people you don't want to talk.

Improve your posture appropriately and an approachable stance can make even difficult conversations flow more smoothly.

Manifest constructive attitudes and beliefs. The attitudes you bring to communication will have a huge impact on the way you compose yourself and interact with others. Choose to Be Honest, Be Patient, Be Optimistic, Be Sincere, Respectful, and Accepting of Others. Be Sensitive to Other People's Feelings and Believe in Others' Competence.

Develop effectively. First, try to be a Good Listener, not only should one be able to speak effectively, one must listen to the other person's words and engage in communication on what the other person is speaking about. Avoid the impulse to listen only for the end of their sentence so that you can blurt out the ideas or memories your mind while the other person is speaking.

Using Your Words

Enunciate your words. Speak clearly and don't mumble. If people are always asking you to repeat yourself, try to do a better job of articulating yourself in a better manner.

Pronounce your words correctly. People will judge your competency through your vocabulary. If you aren't sure of how to say a word, don't use it. Improve your vocabulary by reading new words in daily routine.

Use the right words. If you're not sure of the meaning of a word, don't use it. Grab a dictionary and start a daily habit of learning one new word per day. Use it sometime in your conversations during the day.

Slow your speech down. People will perceive you as nervous and unsure of yourself if you talk fast. However, be careful not to slow down to the point where people begin to finish your sentences just to help you finish.

Develop your voice. A high or whiny voice is not perceived to be one of authority. In fact, a high and soft voice can make you sound like prey to an aggressive coworker or make others not take you seriously. Begin doing exercises to lower the pitch of your voice. Try singing, but do it an octave lower on all your favorite songs. Practice this and, after a period of time, your voice will begin to lower.

Animate your voice. Avoid a monotone and use dynamics. Your pitch should raise and lower periodically. Radio DJ's are usually a good example of this.

Use appropriate volume. Use a volume that is appropriate for the setting. Speak more softly when you are alone and close. Speak louder when you are speaking to larger groups or across larger spaces.

Except what are mentioned above, here are some tips which will help you to improve communication skills:

Tips

Try to speak fluently and try to make sure people can hear you when you speak.

A good speaker is a good listener.

Do not interrupt or talk over the other person—it breaks the flow of conversation. Timing is important.

Use appropriate volume for your conversation setting.

Get feedback from your receiver(s) to ensure you were properly understood during your conversation.

Have confidence when talking, it doesn't matter what other people think.

Make sure you're using proper grammar.

Don't over-praise yourself in front of your audience.

Avoid thinking that whatever you say is always correct.

Make eye contact when speaking and listening.

If you want good communication skills, first be confident and do not stammer in front of people. Try socializing more with people. This will give you the idea how to talk with different people.

Practice makes your communication get better and better.

To improve your body language, practice what you're going to say in front of a mirror.

Practice speaking in public places.

In a word, there are many methods to improve communication skills, as long as we grasp the skills, it will be easier for us to communicate well. (1143 words)

(Adapted from http://www.ehow.com/how_5067247_manage-verbal-intercultural-communication-effectively.html)

Word list:

1. mechanism ['mek(ə)nɪz(ə)m]

    n. 机制；原理，途径；进程；机械装置；技巧

2. modify ['mɒdɪfaɪ]

    vi. 被修饰；修改

    vt. 改变，减轻，减缓；[语] 修饰，(用变音符号) 改变

3. hesitant ['hezɪtənt]

    adj. 踌躇的；犹豫的，迟疑的；吞吞吐吐的

4. trick [trɪk]
    n. 戏法，把戏；计谋；诀窍；骗局；恶作剧
    vt. 哄骗，欺骗；打扮
    adj. 弄虚作假的；有诀窍的；欺诈的
5. hunch [hʌntʃ]
    n. 预感，直觉；肉峰
    v. 隆起；向前移动
6. stance [stæns]
    n. 态度，立场；站姿，被放置的姿势；位置；（运动员的）始发姿势
7. competence [ˈkɒmpɪtəns]
    n. 能力；技能；相当的资产
8. mumble [ˈmʌmbl]
    vt. & vi. 咕哝；抿着嘴嚼
    n. 含糊的话；咕哝
9. manifest [ˈmænɪfest]
    vt. 显示，表明；证明；使显现
    adj. 明白的，明显的
    n. 货单；旅客名单
10. monotone [ˈmɒnətəʊn]
    n. 单调的语调，单调的声音
    adj. 发单调音的；单色的
    vt. 单调地读
11. animate [ˈænɪmeɪt]
    vt. 使有生气；驱动；使栩栩如生地动作；赋予……以生命
    adj. 有生命的，活的；有生气的，生气勃勃的
12. dynamic [daɪˈnæmɪk]
    adj. 动态的；动力的，动力学的；充满活力的，精力充沛的；不断变化的，充满变数的
    n. 动态；动力，动力学；活力

Task 1 Reading comprehension

Exercise One：Work with your pantners and decide whether the following statements are true (T) or false (F) according to what you have learned in the passage.

1. _____ The ability to communicate effectively is important in relationships.
2. _____ To improve your body language, practice what you're going to say in front of a mirror.
3. _____ Have confidence when talking, but it does matter what other people think.
4. _____ Improve posture and an approachable stance cannot make even difficult conversations flow more smoothly.
5. _____ Grammar is not important in dialogues.
6. _____ A good speaker is a good listener.
7. _____ People can communicate without using body language.
8. _____ looking into the eyes of the person with whom you are conversing can make the interaction more successful.
9. _____ Multiple factors can influence nonverbal communication.
10. _____ We should avoid touching others while talking.

Exercise Two: Choose the right answer according to your understanding of this passage:

( ) Which of the following is not mentioned by the writer?

A. Practice speaking in public places.

B. Always thinking that whatever you say is always correct.

C. Make eye contact when speaking and listening.

D. Use appropriate volume for your conversation setting.

Exercise Three: Fill in the blanks with the words given below and change the form when necessary.

contribution   authority   sensitive   pitch   engage

impact   interrupt   worthwhile   modify   aware

1. The attitudes you bring to communication will have a huge _____ on the way you compose yourself and interact with others.

2. Do not _____ or talk over the other person—it breaks the flow of conversation.

3. A high or whiny voice is not perceived to be one of _____.

4. One must listen to the other person's words and _____ in communication on what the other person is speaking about.

5. Be confident in knowing that you can make worthwhile _____ to conversation.

6. Begin doing exercises to lower the _____ of your voice.

7. Be _____ to other people's feelings and believe in others' competence.

8. Be _____ of what your body is saying. Body language can say so much more than a mouthful of words.

9. What is important or _____ to one person may not be to another and may be more so to someone else.

10. We use communication to establish and _____ relationships.

Task 2 Case study

Case 1: Shoes for Street Walking

It is said that in Rome, in front of a shoe store, there was such a sign to attract English-speaking customers: Shoes for street walking. Come in and have a fit. The sign caught the attention of many English-speaking tourists, but not to look at the shoes displayed in the windows, but to read the sign and then break out into laughter. The Italian shop owner did not realize that "a street walker" means a prostitute, while "to have a fit" does not mean to have a try, but to become suddenly and violently angry or upset. No wonder the amusement and laughter! (Deng Yanchang et al., 1989)

Questions for discussion:
1. Why did the Italian shop owner make such a blunder?
2. If you were the shop owner, how would you change the sign to attract customers?

Case 2: A Misunderstanding Caused by a Joke

Roger was the Personnel Executive of a larger American multinational firm. In 1996, Roger was working in Brazil to help promote their business. One evening, there was a party, attended by both his employees from the United States and many Brazilian business people. At the party, Roger bumped into Rosalita, a Brazilian woman he had known for some time. Roger generally had a very good impression on Rosalita and always felt at ease with her, so that he felt free to tell jokes and share personal thoughts, and talk about Brazil and Brazilian life without having the jitters of offending Rosalita. During the party, Rosalita said to Roger, "I'd like to introduce you to one of my good friends, she is a very capable woman and is presently thinking of working in a joint venture so she can provide a better living for her large family. She is very much interested in your company." Hearing that, Roger smiled and replied, "OK, but I just hope I don't get hustled." Unfortunately, Roger's reply made Rosalita quite upset. Very soon she excused herself as politely as she could, and did not speak with Roger for the rest of the evening.

Questions for discussion:

1. Why was Roger confused by Rosalita's behavior? Could you give him an explanation?

2. Do you know what happened between Roger and Rosalita?

III After-tasks

Task 1 Movie and culture discussion *The Joy Luck Club*

The Joy Luck Club is a stunning literary achievement, it explores the tender and tenacious bond between four daughters and their mothers. The daughters know one side of their mothers, but they don't know about their earlier never-spoken of lives in China. The mothers want love and obedience from their daughters, but they don't know the gifts that the daughters keep to themselves. Heartwarming and bittersweet, this is a novel for mother, daughters, and those that love them. The reality requires the second generation to revalue and look for their cultural root. Through the cultural conflict with Chinese mothers, American daughters recognize the root of Chinese tradition and its cultural heritage. The conciliation between the mothers and the daughters by the end of the novel symbolizes the harmonious coexistence of the Chinese culture and the American culture.

There are several phenomena we can't ignore. First, it reflects the differences between traditional Chinese way of education and American education methods. Chinese mothers expect their children to bring them honor, they criticize more and praise less. Chinese parents are more caring, protective. They prefer collectivism-oriented culture value, mutual responsibility and obligation between family members. They always make all arrangements for their children and have high expectations for their children. While American parents like to encourage children to try new things, make their own choices, think independently and creatively, and to do what they want to do. In the way of expressing love, Americans like to hug and kiss and say "I love you." "I'm so proud of you.", while Chinese parents like to cook various delicious food, or use bugging, warning and criticism to show their love to children. Second, it reflects a Taoism philosophy of fatalism which could make people neither fall into great rejoicing when in easy circumstances, not become too sorrowful when in unfavorable situations. Directed by this philosophy of life, the four mothers could forget their misfortunes and all kinds of fears either before or after they came to the USA. Anyway, they could find their happiness. Third, it reflects the mother's good wish for her daughter, "In America I will have a daughter just like me. But over there nobody will say her worth is measured by the loudness of her husband's belch. Over there nobody will look down on her, because I will make her speak only perfect American English. And over there she will always be too full to swallow any sorrow! The mother's dreams were not totally turned into reality. They met some challenges in America, especially how to deal with the relationship between them and their daughters. Thanks to the philosophy of fatalism, the four mothers could face the problems in front of them and their daughters calmly. Besides, this movies also reflect some traditional Chinese cultures, for example, Chinese Feng Shui; the theory of five elements: gold, wood, water, fire, earth. Rose is "without wood", which means that she tends to listen to others and unable to stand on her own; it also reflects the Chinese spirit culture. In the movie, a spirit helped Lindo run away from her unhappy marriage, and a vengeful spirit blessed Anmei.

After watching it, please answer the following questions:
1. What does the theme of the film show to us?
2. What do you think of Yingying's marriage?
3. What are the cultural mistakes committed by Rich?

Task 2 Extended reading

How to Use Words Effectively in Public Speaking

An effective public speaker clearly expresses an idea in a way that keeps the audience interested. A skilled public speaker can inspire people with words. The best public speakers possess an extensive vocabulary, good knowledge of grammar, correct pronunciation and varied sentence length. The effective use of words in public speaking is a skill that you can learn. Learning a few simple tools, increasing your vocabulary and practicing can greatly improve your use of words in public speaking.

Vary the length of your sentences. Use short sentences to emphasize a point and longer sentences when explaining a point. Simple sentences effectively introduce a topic. Longer sentences help when expanding upon an idea or explaining a concept. There are no strict rules about sentence length. A good rule is to end a sentence when you express a complete idea. Too many short sentences will result in monotonous speech. Sentences that are too long will confuse the audience.

Use varied sentence structure that takes full advantage of the different parts of speech. Sentences that are well-constructed will result in a speech that is easy to understand. Simple and compound sentences and the use of conjunctions can help keep the audience's attention. Introductory and propositional phrases can help clarify your thoughts for better communication of your ideas.

Demonstrate your vocabulary by using synonyms in place of trite expressions. An audience will become bored quickly if your speech contains too many commonly used phrases. Refrain from phrases such as "in other words" and "on the other hand". Learn to use synonyms for common words and phrases to develop your ability to convey your ideas in an attention-grabbing way. An audience will remember a speech that is original.

Tell a humorous story to break the ice or to introduce a subject that may be difficult to discuss. The best public speakers use humor effectively to get the audience's attention and to hold it throughout the speech. Listeners will remember a funny story. According to the Advanced Public Speaking Institute, business leaders and politicians use humor in their speeches because it is effective. Humor helps to get your audience's attention and makes you more likable to your listeners.

Even if you're not interested in a career as a public figure, you may find yourself having to speak publicly in front of a group or crowd. You want to make a good impression and have the audience listen to you, so try these tips to increase your chances of a great public speaking experience. You have to know what you're talking about before you can present the topic to other people if you want them to share your interest. Know your subject well, so that your speech comes across as informative and presented by someone who is comfortable discussing it.

Practice your speech in front of a mirror. Use a timer to make sure you stay within the time frame. Enlist the help of family or friends and have them listen to make sure you avoid awkward pauses or too many "um's". They can also alert you if you appear stiff or uncomfortable. Practice as many times as it takes for you to feel secure in your speech.

Get acquainted with the room you'll be in beforehand. Walk around it, practice speaking in it and stand on the stage or behind the podium to get a feel for it. Get familiar with the microphone or any props you'll use during your speech. Meet and greet the audience beforehand if possible. Stand by the door and greet people as they file into the room. You may feel more comfortable addressing them from a stage if their faces look familiar to you. Visualize yourself giving a great speech and the audience applauding. Sometimes just putting a successful picture in your mind is enough to calm your nerves.

Before opening your mouth to speak, take a calming breath and count to 2 or 3 if needed. You want to speak slowly and not rush through your words. If you find yourself feeling nervous during your speech, stop and breathe before continuing. You want to succeed; your audience wants that too. Believe that you and the group want the same thing—a speech full of information and entertainment. Speak confidently and clearly and your audience will believe that you have the authority to discuss your subject. If you make a mistake while speaking, don't call attention to it. Chances are the audience didn't notice. Take a moment to compose yourself and move on.

Instead of focusing on how many people you're addressing, focus on your message and how important it is. If you concentrate on what you're talking about, you're less likely to worry about how you look or sound.

Finally, learn from this public speaking experience. Afterward, ask yourself what went well and what didn't. Analyze how you can improve for your next speech.

Critical thinking questions:
1. Why do we need public speaking?
2. How to improve the ability of using words in public speaking?
3. If you make a mistake in a public speaking, what will you do?

Section II Verbal Communication

I Pre-tasks

Task 1 Talking with your friends

You and your friends probably have several examples of shorthand words and phrases for reminding one another of events, feelings, or people who populate your relational history. You may also have special nicknames for people known only to you and your partner or close friends.

Questions:
1. What are some examples of these words, phrases, and names, and what do they tell you about your relationships?

2. Have you ever been the "out-of-towner" in a group of friends, where did you not understand shorthand words or phrases and needed them to be explained to you?

Task 2　Analyzing everyday communication

Think about a situation where you overheard two people talking and you could tell—you just knew—that they were not close but that one of them was trying to impress the other and get into a relationship with him or her.

Questions:

1. What did you notice that made you sure you were right about the person doing the "impressing"?

2. How did you know whether or not the other person was impressed?

II　While-tasks

How to Manage Verbal Intercultural Communication Effectively

The global nature of today's business environment requires a whole new set of communication skills for effective intercultural business communication. Ineffective intercultural communication can cost companies money and cause hard feelings among staff but a few simple techniques can finetune communication skills for the global audience instructions.

Assess the language knowledge of your audience, if possible, and plan accordingly. People who don't speak the language will obviously need interpreters.

Use simple words and avoid jargon as much as possible. Big words require more translation and usually involve a complex sentence structure, which can confuse nonnative speakers. Intercultural communication is about being understood so keep it simple.

Repeat key concepts using different words to allow for different levels of vocabulary knowledge and increased comprehension. The first time something is said, nonnative speakers translate it; the second time, they verify their translation is correct; the third time, they actually internalize the message. This is not to say that you should repeat things ad nauseam but you should attempt to work in multiple reviews of important information.

Create visual aids for presentations and include text emphasizing the main idea. Communication is enhanced when you use a variety of methods to reach an audience. Text and pictures give nonnative speakers another way to absorb the message beyond listening. If possible, give audience members copies of the visual aids so they can make notes and follow along.

Be clear and specific. Don't assume. Assign tasks or projects to specific individuals along with due dates. Productive intercultural business communication avoids ambiguity.

Speak and enunciate slowly. Remember, your audience has to translate everything you say, which means they will always lag a few seconds behind; thus, good intercultural business communication allows for a translation time delay.

Check with the audience frequently to be sure there are no questions and that everyone is following the message. Encourage questions or an upraised hand when clarification is needed.

Follow up all verbal communication with written confirmation. This is especially true for action items. Putting things in writing allows nonnative speakers to sit down with a language dictionary and digest information at their own pace. It also avoids confusion about who is responsible for what or what needs to be done as the next step.

Open meetings with a greeting in the participants' native language. Showing respect for someone's culture predisposes them to be open to your message. Effective intercultural communication establishes a tone of respect and uses culture as a bridge to build positive working relationships.

Know what is considered rude and polite in other cultures. For example, presenting business cards with both hands and a shallow bow is considered polite in Asian cultures. This is obviously a great contrast to Americans, who sometimes even casually scoot business cards down the conference table to avoid getting up.

The Advantages of Intercultural Communication

Global interconnectivity has made intercultural communication critical for any organization. Intercultural communication takes place with people of different cultures discussing and communicating. Businesses intending to operate globally should invest in intercultural training for their staff to enjoy the immense benefits. Effective intercultural communication produces benefits such as employee teamwork and productivity.

Productivity and Proficiency

Intercultural communication helps employees from different ethnic backgrounds to communicate effectively with one another. It also guides the management competencies to design policies that incorporate the diversity in the team, allowing every member to be productive and proficient in their tasks. Since employees are well trained in intercultural communication, it eliminates misunderstanding and dissatisfaction that may arise if employees' needs are not put into consideration while developing policies, planning for meetings, and designing incentive schemes. Satisfied employees are able to focus on their duties, thereby increasing productivity.

Teamwork

Intercultural communication fosters teamwork in an organization. It helps staff to understand each other's cultural differences, and to communicate effectively without misunderstanding. With successful intercultural communication, employees understand the influence of culture on people's behaviors and communication tendencies. This enhances teamwork, as colleagues respect one another's cultural background, unique talents and capabilities, which is key to the smooth running of business. Since employees are aware of their colleagues' cultural influences, intercultural communication eliminates stereotyping—a danger to effective communication and team work.

Global Business Edge

Successful intercultural communication gives an organization a global business edge. Training employees in intercultural communication gives an organization successful negotiation skills in the global market of diverse cultures. A company venturing its business in Africa will have a receptive welcome if it understands important cultural factors crucial to business transactions. Some cultural traits important to transacting business in Africa are time, religion, handshakes, communication tactics and respect towards seniors. A company that understands the importance of cross-cultural communication has advantages in launching its business globally over a company that has not invested in it.

Effective Leadership

Intercultural communication also fosters effective leadership in an organization. Modern organizations are composed of diverse people, and managers are expected to lead their teams by creating understanding of the company's policies while accommodating the diverse views of his team. A company that equips its leadership team in intercultural training enables them to motivate their teams, regardless of their cultural background. Intercultural training builds effective communication, which is a step toward effective leadership.

Effective Communication in a Multicultural Workforce

The culture in which a person grows up helps shape his/her identity, personality and values. A person's culture also partially dictates how he/she communicates and interprets messages. Intercultural communication skills are vital in today's globalized business world, where a workforce could comprise employees from various cultures, all with different communication styles.

Basics of Multicultural Communication

Multicultural communication requires an awareness of the principles and viewpoints of people in other cultures. Successful multicultural communicators realize that values are sometimes judged "right" or "wrong" depending on the cultural background, so communication must remain open and flexible. Some communication happens on a nonverbal level—e. g. , physical and facial behavior cues—so communicators should be especially sensitive to these cues.

Cultural Contexts

Multicultural communicators understand the variety of contexts that cultures comprise. For example, even gender can be thought of as a cultural divide, because males and females have different cultural experiences. The divide between gender experience narrows in some cultures and widens in others. Other cultural contexts include race, ethnicity, national or regional origin, physical ability, sexual orientation, social class, religion and age. Each person's individual cultural context provides a unique worldview that enriches the workforce discussion.

Nonverbal Communication

Nonverbal cues help when language is a barrier to communication, though it's important to remember that sometimes gestures mean something different to each culture. Fidgeting while another talks is a sign of impatience across most cultures and may appear rude. For Americans, eye contact is a sign of focused attention, but in many cultures, such as Japanese, Latin American and some African cultures, lowering eyes represents respect for an elder or superior. The "thumbs up" sign gives approval for Americans, but to Greeks it's a vulgar gesture on a par with the "middle finger". Research into appropriate nonverbal communication practices helps keep the multicultural workplace running smoothly.

Language Nuances

Conversational style and subtle variations occur even when no language barrier-exists. For example, Americans accept exaggeration as part of communication, especially in advertising and sales, while the British tend to understate and many Germans will outright reject statements that aren't literally true. While compliments are a positive way to express friendliness, they may be received differently in various cultural contexts. Women may see a compliment as inappropriate, especially if the compliment focuses on an aspect of their physical appearance or dress. Awareness and respect for these nuances help ensure that the intended message is conveyed in the multicultural workforce. (1283 words)

(Adapted from http://www.ehow.com/how_5067247_manage-verbal-intercultural-communication-effectively.html)

Word list:

1. finetune [faɪntjuːn]
   vt. 调整，对进行微调；使有规则
2. jargon [ˈdʒɑːgən]
   n. 行话，行业术语；黑话
3. ad nauseam [ˌædˈnɔːziæm]
   adv. 令人作呕地；（因重复而）令人厌烦地
4. predispose [ˌpriːdɪˈspəʊz]
   vt. 使预先有倾向；使易接受；使倾向于做；使易于患（病）
5. digest [daɪˈdʒest]
   vt. & vi. 消化；整理
   vt. 吸收；领悟；玩味
   vi. 消化；吸收食物；[化学] 加热
   n. 文摘；摘要；法律汇编；罗马法典
6. immense [ɪˈmens]
   adj. 极大的，巨大的；浩瀚的，无边际的；<口>非常好的；弘道

7. eliminate [ɪˈlɪmɪneɪt]

   vt. 排除，消除；淘汰；除掉；<口>干掉

8. trait [treɪt]

   n. 特点，特性；少许

9. vulgar [ˈvʌlgə(r)]

   adj. 庸俗的，俚俗的，粗俗的；一般大众的，老百姓的；粗野的，下流的

10. outright [ˈaʊtraɪt]

    adv. 完全地，彻底地；坦率地，不客气地；即刻，马上

    adj. 完全的，彻底的；直率的；明白的；总共的

11. ethnicity [eθˈnɪsɪtɪ]

    n. 种族地位，种族特点，种族渊源

12. fidgeting [ˈfɪdʒɪtɪŋ]

    v. 坐立不安，烦躁（fidget 的现在分词）

13. nuance [ˈnjuːɑːns]

    n. 细微差别；细微的表情

Task 1 Reading comprehension

Exercise One: Work with your partners, decide whether the following statements are true (T) or false (F) according to what you have learned in the passage.

1. _____ Global interconnectivity has made intercultural communication critical for any organization.

2. _____ Some cultural traits important to transacting business in Africa are time, religion, handshakes, communication tactics and respect towards seniors.

3. _____ If you make a mistake while speaking, you should call attention to it.

4. _____ The British accept exaggeration as part of communication, especially in advertising and sales, while the Americans tend to understate and many Germans will outright reject statements that aren't literally true.

5. _____ The "thumbs up" sign gives approval for Americans, but to Greeks it's a vulgar gesture on a par with the "middle finger".

6. _____ It's important to remember that sometimes gestures mean something different to each culture.

Chapter 3 Verbal Intercultural Communication

7. _____ Big words require more translation and usually involve a simple sentence structure.

8. _____ Intercultural communication helps employees from different ethnic backgrounds to communicate effectively with one another.

9. _____ We use symbols to explain meanings.

10. _____ People learn about communication during lifetime.

Exercise Two: Choose the right answer according to your understanding of this passage:

(　　) Which of the following is NOT mentioned by the writer?

A. The culture in which a person grows up helps shape his identity, personality and values.

B. Women may see a compliment as inappropriate, especially if the compliment focuses on an aspect of their physical appearance or dress.

C. With successful intercultural communication, employees understand the influence of culture on people's behaviors and communication tendencies.

D. Follow up all nonverbal communication with written confirmation.

Exercise Three: Fill in the blanks with the words given below and change the form when necessary.

gender　　vital　　enhanced　　attempt　　expanding
compliment　　complex　　eliminates　　diverse　　frequently

1. Big words require more translation and usually involve a _____ sentence structure, which can confuse nonnative speakers.

2. Longer sentences help when _____ upon an idea or explaining a concept.

3. Women may see a _____ as inappropriate, especially if it focuses on an aspect of their physical appearance or dress.

4. Even _____ can be thought of as a cultural divide, because males and females have different cultural experiences.

5. Intercultural communication skills are _____ in today's globalized business world.

6. Since employees are well trained in intercultural communication, it _____ misunderstanding and dissatisfaction.

7. Training employees in intercultural communication gives an organization successful negotiation skills in the global market of _____ cultures.

8. Check with the audience _____ to be sure there are no questions and that everyone is following the message.

9. Communication is _____ when you use a variety of methods to reach an audience.

10. You should _____ to work in multiple reviews of important information.

Task 2 Case study

Case 1: Look out

A foreign student in the US was sitting by a window reading a book. She heard someone yelling "look out", so she stuck her head out of the window. Just then a board hurtled down from above, narrowly missing her. She looked up, half in anger and half in fright. There was a man on the roof doing repairs. "Didn't you hear me call 'look out'?" he demanded. "Yes, and that's what I did," she replied.

Questions for discussion:

1. In this case, what does "look out" mean?
2. Could you give a similar case like this?
3. Can you list some phrases about the word "look"?

Case 2: John, an American from California, has received a very high-paying teaching position in an all-male private school in Saudi Arabia. Because he wants to make a good impression and have his students like him, he goes from student to student, introduces himself, and shakes hands in the same manner he used when he taught in California. The next day the dean of students calls John into his office and asks him to leave the school.

Questions for discussion:

1. Do you know what happened and why?
2. If this same situation happened in China, would John be fired? Why?

III After-tasks

The Pursuit of Happiness

Task 1 Movie and culture discussion *The Pursuit of Happiness*

The Pursuit of Happiness—the title comes from a misspelled schoolhouse mural—has a lot on its mind but mostly this: If America is about the promise of bettering oneself, why does it have to be so freaking hard? In the movie, Jefferson's Declaration of Independence words about happiness kept recurring to Chris Gardner. Every day, Christ had to work hard from morning till night, but still could hardly make a living. Chris saw a bunch of suits, mostly male, pouring out of the Dean Witter Reynolds brokerage firm in downtown San Francisco. They all looked "happy". "Why not me?" Christ wondered. He did have an adorable boy, Christopher, but wife Linda was becoming a scarecrow of overworked anxiety. Finally, his wife left Christ because of life pressure, leaving him and her five-year-old son, Christopher. And naturally, Christ became a single father. With the failure of his business, Christ had no money to pay for the rent, so they were driven away from the flat. They became homeless. They slept in asylum, subway station, public bathroom or anywhere as a temporary shelter. The destitution of life was absolutely depressing, but for his son's future, for his own belief, Christ never gave up and he still strongly believed that happiness would come one day if he worked hard enough today. With his great efforts, Christ won a six-month internship at Dean Witter, but there was no pay at all. So on one hand, Christ had to work hard to make a living; on the other hand, he had to fight for his intern work, since only one of the twenty interns would succeed finally. Besides, he had to take good care of his son after day care. However, Christ made it with his amazing willpower. Christ was unfortunate, for he got a wife who was not understandable at all (though she has her own difficulties) and was in bad luck with his business. But he was very fortunate also, for he got a son who was very thoughtful and tough life experiences always make a great person. This is a story of a stockbroker named Chris Gardner who faced homelessness, poverty, and the responsibility of raising a child singlehandedly for about a year while he held an unpaid internship at Dean Witter Reynolds, becoming a stockbroker. Finally, Chris, through his untiring work and his excellent communication skills despite having a disadvantage of having to take care of his son and having to sell the remaining scanners, received the paid position at Dean Witter Reynolds. Chris then remarks, after he received the job "This part of my life, this little part right here, is called happiness.", and the movie ends as Chris and his son stroll down a street looking happy.

Classic quotations:

1. Chris Gardner: You have a dream, you got to protect it.

克里斯·加德纳：如果你有梦想，就要守护它。

2. Chris Gardner: People can't do something by themselves; they wanna tell you you can not do it.

克里斯·加德纳：当人们做不到一些事情的时候，他们就会对你说你也同样不能。

3. Chris Gardner: You want something. Go get it!

克里斯·加德纳：有了目标就要全力以赴！

4. There is an I in "happiness". There is no Y in "happiness". It's an I.

幸福的幸里面是一个"幸"，不是一个"辛"。或者理解成，Y = Why = 为什么，I = 我。幸福里面没有为什么，只有我。

5. I'm the type of person, if you ask me a question, and I don't know the answer, I'm gonna to tell you that I don't know. But I bet you what: I know how to find the answer, and I'll find the answer.

我是这样的人，如果你问的问题我不知道答案，我会直接告诉你"我不知道"。但我向你保证：我知道如何寻找答案，而且我一定会找出答案的。

6. —What would you say if a man walked in here with no shirt, and I hired him? What would you say?

—He must hare had on some really nice pants.

——如果有个人连衬衫都没穿就跑来参加面试,你会怎么想? 如果最后我还雇用了这个人,你会怎么想?

—— 那他穿的裤子一定十分考究。

7. Don't ever let somebody tell you that you can't do something, not even me.

别让别人告诉你你成不了才,即使是我也不行。

8. You got a dream, you gotta protect it. People can't do something themselves, they wanna tell you that you can't do it. If you want something, go get it. Period.

如果你有梦想的话,就要去捍卫它。那些一事无成的人想告诉你你也成不了大器。如果你有理想的话,就要去努力实现。就这样。

After watching it, please answer the following questions:

1. Can happiness be achieved?

2. Is happiness an influx of certain hormones in the brain, or is it something more divine, unachievable by humans?

3. Is happiness something that is achievable with the smallest of successes, or is it achievable through years of meditation and righteousness, or can it be achieved at all?

Task 2 Extended reading

Different Kinds of Communication

Communication is the purposeful activity of information exchange between two or more participants in order to convey or receive the intended meanings through a shared system of signs and semiotic rules.

Communication takes place inside and between three main subject categories: human beings, living organisms in general and communication-enabled devices (for examp, lesensor networks and control systems). Communication in living organisms (studied in the field of biosemiotics) often occurs through visual, auditory, or biochemical means. Human communication is unique for its extensive use of language.

Verbal communication

Effective verbal or spoken communication is dependent on a number of factors and cannot be fully isolated from other important interpersonal skills such as nonverbal communication, listening skills and clarification. Human language can be defined as a system of symbols (sometimes known as lexemes) and the grammars (rules) by which the symbols are manipulated. The word "language" also refers to common properties of languages. Language learning normally occurs most intensively during human childhood. Most of the thousands of human languages use patterns of sound or gesture for symbols which enable communication with others around them. Languages tend to share certain properties, although there are exceptions. There is no defined line between a language and a dialect. Constructed languages such as Esperanto, programming languages, and various mathematical formalisms are not necessarily restricted to the properties shared by human languages. The communication is two way process instead of one way.

Written communication and its historical development

Over time the forms and ideas about communication have evolved through the continuing progression of technology. Advances include communications psychology and media psychology, an emerging field of study. The progression of written communication can be divided into three "information communication revolutions": Written communication first emerged through the use of pictographs. The pictograms were made in stone, hence written communication was not yet mobile. The next step occurred when writing began to appear on paper, papyrus, clay, wax, etc. with common alphabets. Communication became mobile. The final stage is characterized by the transfer of information through controlled waves of electromagnetic radiation (i.e., radio, microwave, infrared) and other electronic signals.

Communication is thus a process by which meaning is assigned and conveyed in an attempt to create shared understanding. This process, which requires a vast repertoire of skills in interpersonal processing, listening, observing, speaking, questioning, analyzing, gestures, and evaluating enables collaboration and cooperation.

Misunderstandings can be anticipated and solved through formulations, questions and answers, paraphrasing, examples, and stories of strategic talk. Written communication can be clarified by planning follow-up talks on critical written communication as part of the everyday way of doing business. A few minutes spent talking in the present will save valuable time later by avoiding misunderstandings in advance. A frequent method for this purpose is reiterating what one heard in one's own words and asking the other person if that really was what was meant.

Business communication

Business communications is a term for a wide variety of activities including but not limited to: strategic communications planning, media relations, public relations (which can include social media, broadcast and written communications, and more), brand management, reputation management, speech-writing, customer-client relations, and internal/employee communications.

Companies with limited resources may only choose to engage in a few of these activities while larger organizations may employ a full spectrum of communications. Since it is difficult to develop such a broad range of skills, communications professionals often specialize in one or two of these areas but usually have at least a working knowledge of most of them. By far, the most important qualifications communications professionals can possess are excellent writing ability, good "people" skills, and the capacity to think critically and strategically.

Effective communication

Effective communication occurs when a desired thought is the result of intentional or unintentional information sharing, which is interpreted between multiple entities and acted on in a desired way. This effect also ensures that messages are not distorted during the communication process. Effective communication should generate the desired effect and maintain the effect, with the potential to increase the effect of the message. Therefore, effective communication serves the purpose for which it was planned or designed. Possible purposes might be to elicit change, generate action, create understanding, inform or communicate a certain idea or point of view. When the desired effect is not achieved, factors such as barriers to communication are explored, with the intention being to discover how the communication has been ineffective.

Barriers to effective human communication

Barriers to effective communication can retard or distort the message and intention of the message being conveyed which may result in failure of the communication process or an effect that is undesirable. These include filtering, selective perception, information overload, emotions, language, silence, communication apprehension, gender differences and political correctness.

This also includes a lack of expressing "knowledge-appropriate" communication, which occurs when a person uses ambiguous or complex legal words, medical jargon, or descriptions of a situation or environment that is not understood by the recipient.

Physical barriers

Physical barriers are often due to the nature of the environment. An example of this is the natural barrier which exists if staff are located in different buildings or on different sites. Likewise, poor or outdated equipment, particularly the failure of management to introduce new technology, may also cause problems. Staff shortages are another factor which frequently causes communication difficulties for an organization.

System design

System design faults refer to problems with the structures or systems in place in an organization. Examples might include an organizational structure which is unclear and therefore makes it confusing to know whom to communicate with. Other examples could be inefficient or inappropriate information systems, a lack of supervision or training, and a lack of clarity in roles and responsibilities which can lead to staff being uncertain about what is expected of them.

Attitudinal barriers

Attitudinal barriers come about as a result of problems with staff in an organization. These may be brought about, for example, by such factors as poor management, lack of consultation with employees, personality conflicts which can result in people delaying or refusing to communicate, the personal attitudes of individual employees which may be due to lack of motivation or dissatisfaction at work, brought about by insufficient training to enable them to carry out particular tasks, or simply resistance to change due to entrenched attitudes and ideas.

Ambiguity of words/phrases

Words sounding the same but having different meaning can convey a different meaning altogether. Hence the communicator must ensure that the receiver receives the same meaning. It is better if such words are avoided by using alternatives whenever possible.

Individual linguistic ability

The use of jargon, difficult or inappropriate words in communication can prevent the recipients from understanding the message. Poorly explained or misunderstood messages can also result in confusion. However, research in communication has shown that confusion can lend legitimacy to research when persuasion fails.

Physiological barriers

These may result from individuals' personal discomfort, caused—for example—by ill health, poor eyesight or hearing difficulties.

Cultural differences

These may result from the cultural differences of communities around the world, within an individual country (tribal/regional differences, dialects etc.), between religious groups and in organizations or at an organizational level—where companies, teams and units may have different expectations, norms and idiolects. Families and family groups may also experience the effect of cultural barriers to communication within and between different family members or groups. For example: words, colors and symbols have different meanings in different cultures. In most parts of the world, nodding your head means agreement, shaking your head means no, except in some parts of the world.

Critical thinking questions:

1. How many kinds of communications do you know?

2. What are the barriers which can affect human communication? How to overcome them?

3. How can people do to avoid misunderstandings in advance in daily communication?

Chapter 4

Non-verbal Intercultural Communication

1. It's not what he said, but the way he said it.

—English Saying

2. There is language in her eyes, her cheeks, her lips.

—William Shakespeare

Section I What Is Non-verbal Communication?

I Pre-tasks

Task 1 Game playing

Work in groups, each group will get a piece of paper on which you can read a sentence, discuss with groups members and try to show the sentence with body language.

Task 2 What is happening here?

Have you ever encountered the following situations in your culture? Talk with your partner and try to find out in which culture the following situations are most likely to occur.

1. You arrive at the airport an hour before your flight, only to find that there are large crowds pushing their way to the counter. The ticket agent behind the counter serves several people at once, focusing attention on those who have made themselves most noticed.

2. The doctor has told you that he will meet you at the hospital at 10:00 a. m. You have difficulty finding transportation, and finally arrive at 10:45. The doctor is seeing another patient and says that he will not be able to see you now until he can "squeeze you in" among his other appointment. You will probably have to wait until late afternoon.

II While tasks

What Is Non-verbal Communication?

Even though the importance of non-verbal communication has grown rapidly over the last few decades and it is now widely used in media, business, interpersonal relationships, education and politics, many people still pay little attention to non-verbal messages and body signals, concentrating mostly onwords. It is one of the biggest misconceptions to think that what is being said is more important than how it is being said. In reality only 7% of information is sent through words, the remaining 93% of communication is non-verbal. If you fail to read and decode non-verbal messages, you set yourself up for constant misunderstandings and various communication problems.

I am sure that you have heard the expression "*Their actions speak louder than words.* " before. This is very true, because in many situations people tend to hide their feelings behind carefully chosen words. A non-verbal message is a subconscious response of the body. Therefore, it cannot be easily controlled and is likely to be more genuine. As words have limitations, non-verbal communication is more effective in situations where a person has to explain shapes, directions, inner feelings and personalities. Non-verbal signals serve to make the message more powerful and convincing. Try to convince or motivate another person into doing a certain task while keeping your face expression, gestures and tone of voice unanimated. No matter what you say, you will not be able to sound convincing, or motivating. If a message is too emotional or too complex, a separate non-verbal communication channel is needed to transmit this message correctly.

Non-verbal communication helps to clarify misunderstanding and avoid possible communication barriers. Non-verbal communication is not just body language, gestures or facial expressions as many people mistakenly think. It also includes eye contact, touch, spatial distance between two or more people or positioning within a group, kinesics or body movements, appearance, smell, tone of voice and even silence!

Body language

Body language is one of the most important and complicated parts of non-verbal communication. Although many books have been written on this topic, body language is still hard to decode, because it must be interpreted in the context of a person's lifestyle, cultural background, family, education, physical health, and other factors that may be obscure.

Gestures

Gestures are used to express emotions and signify certain feelings. One of the most frequently observed is hand movements, as people often gesticulate with their hands while talking.

Facial expressions

Our face is a highly developed organ that can create more than 7,000 facial expressions. Facial expressions continually change during interaction and should be constantly monitored by the recipient. Even though the meanings of facial expressions may vary in different countries, there are six main types that are the same in all cultures:

Happiness (sincere broad smile, raised cheeks, round eyes)

Anger (lowered eyebrow, tightly pursed lips, intensive stare)

Surprise (wide open eyes, open mouth, raised eyebrows)

Fear (open mouth, round eyes, pale face)

Disgust (wrinkled nose, raised upper lip, lowered eyelids)

Sadness (lowered corners of mouth, sad eyes)

Eye contact

Eye contact is an important feature of social communication. In many cultures it is believed, that even if you can control your facial expressions and body movements, eyes can never lie. This is why in business cultures a fair degree of eye contact is viewed as a sign of a person's openness, honesty and trust. Often, just by eye contact we can signal to another person when to talk or to finish. In interpersonal relationships looking away is often perceived as deviousness and avoidance, while gaze holding, decreased blinking rate and dilated eye pupils show our interest in a partner. Also frequency of eye contact may indicate either interest or boredom.

Chapter 4 Non-verbal Intercultural Communication

Touch

"Haptics" is a non-verbal communication study of touch. The way one person touches another can tell a great deal of information. Even a handshake can tell a lot about the individual's character and social position. In most interpersonal relationships touching can (arm pat) express tenderness, give encouragement and show emotional support. Such physical contacts as embracing, pushing, grabbing, holding another person on the shoulder, patting on the back, ruffling their hair may reflect elements of intimacy, lack of attraction, patronizing or gentleness. The meaning of touch depends highly on the situation, sex, age, culture and one's character. If used improperly it can become a cause of aggravation, communication barriers and mistrust.

Distance and personal space

There are two main types of distance: horizontal and vertical. Horizontal distance determines the distance, which people intuitively feel comfortable with when approaching other and having others approach them. There are four horizontal distance zones:

Intimate distance—from actual touching to 18 inches. It is assigned for intimate relationships and mother- baby relationships. At this distance the physical presence of another is overwhelming. Violation of "our territory", depending on the seriousness may provoke such feelings as discomfort, irritation, anxiety and even anger and aggression.

Personal distance —from 18 inches to 4 feet. This zone is reserved for interactions with good friends, when discussing personal and casual matters.

Social distance —from 4 to 12 feet. This is an appropriate distance for impersonal, social gatherings and business communication.

Public distance —more than 12 feet. At this distance a speaker becomes formal. It is reserved for public speaking and interaction in public places (like parks, supermarkets, or on the street).

The more we get to know the person and the more we like them, the closer we will permit them into our personal space. Vertical distance often indicates a degree of dominance and sub-ordinance in the relationship.

Kinetics

Kinetics (or a study of body movements in space) helps a person to transmit information as well as affecting the feelings of the person doing the moving. Body movements are widely used. As emblems or gestures that have a direct translation to words (e. g. "OK" sign or a thumb up, meaning "Great!"). To reinforce or emphasize words (e. g. "He is THIS tall. ", "The fish was THIS big!"). To show strong feelings through body motions (e. g. jumping and clapping hands from joy, tiptoeing from impatience or anxiety). To control the flow of conversation (e. g. showing with body movements to another person when to start or to stop talking).

Usually people with a more relaxed posture, an open arm and body position and the body leaning slightly forward in the conversation are perceived as more likable, attentive and trustful.

Chronemics

"Chronemics" is the study of the use of time in non-verbal communication. Time perception greatly affects our lifestyle, movements, speed of speech, and the amount of time set for listening. It is also closely linked to a person's social status. The higher the status, the more control the person has over his time. For example, a boss can talk to an employee whenever he chooses to do so, while the employee has to make an appointment to see the boss. In business communication it is very important to remember that various cultures have different perception of time. For example, in North America, Germany or Switzerland, you often hear statements such as, "Time is money. ", "We're running out of time. ", "The deadline for the project is tomorrow. " In South America or Arabian countries people believe that they have "all the time in the world" and the word "deadline" does not exist in their language.

Olfactics

"Olfactics" is a non-verbal communication study of smell. We tend to react to people based on their smell. For both men and women body smell is one of the most important subconscious factors of choosing a life mate. During interaction body odoror too much perfume can make even the most attractive person seem repulsive.

Appearance

Appearance plays an important role in non-verbal communication. Clothes, makeup, accessories, hairstyle, choice of colors and uniforms usually offer signals relating to person's individuality, status, wealth, occupation and even attractiveness.

People we find attractive are perceived as more credible, sociable, successful, interesting, sensitive, kind and popular. However you have to remember that forming stereotypes based on other people's physical characteristics and attractiveness may lead to false assumptions and communication barriers.

Voice

Paralanguage is a non-verbal element of communication that includes rate (speed), pitch (highness or lowness of voice), volume (loudness), and enunciation of vocal speech. A person's character, emotional condition and ability to get a message correctly to a receiver can be revealed by vocal cues. Experimental findings suggest that people tend to listen more attentively to men with deep, low voices and resonant tones as these vocal cues are associated with strength, sexiness and self-confidence.

High pitch voices are associated with rage, nervousness and helplessness, while despair and depression is often vocalized by a lower pitch and slower word pace. People who speak very loud are often perceived by others as aggressive, overbearing and uncompromising. Soft spoken people are viewed as timid, polite and unsure of themselves. When a vocal message contradicts a verbal one, it is considered an indication of sarcasm. For example, a phrase, "Great job!" can either mean a sincere praise or if intoned sarcastically, it has the opposite meaning.

Silence

Silence is also viewed as a part of non-verbal communication that depending on the situation and usage can influence conversation in a positive or negative way. On one hand silence may create tension and uneasiness, while on the other it may give another person time to collect his thoughts and calm down. Silence can also be an indicator of agreement or disagreement, depending on other non-verbal aspects such as facial expression, body language or eye contact. By learning to observe and understand the non-verbal communication process, you can noticeably improve your communication and persuasion skills. You will be able to immediately identify what another person really thinks and change their point of view if necessary.

Word list:

1. obscure [əbˈskjʊə]
    adj. 昏暗的，朦胧的；晦涩的，不清楚的；隐蔽的；不著名的，无名的
    vt. 使……模糊不清；掩盖，隐藏；使难理解
    n. 某种模糊的或不清楚的东西

2. decode [diːˈkəʊd]

    vt. [计][通信] 译码，解码

    vi. 从事破译工作

3. kinetics [kɪˈnetɪks; kaɪ-]

    n. [力] 动力学

4. emblem [ˈembləm]

    n. 象征；徽章；符号

    vt. 象征；用符号表示；用纹章装饰

5. chronemics [krəʊˈnemɪks]

    n. 语言时位学，话轮停顿时位学（语言学研究谈话时轮流发言和停顿的时机选择）

6. repulsive [rɪˈpʌlsɪv]

    adj. 排斥的；令人厌恶的；击退的；冷淡的

7. resonant [ˈrez(ə)nənt]

    adj. 洪亮的；共振的，共鸣的

8. sarcasm [ˈsɑːkæz(ə)m]

    n. 讽刺；挖苦；嘲笑

9. sarcastically [saːrˈkæstɪkəli]

    adv. 讽刺地；挖苦地

Task 1　Reading comprehension

Exercise One：Work with your partners, decide whether the following statements are true (T) or false (F) according to what you have learned in the passage.

1. _____ Speaking is just one mode of communication. There are many others.

2. _____ Environment is one of the studies areas that non-verbal communication covers.

3. _____ Much of our non-verbal behavior, like culture, tends to be elusive, spontaneous and frequently goes beyond our awareness.

4. _____ In some cultures, eye contact should be avoided in order to show respect or obedience.

5. _____ Western women usually like Chinese to touch their babies or small children.

Chapter 4 Non-verbal Intercultural Communication

6. _____ There are three main types of distance.
7. _____ A non-verbal message is a conscious response of the body.
8. _____ A handshake can tell a lot about the individual's character and social position.
9. _____ High pitch voices are associated with rage, nervousness and helplessnes.
10. _____ By learning to observe and understand the non-verbal communication process, one can noticeably improve one's communication and persuasion skills.

Exercise Two: Choose the right answer according to your understanding of this passage:

( ) Which of the following is not mentioned by the writer?

A. One of the most frequently observed gestures is hand morements, as people offen gesticalatewith their hands while talking.

B. Social distance is a distance from 14 to 20 feet. This is an appropriate distance for impersonal, social gatherings and business communication.

C. The more we get to know the person and the more we like them, the closer we will permit them into our personal space.

D. A person's character, emotional condition and ability to get a message correctly to a receiver can be revealed by vocal cues.

Exercise Three: Fill in the blanks with the words given below and change the form when necessary.

sarcasm   signify   concentrate   perception   perceive   identify
dominance   indicator   emotional   Chronemics

1. Many people pay little attention to non-verbal messages and body signals, mostly _____ on words.

2. You will be able to immediately _____ what another person really thinks and change their point of view if necessary.

3. Silence can also be a (n) _____ of agreement or disagreement, depending on other non-verbal aspects such as facial expressions, body language or eye contact.

4. When a vocal message contradicts a verbal one it is considered an indication of _____.

5. Time _____ greatly affects our lifestyle, movements, speed of speech, and the amount of time set for listening.

6. If a message is too _____ or too complex, a separate non-verbal communicationchannel is needed to transmit this message correctly.

7. Gestures are used to express emotions and _____ certain feelings.

8. People who speak very loud are often _____ by others as aggressive, overbearing and uncompromising.

9. _____ is also closely linked to a person's social status. The higher the status, the more control the person has over his time.

10. Vertical distance often indicates a degree of _____ and sub-ordinance in the relationship.

Task 2 Case study

Case 1

Bill had just arrived from the United States to study engineering at a Chinese university. In the first few days he met and moved in with his roommate Zemin. Over the next few days he noticed that female students on campus frequently walked arm-in-arm or even holding hands. He noticed, too, that students of both sexes, but especially the boys, would huddle around newspaper displays in a fashion of close contact. Bill felt rather uncomfortable and wondered how he would respond if one of his classmates were to put his arms around him...

Questions for discussion:
1. Why does Bill feel uncomfortable?
2. Do you often walk hand-in-hand or arm-in-arm with your friends?

Case 2

In 1987, a delegation made up of four Chinese experts went to Pingyong Foreign Language University to train faculty to be top-level simultaneous interpreters for the 13th International Youth Festival. Of the four experts, two are men and two are women. The two men were dressed in suits with ties and the two women were typically dressed in trousers and typical business clothes. Two Korean interpreters came to meet them. These two interpreters repeatedly looked at the Chinese ladies' trousers.

Questions for discussion:
1. Why and what are Chinese ladies assumptions about being looked at?
2. According to the two Korean interpreters, what should the Chinese ladies wear?

II After-tasks

Task 1 Movie and culture discussion Charlie Chaplin swept the world with his silent films

Charlie (1889 ~ 1977), Britain movie actor, direction, producer, on April 16, 1889 was born in London, on December 25, 1977 died at Swiss Corsi Ye. His silent films are very interesting. Non-verbal communication plays an important role in movies, we can find it from many popular movies. So much of our communication is done non-verbally! Of all the types of non-verbal communication, this may be one of the most noticeable. We all examine each others' faces as we talk, gleaning information to confirm that the meaning is received as it is delivered. Smiling is one facial expression that is likely to put other people at ease and make them feel accepted and comfortable. You exude happiness and encouragement when you smile, so try to add it to more of your conversations. Scowling, chewing your lip, and raising your eyebrows can all signal different meanings, so it is important to be aware of how your face looks during a conversation. Smiling is often used to request information or help. Verbal expressions in the states such as "thank you" are often skipped and a smile is used instead. Be aware that smiling could also signal embarrassment. Wiggling the nose may indicate confusion or a desire to have a situation explained. To point at something, a Puerto Rican student may purse their lips and motion toward it with their mouth. In the Chinese culture, a display of good feelings can mask the true feelings of the speaker. May display good feelings when feeling nervous, embarrassed, or criticized. Most with a person in a lower position of a hierarchy, showing respect or consideration to their superiors. Smile is also used to suppress the bad feelings within themselves. Gestures are another one of the types of non-verbal communication. They can add warmth and personality to a conversation. If you're not a big hand gesture person, remember at least to nod your head appropriately. This is an easy way to show that you are listening to, understanding, and connecting with the speaker. The majority of gestures used in the states will be familiar to Puerto Rican students. When giving someone a small item, do not throw it at them or to them. Waving the fingers is a way of asking for someone to come closer. Jabbing, pushing, or pounding on the back are not uncommon among boys who are friends. In China, men usually shake hands when greeting and departing and will sometimes nod their head. Usually, the oldest man will always be greeted first. (Example—Meeting a professor, young man greeting an old man.) Women will also shake hands and not when greeting and departing. Shaking hands is not used between people of different statuses, but only with socially equal people, friends, or businessmen. (Example—Peer in the same class; Two colleagues with the same job title.) In our daily life, "How you walk, talk, stand, and sit sends a lot of messages to others. Think of the times you've felt nervous at a party...your posture most certainly gave you away. Letting your body relax, having fluid smooth movements, and facing your conversation partner all indicate confidence and engaging conversation skills.

Questions:

1. Can you understand the silent film even though the actors didn't speak any words in the film?

2. How can people understand the silent film without dialogues between actors or without any subtitles?

3. Why Charlie's silent films were so popular during that period?

Task 2 Extended reading

Variables in Intercultural Communication Modules

The challenge is that even with all the good will, miscommunication is likely to happen, especially when there are significant cultural differences between communicators. Miscommunication may lead to conflict, or aggravate conflict that already exists. We make quite different meaning of the world, our places in it, and our relationships with others. In accordance to this, intercultural communication can be demonstrated by examples of ideas, attitudes, and behaviors involving four variables (Time and Space—Fate and Personal Responsibility—Face and Face-saving—Non-verbal Communication) as our familiarity with these different starting points increases, we are cultivating cultural fluency—awareness of the ways cultures operate in communication and conflict, and the ability to respond effectively to these differences.

Time and Space

Time is one of the most central differences that separate cultures and cultural ways of doing things. In the West, time tends to be seen as quantitative, measured in units that reflect the march of progress. It is logical, sequential, and present-focused. Novinger calls the United States, for instance, a "chronocracy", in which there is such reverence for efficiency and the success of economic endeavours that the expression "time is money" is frequently heard. This approach to time is called monochronic—it is an approach that favors linear structure and focus on one event or interaction at a time. In the East, time feels like it has unlimited continuity, an unravelling rather than a strict boundary. Birth and death are not such absolute ends since the universe continues and humans, though changing form, continue as part of it. People may attend to many things happening at once in this approach to time called polychronous. This may mean many conversations in a moment (people speak simultaneously), or many times and people during one process (a ceremony in which those family members who have died are felt to be present as well as those yet to be born into the family). A good place to look to understand the Eastern idea of time is India. Differences over time can play out in painful and dramatic ways in negotiation or conflict-resolution processes. It is also true that cultural approaches to time or communication are not always applied in good will, but may serve a variety of motives. Asserting power, superiority, or control over the course of the negotiations may be a motive wrapped up in certain cultural behaviours. Culture and cultural beliefs may be used as a tactic by negotiators; for this reason, it is important that parties be involved in collaborative-process design when addressing intractable conflicts. As people from different cultural backgrounds work together to design a process to address the issues that divide them, they can ask questions about cultural preferences about time and space and how these may affect a negotiation or conflict-resolution process, and thus inoculate the use of culture as a tactic or an instrument to advance power. A polychromic perspective is often associated with a communitarian starting point. The focus on collective, or group, stretching forward and back, animates the polychronic view of time. In more monochromic settings, an individualist way of life is more easily accommodated. Individualists can more easily extract moments in time, and individuals themselves, from the networks around them.

Fate and Personal Responsibility

Another important variable affecting communication across cultures is fate and personal responsibility. This refers to the degree to which we feel ourselves the masters of our lives, versus the degree to which we see ourselves as subject to things outside our control, in other words, how much we see ourselves able to change and manoeuvre, to choose the course of our lives and relationships. Some have drawn a parallel between the emphasis on personal responsibility in North American settings and the landscape itself. The North American landscape is vast, with large spaces of unpopulated territory. The frontier mentality of "conquering" the wilderness, and the expansiveness of the land stretching huge distances, may relate to generally high levels of confidence in the ability to shape and choose our destinies. Now consider places in the world with much smaller territory, whose history reflects repeated conquest and harsh struggles: Northern Ireland, Mexico, Israel, Palestine. In these places, there is more emphasis on destiny's role in human life. Their fatalistic attitude is expressed in their way of responding to failure or accident by saying "ni modo" ("no way" or "tough luck"), meaning that the setback was destined. This variable is important to understanding cultural conflict. If someone invested in free will crosses paths with someone more fatalistic in orientation, miscommunication is likely. The former may expect action and accountability. Failing to see it, they may conclude that the other is lazy, obstructionist, or dishonest. The second person will expect respect for the natural order of things. Failing to see it, they may conclude that the first is coercive or irreverent, inflated in his ideas of what can be accomplished or changed.

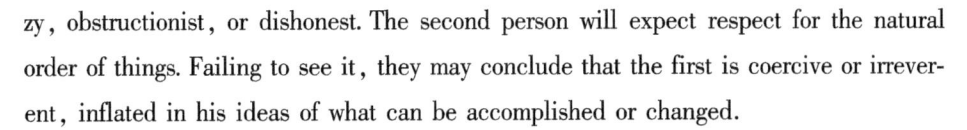

Face and Face-saving

Face is important across cultures, yet the dynamics of face and face-saving play out differently. Face is defined in many different ways. Novinger says it is "the value or standing a person has in the eyes of others...and that it relates to pride or self-respect". Others have defined it as "the negotiated public image, mutually granted each other by participants in communication". In this broader definition, face includes ideas of status, power, courtesy, insider and outsider relations, humor and respect. In many cultures, maintaining face is of great importance, though ideas of how to do this vary. If I see myself as a self-determining individual, then face has to do with preserving my image with others and myself. I can and should exert control in situations to achieve this goal. I may be comfortable in a mediation where the other party and I meet face to face and frankly discuss our differences. If I see my primary identification as a group member, then considerations about face involve my group. Direct confrontation or problem-solving with others may reflect poorly on my group, or disturb overall community harmony. I may prefer to avoid criticism of others, even when the disappointment I have concealed may come out in other, more damaging ways later. When there is conflict that cannot be avoided, I may prefer a third party who acts as a shuttle between me and the other people involved in the conflict. Since no direct confrontation takes place, face is preserved and potential damage to the relationships or networks of relationships is minimised.

Non-verbal Communication

Its importance is multiplied across cultures. This is because we tend to look for non-verbal cues when verbal messages are unclear or ambiguous, as they are more likely to be across cultures (especially when different languages are being used). Since non-verbal behavior arises from our cultural common sense—our ideas about what is appropriate, normal, and effective as communication in relationships—we use different systems of understanding gestures posture, silence, special relations, emotional expression, touch, physical appearance, and other non-verbal cues. Cultures also attribute different degrees of importance to verbal and non-verbal behavior. Low-context cultures like the United States and Canada tend to give relatively less emphasis to non-verbal communication. This does not mean that non-verbal communication does not happen, or that is unimportant, but that people in these settings tend to place less importance on it than on the literal meanings of words themselves. In high-context settings such as Japan or Latin America, understanding the non-verbal components of communication is relatively more important to receiving the intended meaning of the communication as a whole. Some elements of non-verbal communication are consistent across cultures. For example, research has shown that the emotions of enjoyment, anger, fear, sadness, disgust, and surprise are expressed in similar ways by people around the world. However, differences are also to be recognised. For instance, it may be more social acceptable in some settings in the Western for women to show fear, but no anger, and for men to display anger, but not fear. At the same time, interpretation of facial expressions across cultures is difficult. In the East, for example, a facial expression that would be recognised around the world as conveying happiness may actually express anger or mask sadness, both of which are unacceptable to show overtly.

Critical thinking questions:

1. Some people think cultural approaches to time or communication are not always applied in good will, but may serve a variety of motives, what do you think about it?

2. How important is face in intercultural communication? Can you think of some examples about how do you save face in daily communication?

3. Somebody say "time can speak", can you use examples to explain how time speaks?

Section II What Are the Universal Gestures?

I Pre-tasks

Task 1 Talking without saying

The figures in the picture are not talking to anyone, but they are telling us something. What are they trying to say? Try to answer the following questions: Someone says, "When you speak, you communicate. When you don't speak, you may still be communicating." Do you agree? Why or why not?

Task 2　Handshakes around the world

Look at the following captions and pictures of handshakes. Match the caption with the corresponding picture. Please talk with your partner and try to explain why there are different handshakes around the world.

1. Introduce yourself by name with a firm handshake.

2. If you are a woman, shaking a man's hand, offer your hand first; women do not shake hands with other women.

3. Gentle handshakes; shake only if you're the same gender.

4. Don't shake hands with the opposite sex, unless it's a business situation; a man should kiss a woman's hand.

5. Light handshake; after shaking hands, do not stand or speak too close.

6. Shake hands with everyone and use a title—such as Ms. or Mr.—followed by his or her last name.

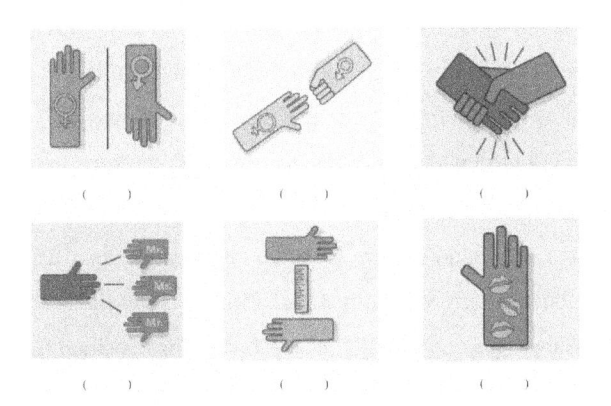

II While-tasks

List of Gestures

Gestures are a form of non-verbal communication in which visible bodily actions are used to communicate important messages, either in place of speech or together and in parallel with spoken words. Gestures include movement of the hands, face, or other parts of the body. Physical non-verbal communication such as purely expressive displays, proxemics, or displays of joint attention differ from gestures, which communicate specific messages. Gestures are culture-specific and can convey very different meanings in different social or cultural settings. Gesture is distinct from sign language. Although some gestures, such as the ubiquitous act of pointing, differ little from one place to another, most gestures do not have invariable or universal meanings but connote specific meanings in particular cultures. A single emblematic gesture can have very different significance in different cultural contexts, ranging from complimentary to highly offensive.

This list includes links to Wikipedia pages that discuss particular gestures, as well as short descriptions of some gestures that do not have their own page. Not included are the specialized gestures, calls, and signals used by referees and umpires in organizedsports. Police officers also make gestures when directing traffic. Mime is an art form in which the performer utilizes gestures to convey a story. Charades is a game of gestures.

Single handed gestures

A-ok or Okay, made by connecting the thumb and forefinger in a circle and holding the other fingers straight, may signal the word okay. It is considered obscene in Brazil and in Iran, being similar to the Western extended middle finger with the back of the hand towards the recipient. Abhayamudra is a Hindu Mudra or gesture of reassurance and safety. Apology hand gesture is a Hindu custom to apologize in the form of a hand gesture with the right hand when a person's foot accidentally touches a book or any written material (which is considered as a manifestation of the goddess of knowledge Saraswati), money (which is considered as a manifestation of the goddess of wealth Lakshmi) or another person's leg. The offending person first

Okay sign

touches the object with the fingertips and then the forehead and/or chest.

Beckoning sign

In North America or Northern Europe a beckoning sign is made with the index finger sticking out of the clenched fist, palm facing the gesturer. The finger moves repeatedly towards the gesturer (in a hook) as to draw something nearer. It has the general meaning of "come here". In Northern Africa (Maghreb), calling someone is done using the full hand. In several Asian and European countries, a beckoning sign is made with a scratching motion with all four fingers and with the palm down. In Japan, the palm faces the recipient with the hand at head's height.

Before "bunny ears", people were given cuckold's horns as an insult by sneaking up behind them with two fingers (c. 1815 French satire). Bellamy salute was used in conjunction with the American Pledge of Allegiance prior to World War II.

Hand of benediction and blessing

The benediction gesture (or benedictio Latina gesture) is a raised right hand with the ring finger and little finger touching the palm, while the middle and index fingers remain raised. Taken from Ancient Roman iconography for speaking (an example is the Augustus of Prima Porta where the emperor Augustus assumes the pose of an orator in addressing his troops), often called the benediction gesture, is used by the Christian clergy to perform blessings with the sign of the cross; however Christians keep the thumb raised—the three raised fingers (index, middle, and thumb) are frequently allegorically interpreted as representing the three Persons of the Holy Trinity. The hand's shape is said to partially spell the name of Jesus Christ in Greek.

Blah-blah

The fingers are kept straight and together, held horizontal or upwards, while the thumb points downwards. The fingers and thumb then snap together repeatedly to suggest a mouth talking. The gesture can be used to indicate that someone talks too much, gossips, is saying nothing of any consequence, or is boring. Check, please. This gesture, used to mean that a dinner patron wishes to pay the bill and depart, is executed by touching the index finger and thumb together and "writing" a checkmark, circle, or wavy line (as if signing one's name) in the air. To signal for the bill in Japan, although not widely used by younger people, both hands are raised, with the two index fingers forming an "X". This is to signal the "end" of a meal which is called "Shime (〆 (しめ))" in Japanese. The crossed fingers represent this sign resembling an "X".

Chinese number gestures are a method of using one hand to signify the natural numbers one through ten. Clenched fist is used as a gesture of defiance or solidarity. Facing the signer, it threatens physical violence (i. e. , "a thumping").

Aclenched fist

Kennedy's gesture seen here with Nikita Khrushchev.

Clinton thumb

The gesture dubbed the "Clinton thumb" after one of its most famous users, Bill Clinton, is used by politicians to provide emphasis in speeches. This gesture has the thumb leaning against the thumb-side portion of the index finger, which is part of a closed fist, or slightly projecting from the fist. An emphatic, it does not exhibit the anger of the clenched fist or pointing finger, and so is thought to be less threatening. This gesture was likely adopted by Clinton from John F. Kennedy, who can be seen using it in many speeches and images from his political career.

Crossed fingers are used to superstitiously wish for good luck or to nullify a promise. Cuckoo sign, touched or screw loose. In North America, making a circling motion of the index finger at the ear or side of the head signifies that the person "has a screw loose", i. e. , is speaking nonsense or is crazy. Cuckold's horns are traditionally placed behind an unwitting man (the cuckold) to insult him and represent that his wife is unfaithful. It is made with the index and middle fingers spread by a person standing behind the one being insulted. The symbolism has been forgotten but the insult remains "in modern culture as bunny ears". Dap greeting is a form of handshake recently popularized in western cultures, related to the fist bump.

The "fig sign" is an ancient gesture with many uses. Fig sign is a gesture made with the hand and fingers curled and the thumb thrust between the middle and index fingers, or, rarely, the middle and ring fingers, forming the fist so that the thumb partly pokes out. In some areas of the world, the gesture is considered a good luck charm; in others (including Greece, Indonesia, Japan, Korea, Russia, Serbia and Turkey among others), it is considered an obscene gesture. The precise origin of the gesture is unknown, but many historians speculate that it refers to a penis penetrating the female genitalia (to which The Finger also refers). In ancient Greece, this gesture was a fertility and good luck charm designed to ward off evil. This usage has survived in Portugal and Brazil, where carved images of hands in this gesture are used in good luck talismans. The Finger, an extended middle finger with the back of the hand towards the recipient, is an obscene hand gesture used in much of Western culture. The middle finger presumably refers to an erect penis penetrating the female genitalia represented by the curled ring and index fingers. Finger gun is a hand gesture in which the subject uses their hand to mimic a handgun. If pointed to oneself, it may indicate boredom or awkwardness; when pointed to another, it is interpreted as a threat of violence, either genuine or in jest. Fist bump is similar to a handshake or high five which may be used as a symbol of respect.

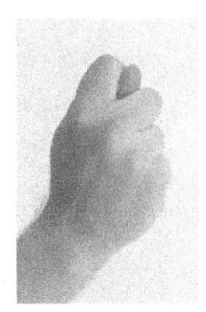

Word list:

1. proxemics [prɒːkˈsiːmɪks]

   n. 近体学; 空间关系学

2. recipient [rɪsɪpɪənt]

   n. 接受者; 容器; 容纳者

   adj. 容易接受的; 感受性强的

3. clergy [ˈklɜːdʒɪ]
   n. 神职人员；牧师；僧侣
4. execute [ˈɛksɪkjut]
   vt. 实行；执行；处死
5. nullify [ˈnʌlɪˈfaɪ]
   vt. 使无效，作废；取消
6. defiance [dɪˈfaɪəns]
   n. 蔑视；挑战；反抗
7. penetrate [ˈpɛnətret]
   vi. 渗透；刺入；看透
   vt. 渗透；穿透；洞察
8. symbolism [ˈsɪmbəlɪzəm]
   n. 象征，象征主义；符号论；记号

Task 1　Reading comprehension

Exercise One：Work with your partners, decide whether the following statements are true (T) or false (F) according to what you have learned in the passage.

1. _____ Pointing with index finger may be used to indicate an item or person.
2. _____ Rubbing both hands together indicates either one feels warm or one is expecting or anticipating something.
3. _____ Applause is an expression of approval made by clapping the hands together to create noise.
4. _____ Kissing hands is a gesture to express positive emotions between friends, relatives, and lovers.
5. _____ In Germany, thumb and forefinger are placed against the cheek means that something is delicious.
6. _____ Cheek kissing, pressing one's face to another person's cheek, may show friendship or greeting.
7. _____ Hand-shaking is a gesture in which the hand is raised and moved left and right, as a greeting or sign of departure.
8. _____ The so-so gesture expresses mild dissatisfaction.

9. _____ Chinese number gestures are a method of using one hand to signify the natural numbers one through ten.

10. _____ Two-finger salute is a salute made using the thumb and index fingers.

Exercise Two: Choose the right answer according to your understanding of this passage.

(   ) Which of the following is NOT mentioned by the writer?

A. A single emblematic gesture can have very different significance in different cultural contexts, ranging from complimentary to highly offensive.

B. A-ok or Okay, made by connecting the thumb and forefinger in a circle and holding the other fingers straight is considered OK in Brazil.

C. Air kiss, conveys meanings similar to kissing, but is performed without making bodily contact.

D. Head shake, indicates a negative reaction to a query or a rejection in English-speaking cultures.

Exercise Three: Fill in the blanks with the words given below and change the form when necessary.

connotation   psychology   performance   melodramatically   disaffirmative

frustration   exasperate   solidarity   parallel   consequence

1. A _____ gesture of distress made by lifting the arm and placing the back of the hand on the forehead.

2. Head bobble is a (n) _____ response or acknowledgement common in India.

3. Facepalm is an expression of _____ or embarrassment made by raising the palm of the hand to the face.

4. Jazz hands are used in dance or other _____ by displaying the palms of both hands with fingers splayed.

5. Mani Giunte is an Italian gesture used when expressing _____ or disbelief by putting both palms together in prayer and moving them down and back up towards your chest repeatedly.

6. The revealing of open palms is seen in animal behavior as a (n) _____ and subconscious behavior inbody language to convey trust.

7. The "blah-blah" gesture can be used to indicate that someone talks too much, gossips, is saying nothing of any _____, or is boring.

8. While doing the so-so gesture, the hand is held _____ to the ground and rocked slightly.

9. Clenched fist is used as a gesture of defiance or _____.

10. Shocker is a hand gesture with a sexual _____.

Task 2　Case study

Case 1: A Misunderstanding of Seating Culture

Occasionally, some Americans will sit with their feet on the desk. Once I went to an American bank to close my account before I left America. While talking with me, the bank manager put his feet with leather shoes onto the desk. When I returned home, I still could not forgive him for such behavior, thinking maybe he looked down on me because of my small savings or for being Chinese. Later I came to know that an American's putting his feet on his desk shows he is comfortable. However, for Latin Americans or Asians, such behavior is rude and arrogant. (Translated from *Intercultural Studies* by Lin Dajin, 1997)

Comment: During World War II, a German Nazi once detected an American spy by his sitting posture. This is somewhat true. One can control one's verbal language to disguise himself consciously. But unconsciously his physical behavior can give him away. We can guess where someone is from by observing his typical and unique behavior and posture, for example, if someone likes to talk and eat with a squatting posture, most likely he is from Shanxi, the Yellow Plateau of China.

Questions for discussion:

1. Is it possible to identify a person by his/her sitting posture?
2. Can you find some examples about seating culture?

Case 2: This Is not a Love Signal

On the campus of a language institute in Beijing, there were overseas students studying English and Chinese. In 1989, a Japanese student, Sawada, came to the institute after studying two years in Australia. His English and Chinese were fairly good. One day, he met a girl on the campus from Holland, who introduced herself as Linda. Both of them were able to communicate in English. Sawada greeted her in Chinese, and Linda responded with a sweet smile and they began to talk in broken Chinese. As they were sitting on a bench, Linda turned her body toward Sawada and seemed to be very happy to have met this Japanese boy. As agreed, they met in Linda's apartment the following day to continue their talk. Observing that Linda was standing and sitting very close to him and looking at him with a sweet smile, Sawada felt she liked him, so he decided to put his arm around her shoulder. But to his disappointment, Linda pushed him away. Sawada thought she was shy, so he attempted a second approach by trying to hug her and kiss her. At this, Linda got very angry and asked him to leave the apartment. Sawada was quite puzzled and did not know why Linda refused him. (汪福祥, 马登阁, 1999)

Questions for discussion:
1. Can you explain why Sawada was turned away?
2. Why Sawada felt very puzzled?

III After-tasks

Please watch the American TV series *Lie to Me*

Task 1 Movie and culture discussion *Lie to Me*

Lie to Me is an American crime drama television series. It originally ran on the Fox network from January 21, 2009 to January 31, 2011. In the show, Dr. Cal Lightman and his colleagues in The Lightman Group accept assignments from third parties (commonly local and federal law enforcement), and assist in investigations, reaching the truth through applied psychology: interpreting micro-expressions, through the Facial Action Coding System, and body language.

In this series, Dr. Lightman and his colleagues tell us how to see through one's fraud, how to know whether a person is honest or not by his/her micro-expressions. Dr. Lightman can know whether a person is telling lies by looking at his/her eyes, by watching every details of his/her actions, by analyzing a person's voice, or even by shaking hands with the person. There are many methods we can learn from the series. For example, if the expression of fear or surprise lasts over one second on a person's face, the person may be lying; when a person trumps up a succession of things, he/she may describe it vividly in the normal order because he/she has prepared it, but the person can't describe it from the end correctly, because he/she has never prepared it; if one person shows disdain to your question, you touch him on his sensitive spot and maybe your doubt is right; when you try to recall your memory, your eyeball will turn to the left corner, but when you tell a lie, you don't have any time to recall it.

There are many tips we can use to see through lies, a micro-expression is a brief, involuntary facial expression that is shown on the face of humans according to the emotions that are being experienced. Unlike regular pro-longed facial expressions, it is difficult to fake a micro-expression.

There are seven universal micro-expressions: disgust, anger, fear, sadness, happiness, surprise, and contempt. They often occur as fast as 1/15 to 1/25 of a second.

The face is the best indicator of a person's emotions. Yet, it is often overlooked. Dr. Paul Ekman, whose research is the premise of the show *Lie to Me*, has done groundbreaking research on decoding the human face. He has shown that facial expressions are universal. In other words, people in the US make the same face for sadness as indigenous people in Papa New Guinea who have never seen TV or movies to model. He also found that congenitally blind individuals—those blind since birth, also make the same expressions even though they have never seen other people's faces.

Ekman has designated seven facial expressions that are the most widely used and easy to interpret. Learning to read them is incredibly helpful for understanding the people in our lives. If you want to practice reading people's faces, it is important to know the following basic expressions. I would recommend trying the following faces in the mirror so you can see what they look like on yourself. You will also find that if you make the facial expression, you also begin to feel the emotion yourself! Emotions not only cause facial expressions, facial expressions also cause emotions.

Identifying the micro-expressioncan help us understand each of the expressions, specifically the science behind each emotion.

Classical quotations:

1. Eyebrows go up, the person knows the answer to the question they're asking.

眼眉向上抬 表示发问的人知道问题的答案。

2. Micro-expression: expression lasted for less than a fifth of a second.

微表情：持续不到五分之一秒的表情。

3. One-sided shrug shows I've absolutely no confidence of what I just said.

单肩耸动表示我对所说的话极不自信。

4. Surprise lasts for less than a second when it comes across face.

惊讶的表情不会超过1秒。

5. Oblique eyebrows show sadness.

眉毛倾斜代表悲伤。

6. People got the slightest head nod "yes" before they shook their head "no".

摇头之前先轻轻地点一下头，是谎言。

7. Tension: He had his left hand in his pants pocket, pressed against his leg the whole time.

左手一直插在裤袋里顶着大腿，说明紧张。

8. When you are lying, it's hard to tell a story backwards, because there's no real memory of what happened. Liars rehearse their stories in order. They don't think to rehearse them backwards.

撒谎时，很难把事情倒叙说出来，因为都是编的。撒谎者按顺序编故事，从没想过倒过来顺一遍。

9. Fear, anger, and sexual arousal can make pupils dilate.

害怕、愤怒、性欲能使人的瞳孔放大。

10. In a fake smile, there is no eye wrinkling.

假笑时，眼角是没有皱纹的。

After watching it, please try to answer the following questions:

1. When some people use negative emotion words every time, what do they indicate?

2. Which special facial expression will appear on the face when someone shows his disgust?

3. Whose book is the drama based upon?

Task 2 Extended reading

Nonverbal Communication in Business

Non-verbal communication in business takes place in many settings: during meetings in conference rooms, in offices, at the hallway, during business travel, at restaurants, golf courses, you name it.

As a start, we will focus now on how people communicate (non-verbally) in an office setting, including a brief discussion regarding business travel. Many of the principles of nonverbal communication in business apply to other settings as well. Non-verbal messages go beyond body language, they also include the messages we send with the clothes we wear, the car we drive, the way we do our hair and so forth. See workplace dress code for more insights on this. On separate pages we discuss a related subject: body language at work, where you can learn the meaning of many gestures used in the workplace; and defensive body language, where you can learn how to quickly read the signs of defensive communication.

During Meetings in Conference Rooms

Who sits where at a conference table. People with the highest ranking tend to sit at the head of the table, preferably the end that faces the door. People second in command will tend to sit close the big boss, preferably to his/her right. In round tables, the highest ranking person will sit in a position that faces the door. Interruptions will depend on the setting. In formal meetings, people will not interrupt as often as in more informal settings. People will wait for the boss to look at them or to give them the go-ahead to speak. In an office, if a manager has a meeting area in addition to his desk, observe how he approaches meeting with you. A manager that meets with you while sitting behind his desk is either trying to keep the meeting short, or tying to assert his authority over you. Or perhaps he/she doesn't feel like getting up from his chair at that moment. Don't give this a whole lot of importance, just observe it. Looking at their watch. When you are meeting with someone who looks at their watch (or tap their feet) every so often, it's a sure bet that they need to cut the meeting short. And perhaps go somewhere, or do something else. To avoid jumping to conclusions, just ask if they need to go and continue the meeting at another time. Even if you are dealing with something that is critical and urgent, you are not getting the person's attention anyway, it's best to continue at another time, when you have the person's full attention. Pounding the table or desk: The person is very likely angry. Except in cases when the person is just trying to look stern. It's easy to know if this is the case because the person's face doesn't show anger, it's calm. Always look for congruence between the various verbal and non-verbal cues.

During Business Traveling

People loosen up their norms and rules of behavior and communication while traveling, that is why so many affairs get started in business trips. Two factors contribute to this relaxation of rules: the first factor is that people socialize during or after the conference. This may include social drinking. The second factor is that the setting is removed from the usual office environment, so the line between people's business and private personae become blurred. If you travel often, you already know what I'm telling you. If you don't travel as often, you may be taken by surprise by this relaxation of norms during business travel. It's tempting to enjoy being free of norms but it's not advisable to let it all hang out. After all, you are coming back to the office on Monday, the structure and rules will be there waiting for you to fit right back in.

During Job Interviews

When you go to a job interview, you could be facing one person or a panel of interviewers. The interviewer (s) will be looking for signs of confidence, reliability, openness, and authenticity in your communication. Both, the interviewers' and the candidate's body language will be aimed at conveying a specific message. The interviewers on their end may be trying to appear as approachable, knowledgeable and objective. The candidate will be trying to appear knowledgeable, trustworthy and likable. Non-verbal behavior and body language play a big part during an interview. Whether you are an interviewer or a candidate, make sure you read about job interview body language if an interview is in your horizon.

But we have to notice that non-verbal communication can be ambiguous. For example, you may engage in a random gesture (such as swatting a fly off your arm) and someone may see that action and assume you are waving at them. Part of the ambiguity we have been talking about exists because non-verbal communication can be contextual. The ambiguity of context is clearly seen if someone brushes against you in an elevator: was it merely an accident or was it an opportunistic sexual act? Our point should be obvious: when you use or interpret non-verbal communication, you need to be aware of the ambiguous nature of this form of interaction. As Osborn and Motley tell us, Meanings and interpretations of non-verbal behaviors are often on very shaky ground, we saw that "shaky ground" when some people, both in and out of the media, interpreted a fist bump exchanged by Democratic presidential candidate Barack Obama and his wife Michelle as a "terrorist greeting" instead of a simple sign of affection between a husband and wife.

The issue of the contextual nature of non-verbal communication might simply be an adjunct to our last point, in that it is once again calling your attention to the idea that "different situations or environments produce different non-verbal messages". Personal observations will tell you that you behave differently at a club than you do in the lobby of a bank. It is the setting that offers norms and guidelines for your interpersonal actions. When engaged in an intercultural interaction, keep this notion of context in mind as you try to decide the meaning behind the non-verbal cues you are receiving.

Reading and interpreting non-verbal communication in business is a skill worth mastering for more effective communication in the workplace. Just keep in mind that you have to look at non-verbal cues together with other message cues. (1056 words)

(Adopted from http://www.people-communicating.com/non-verbal-communication-in-business.html)

Critical thinking questions:

1. Except what you have read from this passage, can you list other settings in which non-verbal communication in business takes place?

2. How can a person pay attention to the non-verbal communication during business traveling?

3. If you were a job interviewer, how would you use non-verbal communication to help you get the job?

Chapter 5

Daily Life Differences in Intercultural Communication

1. When in Rome, do as the Romans do.

   —English Proverb

2. By nature people are nearly alike, by practice they get to be wide apart.

   —Confucian Saying

Section I How do people communicate in daily life?

I Pre-tasks

Task 1 Cultural puzzles

Read the following situations and choose the appropriate answers. There may be more than one possible answer for each cultural puzzle.

1. What would you do if you gave your American boss an expensive gift and he or she said, "I'm sorry. I really can't accept this gift."

   A. You could say: "If you don't accept this gift, I'll quit." or "I won't take this class anymore."

   B. You could try to find out his or her reasons for not accepting the gift.

   C. You can insist many times on giving the gift until he or she accepts it.

2. What would you do if you met a woman and you didn't know if she should be called "Mrs." "Miss" or "Ms."?

A. You could use "Ms.".

B. You could try not to use her name.

C. You could check the woman's left hand to see if she's married.

Task 2 Interview

Locate someone from a culture different from your own, and interview him or her regarding the characteristics of a successful communicator in that culture. Include some of the following questions in your interview:

1. What are the elements of credibility within your culture?

2. What communicative behaviors are least desirable in your culture?

3. What communication skills are most valued in your culture?

II While-tasks

Cultural Differences in Daily Communication between China and the US

With the developing of sciences and technologies, people with different cultural backgrounds are communicating more and more frequently. People with different lifestyles, ways of thinking, behaviors and values are interacting more with each other. With more cross-cultural communication, because of cultural differences, misunderstandings may arise, although the language used in communication may be faultless. As cultures are diverse, so languages are diverse. It is only natural then that differences in languages can create differences in communicating between cultures and across cultures. Understanding is not always easy. It is therefore very important to be aware of and understand culture differences, only with that will someone know how to respect other cultures and how to use their languages well when communicating with them. Agreement about a simple meaning of culture is not in sight. Various definitions of culture reflect differing theories for understanding—or criteria for evaluating—human activity. Sir Edward B. Taylor writing from the perspective of social anthropology in the UK in 1871 described culture in the following way: "Culture or civilization, taken in its wide ethnographic sense, is that complex whole which includes knowledge, belief, art, morals, law, custom, and any other capabilities and habits acquired by man as a member of society." Culture consists of all the shared products of human society". This means not only such visible things as cities, organizations

Chapter 5　Daily Life Differences in Intercultural Communication

and schools, but also non-material things such as ideas, customs, family patterns, languages. To simplify, culture refers to the entire way of life of a society, "the ways of a people". Language is a part of culture and plays a very important role in it. Some social scientists consider it the keystone of culture. Without language, they maintain, culture would not be possible. On the other hand, language is influenced and shaped by culture, it reflects culture. In the broadest sense, language is the symbolic representation of a person, and it comprises their historical and cultural backgrounds as well as their approach to life and their ways of living and thinking. What needs to be stressed here is that culture and language interact, and that the understanding of one requires the understanding of the other.

Brief Introduction to Daily Communication

Communication, namely the interaction between people, usually refers to the two and two or more people through the language and behavior to communicate express opinionsand emotions. The human communication is not only a linguistic phenomenon, but also a cultural phenomenon. It is no doubt that communication is of great importance in our daily life. People cannot live without communication. Communication is everywhere. Daily communication is very important to our human the vehicle by which people initiate, maintain, and terminate their relationships with others. If you want to communicate well, the first thing you should do is to understand different cultures. The cultures between China and the US are distinguished by a rather large scale of elements and the people's communication in daily life is also not the same. We should get to learn how to coordinate the different cultures. For example, their forms of address, greetings, farewells and so on. Only in this way we can communicate successfully with other people who come from the different countries.

Forms of Address

The trend is for Americans to address others by using first names such as Bill or Jean rather than the more formal method of address such as Mr. Smith or Miss Jones. This also applies even when people meet for the first time. It is also common when young children address older people, including their grandparents. This is not considered a sign of disrespect but as an accepted cultural norm. People of different social status also do the same, for example, students often call their professors by their first name. This is not regarded as a sign of familiarity or disrespect, but rather, as an indication that the relationship between professor and student is affable and has a sense of equality. The Chinese custom in this aspect certainly seems to counter what is practiced in the United States. In China, seniority is paid respect, with the affability and equality of the American professor and student relationship absent. It is expected for the junior to address the senior in a formal and proper way. The reaction of a grandparent being called by their first name by a grandchild or a teacher/lecturer being addressed in first name terms by a student would be one of shock and result in possible displeasure and probable reprimand. The old traditional hierarchical structure in Chinese society has helped maintain this respectful form of addressing others. Two prefixes used in Chinese which do however embody a less formally and more friendly form of address are *Lao* and *Xiao*, but in comparison to American, formal address is what is expected in China. Chinese often extend kinship terms like *da ye*, *da ma* and *a yi* to people not related by blood or marriage. These terms are used after surnames to indicate politeness and respect. In America, however, the name alone would ordinarily be enough. The English equivalents of the above mentioned kinship terms are not used. With relatives it is the first name that is normally used and the relationship is omitted. Other terms used in addressing people in China are gingham shush and hush aye. Using these terms in the English form in addressing Americans would sound odd to the American ear. Another common Chinese form of address is the use of a person's title, office or occupation such as "张校长" "马经理". To use these forms of address is far from normal in America though in certain occupations titles are used, particularly in establishment occupations such as law, government and armed forces e. g. Judge, President and General.

Greeting and Farewell

Americans have many forms of greeting someone, including "Good morning", "Good evening!", "Hello!", "Hi!". The equivalents most commonly used in China, particularly in urban areas, are "你好" or "您好". But traditional greetings in China can still be heard which differ a lot from America. Two typical greetings—translated into English are "Have you eaten yet?" Or "Have you had your lunch?". Addressing an American using these questions would probably be taken literally —The reply would probably be yes or no. In fact it would most probably be interpreted as an invitation to come for a meal or an invitation to come to someone's home for a meal. The greeting would be misunderstood. Similar Chinese greetings literally translated are "Where are you going?" and "What are you doing?" Addressing Americans in these ways would be looked upon as intruding into personal matters. In general, they would feel uncomfortable if someone approached and addressed them in such a way. They would most likely react by saying "Mind your own business" or indeed saying something very rude! So, what is meant by the Chinese as a form of greeting and not as a genuine question is seen by Americans as a rude question. When Americans part from a friend or friends, the usual remarks are bye, goodbye, see you soon, or so long, take care, often accompanied by a smile. This would be done after an informal meeting or an evening spent in each other's company or when leaving someone's home after dining with them. For strangers or people who may not see each other again, the greeting may be more formal and they may say "It's nice to have met you.", or "Nice meeting you." take care, and to accompany this with a handshake. Terms used when Chinese part, differ. On accompanying a guest to the door, an indication of the esteem for a guest is shown by the distance between host and guest, accompanied by the host saying: "请留步". Final parting remarks include "慢走" "走好" "慢点骑". Such remarks used in America would sound strange and indeed pointless. It can be seen that Americans tend to have less formal ways and a more relaxed attitude in greeting and parting from others. They tend to avoid commenting on the personal aspects of someone's life. In doing this they tend to respect the privacy of the individual, it is their American culture of individualism.

Compliments and Praise

Both cultures use compliments to people on many aspects such as intelligence, talents, and personal qualities and on material possessions. However, compliments can be interpreted in different ways and reacted to in different ways. An example is of a Chinese student in America who is complimented about her new dress by an American student. She may result, may feel happy but also embarrassed and so replies in a typical Chinese fashion, "It's just an ordinary dress I bought in China." The American however may then feel that her taste in clothing is questionable and so feel uncomfortable that she praised the dress in the first place. Another example can be illustrated by the American who teaches in China and invites the Chinese art teacher to give him advice on a new painting he is creating. The Chinese teacher makes some suggestions and then says, "I really don't know much about the subject." The American may interpret this as the art teacher "fishing for a compliment", even though the teacher's remarks may be very sincere. It would then necessitate a response from the American such as "Oh, come on, I know you are an expert on Chinese art". This appears as a forced compliment and can lead a bad taste in the mouth. In fact, Chinese people value modesty highly and think it bad taste and impolite to accept compliments without showing modesty. In American families it is common for members to praise each other. The person praised feels good. Mothers may talk about their children to others and praise their abilities, their marks and grades at school and their skills at sport. Sometimes this praise is not justified. The culture praises success. This praise is also given to the husband, wife or partner who shows success at work and who receives promotion or honors. Praise is a very public matter in America to be seen by all. In China, however, this would be considered bad taste. One simply does not praise members of one's own family in front of others even if they have shown great success in something. One taboo in China is the complimenting of another man's wife. Such a remark as you have a lovely wife could be regarded as something almost indecent particularly to older people. In America such a compliment, however, is a common and acceptable remark to make. It should be noted however that with equality between male and female in America, such remarks are now less made and indeed becoming less acceptable especially by feminists. Compliments in America are usually acknowledged with a thanks and in China with a reply that suggests not being worthy of the praise.

Thanks and Response

"Thank you" is widely used in English to show gratitude in such cases as being invited, helped, given a gift, etc. Cultural differences exist between China and the US in how to express thanks and responses. In fact, "Thank you" is uttered in English for more than acknowledging favor or gratitude, and it is often a means to show politeness. On many occasions, the English use this utterance while the Chinese may say "辛苦您了" or do not say a word at all but just smile or nod. As a matter of fact, "Thank you" is used more widely by westerners than Chinese use "谢谢", for minor favors like borrowing pencil, asking directions, requesting someone to pass on a message, receiving a telephone, etc. "Thank you" not only shows politeness but also carries a person's grateful feeling for those who offer help. Without using expres-

Chapter 5 Daily Life Differences in Intercultural Communication

sions of gratitude, misunderstandings may arise because the help seems to be taken for granted and is not appreciated, For the US, each person is an equal individual, whether he is a family member or not. In Chinese, "谢谢" is not frequently used between intimate friends and family members because it may imply a certain distance between the addresser and the addressee. Native speakers may respond to "Thank you" by saying: You are welcome./It is my pleasure./Not at all./Don't mention it./That's all right. While Chinese people may say: "这是我应该做的", which may convey to Americans the message that the Chinese did not really want to do it, or than he/she did it only because it was his/her duty.

Word list:

1. individualism [ˌɪndɪˈvɪdjuəlɪzəm]
   n. 个人主义,利己主义;自由放任主义;个性,独特性;不干涉主义
2. compliment [ˈkɒmplɪmənt]
   n. 恭维;敬意;道贺,贺词;致意
   vt. 称赞;向……道贺;向……致意
3. indecent [ɪnˈdiːsnt]
   adj. 粗鄙的,猥亵的;不适当的,不合适的;不礼貌的;不得体的
4. necessitate [nɪˈsesɪteɪt]
   vt. 使……成为必要,需要;强迫,迫使
5. affable [ˈæfəbl]
   adj. 和蔼的;友善的;平易近人的;(天气)宜人
6. gratitude [ˈɡrætɪtjuːd]
   n. 谢意;感激,感谢;感激的样子;恩义
7. utterance [ˈʌtərəns]
   n. 说话;表达;说话方式;发言
8. intimate [ˈɪntɪmət]
   adj. 亲密的,亲近的;私人的,个人的;内部的;直接的
   n. 至交;密友
   v. 暗示,提示;宣布,通知
9. imply [ɪmˈplaɪ]
   v. 暗示;意味;隐含;说明,表明

Task 1　Reading comprehension

Exercise One: Work with your partners, decide whether the following statements are true (T) or false (F) according to what you have learned in the passage.

1. _____ With more cross-cultural communication, misunderstandings may arise.
2. _____ The cultures between China and the US are distinguished by a rather large scale of elements.
3. _____ It's OK a grandparent being called by their first name by a grandchild or a teacher/lecturer being addressed in first name terms by a student in China.
4. _____ Compliments in America are usually acknowledged with a thanks and in China with a reply that suggests not being worthy of the praise.
5. _____ "Thank you" not only shows politeness but also carries a person's grateful feeling for those who offer help.
6. _____ In Chinese families it is common for members to praise each other.
7. _____ Communication usually refers to the two and two or more people through the language and behavior to communicate express opinions and emotions.
8. _____ Without language, they maintain, culture would not be possible.
9. _____ "Thank you" is uttered in English only for acknowledging favor or gratitude.
10. _____ Remarbs, such as "慢走""走好""请留步", used in America would sound strange and indeed pointless.

Exercise Two: Choose the right answer according to your understanding of this passage.

Which of the following is NOT mentioned by the writer?

A. It is very important to be aware of and understand culture differences, only with that will someone know how to respect other cultures and how to use their languages well when communicating with them.

B. The human communication is not only a linguistic phenomenon, but also a cultural phenomenon.

C. The old traditional hierarchical structure in Chinese society has helped maintain this respectful form of addressing others.

D. "Thank you" is uttered in English only to show gratitude.

Exercise Three: Fill in the blanks with the words given below and change the form when necessary.

terminate   convey   frequently   misunderstanding   gratitude
compliment   interpret   individualism   compliment   utter

1. "Thank you" is widely used in English to show _____ in such cases as being invited, helped, given a gift.

2. Chinese people value modesty highly and think it bad taste and impolite to accept _____ without showing modesty.

3. Americans tend to avoid commenting on the personal aspects of someone's life to respect the privacy of the individual their American culture of _____ .

4. Daily communication is very important to our human by which people initiate, maintain, and _____ their relationships with others.

5. People with different cultural backgrounds are communicating more and more _____ .

6. In China it is a taboo to _____ another man's wife.

7. When Chinese say "这是我应该做的", it may _____ to Americans the message that the Chinese did not really want to do it.

8. "Thank you" is _____ in English for more than acknowledging favor or gratitude.

9. Because of cultural differences, _____ may arise.

10. People from different cultures may _____ same expressions in different ways.

Task 2   Case study

Case 1: Feeling Left-out

After graduating from Beijing International Studies University, Chen Liang pursued an MA program at a university in Boston, the US Early in the program he made friends with some of the American students studying in the same program. One day after class, his American friend, Dick, asked Chen to join him in the university cafeteria. On their way they ran into Dick's girlfriend, Lisa, who was on her way to a lecture. Walking shoulder to shoulder, Dick and Lisa carried on an intimate conversation, as if they hadn't seen each other for ages. Meanwhile, Chen Liang was walking behind them, not taking part in the conversation. When they were nearing the cafeteria Lisa said she had to leave for the lecture. Dick embraced her and gave her a long and passionate kiss. Seeing this, Chen turned away and walked off toward the cafeteria, when Dick looked up, he saw Chen walking into the cafeteria. Dick was puzzled as to why Chen didn't wait for him, and went to the cafeteria alone. （汪福祥，马登阁，1999）

Questions for discussion：

1. Could you explain to Dick why Chen Liang walked into the cafeteria without waiting for him?

2. If you were Chen Liang, how would you do in such a situation?

Case 2：Kindness can kill

As a college professor of English, Mr. Wang was in constant contact with people from English-speaking countries. Therefore, he was often asked to help introduce foreign businessmen interested in investing in China. One day, a country magistrate came and presented him with some documents concerning a project. He asked the professor to keep an ear open for potential investors. The professor agreed that it was a very good project, but the sum of money being sought was staggering. Afterwards, the professor met with several foreign businessmen, among which an Australian seemed very interested in the project. Through several phone calls, he arranged a meeting between the magistrate and the investor. Realizing that a big opportunity presented itself, the magistrate assured the professor of their one hundred percent "cooperation", and told the professor that they would do whatever possible to please that investor. When the big day arrived, the investor and the magistrate met in a reception room, where about 15 other local officials were eagerly waiting. After a customary greeting and some details regarding the project, the magistrate showed the investor around the project site and its beautiful surroundings. The investor was very pleased with the project prospects and the location of the joint venture, and the atmosphere was encouraging for both the investor and the magistrate. At 11:30, they were driven to the best hotel in the country, where they were seated in an extravagantly decorated restaurant. After a couple of minutes, the first course was served. The second followed, then the third. Before the third course was replaced by the fourth, the investor jokingly said that their food was enough to feed an army. Misjudging the investor's joke as a compliment, the magistrate kept encouraging him to eat slowly so that he could taste all the delicacies that were specially prepared for him. Although the professor had food arrived up and both the magistrate and the local officials displayed a kind of hospitality that had made the investor almost ill. At about 2:00 P. M., the investor customarily thanked the magistrate for his hospitality and left the county. But to the magistrate's bewilderment and disappointment, that was their first and last. (Ibid)

Questions for discussion:

1. Why did the Australian investor not come back for the project that he earlier showed a great interest in?

2. Why did misunderstanding happen?

III After-tasks

Task 1　Movie and culture discussion *Crash*

Crash tells interlocking stories of whites, blacks, Latinos, Koreans, Iranians, cops and criminals, the rich and the poor, the powerful and the powerless, all defined in one way or another by racism. All are victims of it, and all are guilty of it. The result is a movie of intense fascination; we understand quickly enough who the characters are and what their lives are like, but we have no idea how they will behave, because so much depends on accident. Most movies enact rituals; we know the form and watch for variations. *Crash* is a movie with free will, and anything can happen.

The film is about racial and social tensions in Los Angeles, California. The film reflects the cultural conflicts among whites, blacks, Asians and Latin Americans. As is known to all, the United States is an immigrant country. And after centuries of development, the United States has become a multicultural country. Therefore, to some extent, the movie is a mirror of the multicultural society in the United States.

As a low cost movie, that *Crash* can get the Oscar award reflects the success of the film from the side. The film sets the story in Los Angeles, where the cultural conflicts phenomenon is very common. These years, we can express our moods freely and we have the rights to do what we think is right, especially in America which is famous for freedom and democracy. Therefore, we get selfish step by step and we just pursue what we want or what can meet our desire. *Crash* tells us some ordinary people's stories. In this movie, many plots connote racial discrimination. The gap between the black and the white still exists despite the abolishment of the slavery. However, this racial discrimination not only happens between the white and the black but also exists among people of different countries like Mexicans, Chinese, Arabians and so on. The white try their best to play the role of respecting the people of color, but in their heart, they discriminate against the people of color. The black suffer the discrimination from the white while at the same time they look down upon other people of color. Discrimination is almost common, which the movie reflects. But as a member of the earth, we are the same. Everyone should try to forgive others and admonish ourselves to avoid making prejudices. Love can reduce this kind of discrimination and make society more harmonious whether in America or in other countries. *Crash* is a real microcosm of contemporary American society, highlighting the conflicts and contradictions among multiethnic culture. Conflicts between African Americans and whites constitute the movie's main conflict in the movie. In my opinion, to avoid cross-cultural conflict, not only do we need to understand the concept of cross-cultural communication, but also to cultivate our cross-cultural competence. In the wave of globalization sweeping all areas of social life in the 21st century, there are indications that the collision of different nationalities, different cultures, and different religions and so on will become an important factor which affects the stability of the world. From the consideration of national interests and long-term development, we must take part in international economic competition actively and learn to respect the values of different cultures.

Please watch the movie Crash and try to answer the following questions:
1. What do you think of racism?
2. What touches you most after watching it?
3. Try to analyze one role from the movie.

Task 2 Extended reading

Necessity of Improving Intercultural Communication

An Internet search on the topic of intercultural communication or cross-cultural communication yields over 100,000 results. In recent years practitioners in a wide variety of fields—scientific cooperation, academic research, business, management, education, health, culture, politics, diplomacy, development, and others—have realized just how important intercultural communication is for their everyday work. Fast travel, international media, and the Internet have made it easy for us to communicate with people all over the world. The process of economic globalization means that we cannot function in isolation but must interact with the rest of the world for survival. The global nature of many widely diverse modern problems and issues such as the environment, governance of the Internet, poverty and international terrorism call for cooperation between nations. Intercultural communication is no longer an option, but a necessity.

Because important decisions in business, politics, education, health, and culture these days usually effect citizens of more than one nation, the question of whether communication between people of different nations is effective and whether all parties emerge with the same understanding is of crucial importance. Individuals who deal with people from other cultures want to learn how to improve their performance through improving their communication skills. Numerous resources have sprung up to meet this emerging market in the business, academic and international relations communities: leading authors have written books and articles on the topic; business services provide consultation for improving the conduct of international business; universities and other educational institutions offer programs or degrees in Intercultural Communication; and researchers have established international journals and academic societies specializing in research on intercultural communication. In fact, intercultural communication has become a business in itself. Following are just a few examples.

Richard Lewis Communications is a company owned by the author of the popular *When Cultures Collide: Managing Successfully Across Cultures* (London: Nicholas Brealey, 1993). They offer business consultancy, run "cross-cultural training" courses and workshops, publish papers and workbooks, and develop software for intercultural communication. The website advises:

> *Working in a global team and dealing with business partners or customers across cultures raises challenges and demands new attitudes and skills. Our experience shows that without the right approach, cultural differences greatly reduce effectiveness in the early stages of a relationship. But active management of the internationalization process and a conscious effort to acquire new skills will release fresh sources of competitive advantage.*

The University of British Columbia Center for Intercultural Communication offers International Relocation Programs to prepare people for moving abroad to work, International Meeting Facilitation, Youth Internship Programs abroad, training for government officials involved in international development, community outreach and advocacy, and certificate and MA level programs in Intercultural Relations. They describe their work in this way:

> *In a world that is increasingly interconnected, the success of organizations and their people depends on effective cross-cultural communication. At the Center for Intercultural Communication, we help our clients adopt a truly global perspective in order to work effectively across cultures. Program participants acquire cross-culturalknowledge, build intercultural expertise, and develop global capabilities in order to maximize value and minimize the risks associated with being involved in*

Chapter 5　Daily Life Differences in Intercultural Communication

international activity.

Intercultural Communication is an academic journal specializing in the topic. From their policy statement:

> *The world today is characterized by an ever growing number of contacts resulting in communication between people with different linguistic and cultural backgrounds. This communication takes place because of contacts within the areas of business, military cooperation, science, education, mass media, entertainment, and tourism, but also because of immigration brought about by labor shortage or political conflicts. In all these contacts, there is communication which needs to be as constructive as possible, without misunderstandings and breakdowns. It is our belief that research on the nature of linguistic and cultural similarities and differences here can play a positive and constructive role.*

Intermundo—the Culture Network describes itself as the leading "intercultural network on the Internet". They publish articles on various aspects of intercultural communication and current affairs, reviews of books on intercultural communication, information about relevant conferences, educational videos, and run online discussion forums.

Why is it important to improve intercultural communication? Lack of knowledge of another culture can lead, at the best, to embarrassing or amusing mistakes in communication. At the worst, such mistakes may confuse or even offend the people we wish to communicate with, making the conclusion of business deals or international agreements difficult or impossible.

> *I do not want my house to be walled in on all sides and my windows to be stuffed. I want the cultures of all the lands to be blown about my house as freely as possible. But I refuse to be blown off my feet by any.*
> 　　　　　　　　　　　　　　　　　　　　　　　—*Mahatma Gandhi.*

Donnell King of Pellissippi State Technical Community College provides some examples from the advertising world of how simply translating words is not enough—deeper understanding of the other culture is necessary to translate meaning effectively: A General Motors auto ad with "Body by Fisher" became "Corpse by Fisher" in Flemish. A Colgate-Palmolive toothpaste named "Cue" was advertised in France before anyone realized that *Cue* also happened to be the name of a widely circulated pornographic book about oral sex. Pepsi Cola's "Come Alive With Pepsi" campaign, when it was translated for the Taiwanese market, conveyed the unsettling news that, "Pepsi brings your ancestors back from the grave." Parker Pen could not advertise its famous "Jotter" ballpoint pen in some languages because the translation sounded like "jockstrap" pen.

Understanding cultural norms and rules such as the way we are expected to greet others, the way we are expected to dress, the way we are expected to eat, and the way we are expected to answer questions are also important in improving communication with people from other cultures. For example, if you greet an American by asking him or her "Where are you going?" or "Have you eaten yet?", the American might feel very uncomfortable because asking these questions could be interpreted as an invasion of privacy. But in Chinese culture, these are appropriate greetings which do not invade the other person's privacy.

What are mentioned above illustrate the importance of improving the ability of intercultural communication. No matter what kind of job we do, or what situation we are in, if we want to overcome culture barriers and communicate effectively, it's very necessary to improve the ability of intercultural communication. (1060 words)

(Adapted from http://www.diplomacy.edu/language/intercultural-communication)

Critical thinking questions:

1. According to this passage, why is it important to improve inter cultural communication?

2. If you worked in a global team dealing with business partners or customers across cultures, how would you deal with them?

3. Except the examples mentioned in the passage, can you think of other examples about intercultural communication in advertising world?

Chapter 5 Daily Life Differences in Intercultural Communication

Section II Cross-culture in daily life

I Pre-tasks

Task 1 Situation analysis

Read the following situation and choose the appropriate answer (s). There may be more than one possible answer.

Situation: An American, Diane, invited her Japanese friend, Michiko, to come to her house one afternoon. Michiko couldn't come and said, "No, I can't come, please invite me again to your house." Diane was surprised by what Michiko said.

Why do you think Diane was surprised?

A. Diane thought that Michiko didn't want to come to her house because she said, "No, I can't come." She couldn't understand why Michiko added "invite me again" when it seemed that she didn't want to visit her.

B. When Michiko said that she couldn't come, Diane thought Michiko would invite her in return. She was waiting for Michiko to say, "Why don't you come to my house in a couple of days?"

C. Diane thought Michiko was rude for not explaining why she couldn't come and asking directly for another visit.

Task 2 Dialogue analysis

Read the following dialogue and tell whether you can fully understand the humor or not.

A: Do you know anything about Professor Cornposture?

B: Oh, he's the world's leading expert in ballistic missiles, he won last year's Nobel Prize in Physics and he's head of the Science Department at Yale. Why do you ask?

A: He asked me to lend him five shillings.

II While-tasks

How to Avoid Misunderstandings

Every once in a while you get into an argument. After a short time, your opponent du jour, sometimes even yourself, would step back and talk about misunderstanding and eventually end or postpone the fight. Why do you think you always run into misunderstandings? Misunderstanding is failing to interpret correctly. You interpret best what is least definitive. Your misunderstandings are signs of mismatches, even cracks within your reality. Misunderstanding is—more often than not—a mismatch between actual content and perceived way of delivery. While the content is almost never touched, fighting erupts over the presentation of the message. Misunderstanding is not about failing to receive all of the information. Misunderstanding is about receiving too much information to make sense of within your own context at this very moment. Let's examine the various levels of details and the respective perception involved. The problem is hidden in the details, in fact, the problem is the details. The more specific the provided details, the more you will have to adapt your imagination and the resulting expectation to the message received.

Computer-generated film delivers only as many defails as needed to sufficiently communicate a given story. When you see a panorama shot, for example, you get a very rough scenery with minimal amounts of details. Your mind takes over the decoration part and makes you perceive a rich scenery when in fact, you barely receive enough stimulation to not get overwhelmed. You appreciate the details because you are not fed them but instead, you create them yourself. Your mind completes the picture and as you zoom in and immerse yourself in the story, your mental experience matches and ultimately exceeds the actually seen imagery. The more details a situation provides, the more specific it is and the higher the chance of not exactly matching your preconceived interpretation. The most vague and unspecific arbitrary message reaching you comes with the opportunity to have you custom-color the pale information and personalize it with your own expectation. You are amazed by the highly targeted content that was destined only and especially for you. The same words delivered to you being in positive, allowing mode of expectation make you happy and leave you full of joy, in contrast, when received expecting an insult, you will get just that.

Chapter 5 Daily Life Differences in Intercultural Communication

To counter and prevent misunderstanding, two courses of action are implicit. (1) Communicate as detailed as possible, including all possible misconceptions and discuss every single instance of being potentially unclear. Reiterate what you intend to communicate as often as you think is necessary to make your point bullet-proof. (2) Communicate with brevity and in generic terms in order to allow the recipient to fill in the positive or negative touch of the message. Your job is to predict the best moment for the message to arrive. The first option—reiterating endlessly—is what most people do most of the time only to run into even more arguments. The second option—let the recipient fill in his expectation—is the smarter choice, leading to less arguments and ultimately eliminating fights over conflicting perceptions.

"Why do they keep misunderstanding me?" We often hear people complain. Misunderstanding seems to be one of the most disturbing issues in interpersonal relationships. We often see how it undermines the harmonious relationships between people. Several factors contribute to misunderstanding. Firstly, people with different personal and cultural backgrounds may have diverse perspectively in interpreting one behavior. Secondly, the language we use as a vehicle of conveying thought can be ambiguous, and various ways of decoding words may result in barriers in communication. Thirdly, misunderstanding occurs because of a lack of mutual trust. If you have prejudice against someone, whatever he says may sound intentioned to you. Having gone so far in the exploration of the causes of misunderstanding, we can easily arrive at the ways to avoid them. Firstly, we should be broad minded and be tolerant of the differences among people. Secondly, we should be accurate and appropriate in our handle of language, avoiding misleading words. Thirdly, we should be constructive and patient in dealing with people. If we try hard enough, there will be more understanding and less misunderstanding in this world.

One thing it's vital to understand is the need for clear, unambiguous communication. Here's why. The communication process is a simple one to understand, but a very difficult one to operate successfully. Here's the process: (1) You think of a message you wish to communicate to another person (or a group of people). (2) You then translate the message into a deliverable format—and the message may already have changed in some way from the one you thought of. (3) You deliver your message—whether written or spoken, in person or at the end on a telephone line. (4) The person receiving the message hears or listens to part, all or none of it. (5) The receiver then translates your message into what they think you think you meant to say.

The problems with the process being successful are many. For example:

1. Simply not hearing part of the message.

2. Hearing, but not actually listening to the content of a communication.

3. Taking a different meaning or understanding from the message.

4. Interpreting a message—hearing what the person wants to hear rather than what is actually said.

5. Trying to read the sender's mind rather than simply listening to what is communicated.

6. Being distracted during the receiving process, e. g. by outside noise, looking at other work etc.

Filtering the message through their beliefs, feelings, impressions etc. It's absolutely vital, therefore, to make your communication with others as simple and clear as possible. And, remember this—if you are the communicator, it's your job to make sure your audience understand exactly what you want them to. Never assume!

Word list:

1. mismatch ['mɪsmætʃ]
    n. 错配；不协调
    vt. 使配错
2. panorama [pænə'rɑːmə]
    n. 全景，全貌；全景画；概论
3. decoration [dekə'reɪʃ(ə)n]
    n. 装饰，装潢；装饰品；奖章
4. arbitrary ['ɑːbɪt(rə)rɪ]
    adj. [数] 任意的；武断的，专制的
5. ambiguous [æm'bɪgjʊəs]
    adj. 模糊不清的；引起歧义的
6. deliverable [dɪ'lɪvərəbl]
    adj. 可以传送的；可交付使用的

Chapter 5 Daily Life Differences in Intercultural Communication

Task 1 Reading comprehension

Exercise One: Work with your partners, decide whether the following statements are true (T) or false (F) according to what you have learned in the passage.

1. _____ Your misunderstandings are signs of mismatches, even cracks within your reality.
2. _____ You interpret worst what is least definitive.
3. _____ Misunderstanding happens when failing to receive all of the information.
4. _____ Misunderstanding is about receiving too much information to make sense of within your own context at this very moment.
5. _____ The more specific the provided details, the more you will have to adapt your imagination and the resulting expectation to the message received.
6. _____ The more details a situation provides, the more specific it is.
7. _____ The communication process is a difficult one to understand, but a very simple one to operate successfully.
8. _____ If you have prejudice against someone, whatever he says may sound intentioned to you.
9. _____ If you are the communicator, it's your job to make sure your audience understand exactly what you want them to.
10. _____ In communication, we should avoid using misleading words.

Exercise Two: Fill in the blanks with the words given below and change the form when necessary.

unambiguous	*exploration*	*mismatch*	*adapt*	*filter*
misconception	*ultimately*	*amazed*	*accurate*	*erupt*

1. Misunderstanding is a _____ between actual content and perceived way of delivery.

2. While the content is almost never touched, fighting _____ over the presentation of the message.

3. The more specific the provided details, the more you will have to _____ your imagination and the resulting expectation to the message received.

4. As you zoom in and immerse yourself in the story, your mental experience matches and _____ exceeds the actually seen imagery.

5. You are _____ by the highly targeted content that was destined only and especially for you.

6. Communicate as detailed as possible, including all possible _____.

7. Having gone so far in the _____ of the causes of misunderstanding, we can easily arrive at the ways to avoid them.

8. We should be _____ and appropriate in our handle of language.

9. One thing it's vital to understand is the need for clear, _____ communication.

10. During communication, one need to _____ the message through their beliefs, feelings, impressions.

Task 2 Case study

Case 1: Low vs. High Context Culture

1. When President George Bush went to Japan with leading American businessmen, he made explicit and direct demands on Japanese leaders, which violated Japanese etiquette. To the Japanese, it is rude and a sign of ignorance or desperation to make direct demands. Some analysts believe it severely damaged the negotiations and confirmed to the Japanese that Americans are barbarians.

2. A Japanese manager in an American company was told to give critical feedback to a subordinate during a performance evaluation. Because the Japanese are used to high context language and are uncomfortable with giving direct feedback, it took the manager five tries before he was direct enough for the American subordinate to understand.

Questions for discussion:

1. Why did the Japanese think that Americans are barbarians?

2. Why was it so difficult for the Japanese manager to tell his subordinate about his poor performance?

Case 2: Different Philosophies

Dr. Richard Lowry, a prominent American engineer, was commissioned by a company in Indonesia to direct (with a local construction supervisor) a bridge-building project in the interior of the country. Before departing, Dr. Lowry studied the Indonesian language and customs of the people he would be working with. He also studied Islamic religion since he knew that the Indonesian supervisor was a devout Muslim. Although he adjusted well to the local community, there were aspects of his work to which he had trouble adapting. Material never seemed to be available when it was supposed to be. Workers seldom showed up on time for work, and when they did, they were slow to get started. The relationship with the Indonesian supervisor was far from perfect. They could not seem to agree on a schedule for the arrival of goods. In fact, it did not seem that his partner even cared about completing the project at the desired time. Midway through his three-month assignment Dr. Lowry became so frustrated and moody he became less productive, kept to himself and he frequently thought about returning home. (汪福祥,马登阁,1999)

Questions for discussion:

1. What is the primary cause for the problem above?

2. Does it result from their different philosophies on management or different world views?

III After-tasks

Task 1 Movie and culture discussion *Pushing Hands*

The movie *Pushing Hands* tells a story about Master Chu, a retired Chinese Tai-Chi master, who emigrates from Beijing to live with his son Alex, American daughter-in-law Martha, and grandson in a New York City suburb. Martha's second novel is suffering from severe writers' block brought on by Chu's presence in the house. Alex must struggle to keep his family together as he battles an inner conflict between cultural tradition and his modern American lifestyle. The grandfather is increasingly distanced from the family as a "fish out of water" in Western culture. The film shows the contrast between traditional Chinese ideas of Confucian relationships within a family and the much more informal Western emphasis on the individual. The friction in the family caused by these differing expectations eventually leads to the grandfather moving out of the family home (something very alien to traditional expectations), and in the process he learns lessons (some comical, some poignant) about how he must adapt to his new surroundings before he comes to terms with his new life.

The title of the film refers to the pushing hands training that is part of the grandfarther's Tai-Chi routine. Pushing hands is a two person training which teaches Tai-Chi students to yield in the face of brute force. Tai-Chi Chuan teachers were persecuted in China during the "Cultural Revolution", and the grandfather's family was broken up as a result. He sent his son to the West several years earlier and when he could he came to live with his family with the expectation of picking up where they left off, but he was unprepared for the very different atmosphere of the West. *Pushing Hands* thereby alludes to the process of adaptation to culture shock felt by a traditional teacher in moving to the United States.

Questions:

1. Why do you think this movie is named *Pushing Hands*?

2. Why there are so many misunderstandings between Master Chu and his daughter-in-law?

3. What caused his son to appreciate him and remember why he got his father to live together in the first place in a tear jerking scene and finally they worked out a solution?

Chapter 5 Daily Life Differences in Intercultural Communication

Task 2 Extended reading

How to Overcome Culture Shock in a Foreign Country

It is common to experience culture shock when living in a foreign country for an extended period of time. Culture shock is defined as the feeling of disorientation, insecurity, and anxiety one may feel in unfamiliar surroundings. Values, behaviors, and social customs we routinely take for granted may no longer serve us in our new environment. By adapting to a foreign culture, you can overcome your culture shock and develop meaningful relationships with those around you, rather than feeling anxious and confused in your new space.

Steps

Step 1. Open mind. Do not automatically perceive anything that is different to be "wrong". Withholding judgment will allow you to be an objective observer and will facilitate the process of cross-cultural understanding. Also, if you are going to a country with which you know close to nothing about, do a little background information. As you learn about the country in which you are going to, keeping an open mind is necessary, and, who knows, you may find the reason for something you may not understand.

Step 2. Make an effort to learn the local language. This increases your communication skills and it helps you to integrate with the local community. It also demonstrates your interest in the new country.

Step 3. Get acquainted with the social conduct of your new environment. Do not assume or interpret behavior from your own cultural perspective or "filter". Behavior is not data. For example, Americans often use the phrase "How are you?" to mean "hello" or "I acknowledge your presence as I pass you in the hall". A foreigner may wonder why Americans don't respond in detail to this question about one's well-being. Thus they may interpret the behavior of walking away before one has a chance to respond to the question to be "uncaring" "superficial" or even "rude". An American knows otherwise and would probably not be offended that someone did not take the time to respond to this question. Remember: If in doubt, check it out!

Step 4. Do not take cultural familiarity or knowledge at face-value. Even as you become more savvy about rituals, customs and protocol in your new environment, be careful not to attribute an explanation or rationale to what you now believe you know. A little bit of knowledge can be misleading. Psychologist Geert Hofstede wrote that "culture" is like an onion that can be peeled, layer by layer, to reveal the content. It takes a long time to really understand a culture in its social and historical context.

Step 5. Make sure you get to know people in your new environment. Respectfully ask questions, read newspapers, and attend a variety of festivals and events.

Step 6. Try to achieve a sense of stability in your life. Establishing a routine will give you a feeling of safety.

Step 7. Most importantly, maintain a sense of humor! Don't be too hard on yourself if you make a cultural gaffe or don't know what to do in a social situation. Laugh at yourself and others will laugh with you. Most individuals will admire your tenacity and effort to understand their ways, especially if you are devoid of judgment and cultural comparisons that subtly and perhaps unconsciously convey a veil of superiority.

Tips

- Be patient. It takes time to adapt to new surroundings, a new culture and a new lifestyle.
- It's always good to keep in touch with family and friends back home. However, spending too much time communicating with them can exacerbate homesickness and delay the acculturation process.
- When one experiences culture shock, it is natural to withdraw to the comfort of what is familiar. Try not to give in to the temptation to isolate yourself.

Critical thinking questions:

1. Have you ever experienced culture shock? Share your experience with your classmates.

2. Why do you think culture shock happen?

3. Except the points mentioned above, can you think of other methods to avoid culture shock?

Chapter 6

Value Differences in Intercultural Communication

君子和而不同，小人同而不和。

——孔子《论语·子路》

Your beliefs become your thoughts. You thoughts become your words. Your words become your actions. Your actions become your habits. Your habits become your values. Your values become your destiny.

—Mahatma Gandhi

Section I What Is Value?

I Pre-tasks

Task 1 Who is the real hero?

Look at the following two pictures. Think about what the two pictures imply in terms of teamwork and individualism. Then talk with your partner(s) about the different approaches between the East and the West.

Task 2 Mobility

The number of migrant workers is increasing day by day. They flood into big cities in search of fortune and opportunities. What do people think of the migrant workers? Do you think mobility is a good thing and why?

II While-tasks

Something of Value

The most American form of skyscraper is quite similar to the most American form of jazz. In each, when one has finished, one just stops. On a skyscraper there is no elaborate roof, no tower or temple perched atop. Similarly, jazz also stops abruptly when the end is reached. There is no advance warning that the end is in sight, no Beethoven-like elaboration of the conclusion. We may also notice that American conversations, in contrast to those in many societies, seem to just stop when they are concluded. Even American friendships are also said to "just stop" when it is felt there is no longer any reason to continue them. An American high school senior wrote in his school yearbook, "Good-bye, I'll never see you again."

Concerning values differences, students may ask the questions like: What is Chinese about China, what is French about France, what is Russian about Russia? It assumes that any culture manifests in many ways its special character. Any traveler recognizes this when he says: "How French!" "How very German!" "How Canadian!" But the students are more interested in what is reflected within the form, and not in the form itself.

Definitions

"A system of values," Ethel Albert writes, "... represents what is expected or hoped for, required or forbidden. It is not a report of actual conduct but is the system of criteria by which conduct is judged and sanctions applied." As Professor Albert notes, few languages have a general term equivalent to value, and while some rules of conduct may be explicit ("You must always..." "You must never...!"), most value interpretations must be abstracted from diverse sources. These include child-rearing patterns, folk tales, linguistic data, tacit codes of social interaction, law and much more.

The value of informality so characteristic of much of the United States, for example, is revealed in many forms: verbally, in such expressions as "Don't stand on ceremony." and "Make yourself at home."; non-verbally, as in the preference of casual clothes (tuxedoes may be rented if needed), and the relative lack of calling cards and company lapel pins; in forms of address, with the preference for first names and awkwardness toward titles; in architecture, with the loss of parlors and the increase of recreation rooms in homes, or the change of bank architecture from Greek temples to the friendly neighborhood savings and loan.

According to Clyde Kluckhohn, an anthropologist who has written extensively on value theory, about the only defining point about values which is generally agreed upon is that they have to do with normative as opposed to existential propositions. That is, values have to do with what is judged good or bad, right or wrong. Statements based on values describe the ideal, the standards by which behavior is evaluated, they do not necessarily describe the actual behavior.

Statements about what is true and false are commonly labeled beliefs. This difference between beliefs and values is not always easy to maintain according to Kluckhohn.

What are the differences between values and preferences? Preferences are the sort of thing that poll takers are so often surveying: the preferred political candidate, the woman admired, or the brand preferred (market research). Within a single culture, differences exist. So we may never be sure of what or whom is preferred at a specific moment. On a US college campus, there may be many preferences in choice of majors, but the values underlying all of the preferences may be similar—the values of education or even that of getting away from home.

One difficulty with defining values is that of time-span. Fads and fashions are best regarded as preferences, however, enduring or classic they may seem to be. But what of the value of the nuclear family? What of countless morals in folk and fairy tales? These change as well. A cartoon in the *New Yorker* shows a "hip" father reading the end of a fairy tale to his child: "And they lived happily for some time." The concept of values must be based on a wide time-span, just as that of culture.

Value lists

The most frequent means of presenting values is through simple lists. The Boy Scout oath is a kind of list of values for a scout, and lists of values for a culture can be as stark and abstract as that of the scouts. We may read, for example, that Americans value equality, fair play, progress and self-reliance, often without reading any explanation of how such values function. Such a list may be convenient and accurate to someone familiar with the culture described, but it may be misleading to someone who has no other information to rely upon.

However, the list has disadvantages as well. For example, in the past sociological surveys of desired traits in prospective marriage partners, "cleanliness" has ranked very high in the United States, in parallel studies in Mexico it has ranked relatively low. Should cleanliness be included in a list of values in the United States? If so, how should we distinguish between that value here and "cleanliness" in a nation like Japan, where cleanliness has aesthetic and spiritual significances far different and much more evident than in the United States.

Value orientations

Florence Kluckhohn and her associates at Harvard developed the concept of value orientations. In this approach, it is assumed that there are universal problems and conditions which men in all societies face and only a limited number of solutions to these problems. Each of these possible solutions is called a value orientation. As a social scientist, she believed that these orientations could be tested empirically, with the orientations operated in hypothetical situations and presented in questionnaire form. The results would give in rank order the dominant and minority value orientations within the culture tested.

An example from Kluckhohn will serve to illustrate this approach. Every society must consider the relationship between a person and his environment. One possibility is for a person to see himself as the master of that environment, with nature viewed as something to be exploited. Another possibility is the reverse of this: for the person to see himself at the mercy of natural and supernatural forces. Yet a third possibility is for the person to view himself as a part of nature, neither master nor slave, but as one who must live in harmony with his surroundings. With these three possibilities, hypothetical problems with possible solutions which correspond to each of the alternative value orientations can be posed, surveys can be taken, and the results can be computed and analyzed. The result is the value orientations for that society listed in rank order, from most characteristic to least characteristic.

The self

"Self" is an important word. We carry with a sense of who we are and what we should be and what we want to be, and if our behaviors does not always match our image we may say, "I am not myself." or "Excuse me for last night, I was not myself." In the literature of psychology, the word "self" occupies an important place, we speak of self-concepts, self-image, self-actualization. In everyday codes of behaviors we may praise the man who is selfless and warn the one who is selfish or self-centered.

The meaning of self, how an individual is classified and distinguished from his family and society differs considerably across cultures. Here we will consider three sets of value orientations:

Individualism—interdependence

1. individualism   2. individuality   3. interdependence

Age

1. young   2. the middle ages   3. old age

Sex

1. equality of the sexes   2. female superiority   3. male superiority

Individualism—interdependence

A national flag is probably the worst place to find appropriate expressions of its culture, but in the case of the stars and stripes, some values of the United States are graphically described. With the thirteen stripes marking the nation's original colonies, and the field of stars counting out the additions to the union, the US flag marks its nation's growth through quantification from a fixed beginning. This is also important in the Americans' personal assessment of self. What is illustrated here is the sense of individualism symbolized by the individual stars. Each state, large or small, old or relatively new in its addition to the union, is given an identical representation in the field. Politically, the idea of each state being independent but equal may be outmoded, but as a model of values related to the self, the image is quite similar. What marks individualism in the United States is not so much the peculiar characteristics of each person but the sense each person has a separate but equal place in society. This fusion of individualism and equality is so valued and so basic that many Americans find it difficult to relate to contrasting values in other cultures where interdependence, complementary relationships, valued differences in age and sex greatly determine a person's sense of self.

Individuality is different and appears to be much more the norm in the world than US-style individualism is. Individuality refers to the person's freedom to act differently within the limits set by the social structure. Compared to the United States, many other cultures appear to be much more tolerant of "eccentrics" and "local characters". This confusion of individualism with individuality at first appears paradoxical: we might suppose that a society which promises apparently great personal freedoms would produce the greatest number of obviously unique, even peculiar people, and yet for more than a century visitors to the United States have been struck by a kind of "sameness" or standardization. As one writer interpreted it, the US freedom allows everybody to be like everybody else. ❶

For the children growing up in the United States, these values of equality and independence leading to individualism are introduced and reinforced in many ways. At a very early age—too early from the point of view of persons in many other societies—children are encouraged to make their own decisions and to contribute their suggestions for the plans of the entire family. What foods to eat, where to go on vacation, even whether or not to "join the family" on special occasions are frequently posed as individual choices. If a group decision is made, it may be determined by a "vote", with children and parents having or appearing to have equal parts in the vote. Important social changes in the United States are also related to this principle, even when they appear to run counter to the cherished American institutions; thus the college drop-out, the divorcee, the gap between generations, and even the lack of gun control laws, all may be rationalized directly or indirectly in terms of these values.

---

❶ F. R. Kluckhohn, *Variations in Value Orientations*, P. 23.

Another expression of the distinction between individuality and individualism may be seen in attitudes toward voting. Votes are individual, but the majority rules, and those in the minority feel obliged to support the winning candidate. Compared historically and throughout the world at present, there are remarkably few people in the United States who refuse to go along with the outcome of voting. An enormous number of decisions are put to a vote and the outcome is determined according to the will of the majority.

The term interdependence is used to identify the pattern where the self is largely determined by a person's current relationship to others in the social structure.

Three alternative individualization categories are thus appropriate: individualism, where each self is regarded as equally independent but voluntarily allied with others for specific purposes, which is the characteristic of the dominant values in the United States. Individuality, where persons are interdependent and more strictly limited and shaped by more specific social categories, such as age, sex, family, tribe, and yet within these constraints are allowed individual freedom of expression and behavior; and interdependence, where a person's concept of self almost always involves a consciousness of his place in society and his relationship to another or others with whom he interacts.

Age

The meaning of age is as old as a concern as the riddle of sphinx. There are obvious cultural differences in what is considered too-old-to or too-young-to marry or rule or fight: Brief news items in almost any newspaper daily demonstrate some of the more obvious cultural differences, such as sixty-year-old man marrying twelve-year-old girl. But the more subtle valuations of ages should be noted.

A youth-valuing culture (including the United States) values vigor, idealism, and a freshness that is thought to be dissipated with age. Economically and socially, the "youth market" dictates fashion, language and tastes in popular culture. The social environment which nurtures the values of youth is one of constant change, with new freedoms and new kinds of experiences available every year. So accelerated is the change that a US sociologist in 1970 defined the span of a generation for persons of college age or younger as less than four years.

At the other extreme are the values of age and experience. The value of age had traditionally been the dominant orientation of most cultures in the world, for the elders of societies were the repositories of knowledge as well as the locus of power and authority. Where age is valued it is likely to be expressed in special forms of address—for any old person, regardless of position.

Sex

The previous observation about limits of age adaptability is even more obviously true for values toward sex-role differences. Intercultural organizations such as CARE have in the past had a policy against sending women abroad to represent the organization because most societies are overly male dominated. In more recent years, CARE and other organizations with similar policies have run into their own cultural conflicts between local demands for equality for the sexes and foreign realities where the sexes are not equal.

Male superiority sometimes takes two divergent forms, though both include the distinction between appropriate behaviors for men and women. In one form, the woman's role is to serve the man—including doing hard physical labor, deferring to his judgments and socially subordinating herself in such ways as walking behind him and eating after he has eaten. The romantic tradition of the West is somewhat different: While the man may have the authority, he treats women as the weaker sex and has evolved a pattern of social practices such as standing when a lady enters the room or holding a door for her. In this case, women are treated much like children—weak, immature, less intelligent and more emotional.

Mobility

Technological changes have obviously influenced mobility, but mobility as a value is not found in all societies where the technological possibilities exist. Switzerland is a good example: A person must reside in a city for a period of fifteen years before becoming a "citizen" of that city and only thereafter may proceed to citizenship within the nation. The United States today presents the opposite extreme, the norm appears to be constantly shifting in an effort to better oneself. US expressions such as "the man on the go" or "let's get moving" reflect this orientation. Between these extremes are those values we may call physic mobility, the value of limited or periodic movement (for some specific gain, such as money or education or experience) with the

Chapter 6 Value Differences in Intercultural Communication

expectation of returning to our place of origin. Thus while a migrant worker and a business executive may superficially resemble each other, their values are likely to be different: the migrant worker knows where his home is and where he will return to; the mobile executive's home is where he hangs his hat, and his choice of a location for retirement is likely to be whatever location attracts him along the way.

In intercultural encounters these differences may be very important, the person who travels abroad as a student or adviser or worker is likely to be judged in terms of the values of mobility of his host culture. The traveler may expect to be appraised as a "seeker" or as someone "broadening his horizons", but may find he is mistrusted as an escapist or even one exiled from his community (Note that "exile" as a form of punishment is meaningless in societies like the United States, where moving is valued.).

(Adapted from Condon, John C. "An introduction to intercultural communication", Chapters 3&4)

Word list:

1. interpretation [ɪntɜːprɪ'teɪʃ(ə)n]
    n. 解释；翻译
2. recreation [rekrɪ'eɪʃ(ə)n]
    n. 娱乐；消遣；休养
3. aesthetic [iːs'θetɪk]
    adj. 美的；美学的；审美的，具有审美趣味的
4. orientation [ɔːrɪən'teɪʃ(ə)n]
    n. 方向；定向；适应
5. hypothetical [haɪpə'θetɪk(ə)l]
    adj. 假设的；爱猜想的
6. eccentric [ɪk'sentrɪk]
    adj. 古怪的，反常的
    n. 古怪的人
7. dominant ['dɒmɪnənt]
    adj. 显性的；占优势的；支配的，统治的
    n. 显性

8. accelerate [ək'seləreɪt]
   vt. 使……加快；使……增速
   vi. 加速；促进；增加
9. divergent [daɪ'vɜːdʒ(ə)nt]
   adj. 相异的，分歧的；散开的
10. evolve [ɪ'vɒlv]
    vt. 发展，进化；使逐步形成；推断出
    vi. 发展，进展；进化
11. exile ['eksaɪl]
    n. 流放，充军；放逐，被放逐者；流犯
    vt. 放逐，流放；使背井离乡

Task 1 Reading comprehension

Exercise One: Work with your partners, decide whether the following statements are true (T) or false (F) according to what you have learned in the passage.

1. _____ It is considered rude and impolite for an American high school senior wrote in his school yearbook, "Good-bye, I'll never see you again."

2. _____ According to Ethel Albert, a system of values represents what is expected or hoped for, required or forbidden. It should consist of what is the actual conduct and the system of criteria by which conduct is judged and sanctions applied.

3. _____ The change of bank architecture from Greek temples to the friendly neighborhood savings and loan can indicate that Americans value informality.

4. _____ Some enduring and classic fads and fashions are considered a part of culture.

5. _____ According to the passage, we get to know that Americans value equality, fair play, progress and self-reliance.

6. _____ In Japan, cleanliness has aesthetic and spiritual significances, which is far different and much more evident than that in the United States.

7. _____ A national flag is probably the best place to find appropriate expressions of its culture, like the stars and stripes, some values of the United States are graphically described.

Chapter 6 Value Differences in Intercultural Communication

8. _____ The fusion of individualism and equality is so valued and so basic that many Americans find it difficult to relate to contrasting values in other cultures where interdependence, complementary relationships, valued differences in age and sex greatly determine a person's sense of self.
9. _____ Similar to the United States, many other cultures in the world are also quite tolerant of "eccentrics" and "local characters".
10. _____ A youth-valuing culture, such as that of the United States, Japan and China, values vigor, idealism and a freshness that is thought to be dissipated with age.

Exercise Two: Fill in the blanks with the words given below and change the form when necessary.

> *interpretation   recreation   orientation   hypothetical*
> *accelerate   encounter   horizon   mobility*

1. Prior to the nineteenth century, there were almost no channels of social _____.
2. History is always a matter of _____.
3. This is a (n) _____ example of how a new approach might work.
4. Economic growth will _____ to 2.9 percent next year.
5. All the family members need to have their own interests and _____.
6. If you undertake the project, you are bound to _____ difficulties.
7. It is a multi-dimensional value _____ to construct a harmonious society.
8. By embracing other cultures and genres, we actually broaden our _____, rather than narrow any existing ones.

Task 2 Case study

Case 1

For Americans, time is money. They say, "You only get so much time in this life; you'd better use it wisely." The future will not be better than the past or present, as Americans are trained to see things, unless people use their time for constructive activities. Thus, Americans admire a "well-organized" person, one who has a written list of things to do and a schedule for doing them. The ideal person is punctual and is considerate of other people's time. They do not waste people's time with conversation or other activities that have no visible beneficial outcome.

The American attitude toward time is not necessarily shared by others, especially non-Europeans. They are more likely to regard time as something that is simply there around them, not something they can use. One of the more difficult things many students must adjust to in the States is the notion that time must be saved whenever possible and used wisely every day.

In this context, the fast food industry can be seen as a clear example of American culture product. McDonald's, KFC, and other fast food establishments are successful in a country where many people want to spend the least amount of time preparing and eating meals. As McDonald's restaurants spread around the world, they have been viewed as symbols of American society and culture, bringing not just hamburgers but an emphasis on speed, efficiency and shiny cleanliness.

Questions for discussion:

1. Work with your partner, discuss what punctuality means in China and the United States. If you are invited to a home dinner at 6 p. m., when is the most appropriate time to arrive?

2. What are the differences between Chinese fast food restaurants and McDonald's or KFC?

Case 2

Read the following passage and work in pairs discussing what the reasons for the drop of sales are.

Does a businesslike atmosphere work here?

Ronald, an ambitious young executive, was sent to take over the Sales Branch of an American company in San Paulo, Brazil. He spent a few weeks learning routines and getting familiar with the new surroundings and was somewhat disturbed by the informality and lack of discipline that seemed to take place in the office. People seemed to indulge in excessive socializing, conversations seemed to deal with more personal than business matters, and no one seemed to adhere to their set schedules. Once Ronald had formally taken over, he resolved to do something about this problem and called the staff together for a meeting. He told them bluntly that work rates and schedules would have to be adhered to and demanded a more businesslike atmosphere. Over the next few

Chapter 6 Value Differences in Intercultural Communication

months he concentrated on improving office efficiency, offering higher bonuses and incentives to those who worked well and private warnings to those who did not. By the end of the first quarter he felt he had considerably improved the situation, but was surprised to find that sales figures had dropped since his takeover.

Questions for discussion:

1. According to your understanding, is sales figures supposed to increase after Ronald took measures to make the working environment more businesslike?
2. What causes the sales figures to drop and why?
3. If you were Ronald, what could you do to remedy the problem?

III After-tasks

Task 1 Movie and culture discussion *Flipped*

Flipped is a 2010 American romantic comedy-drama film directed by Rob Reiner and based on Wendelin Van Draanen's novel of the same name. It began a limited release in the United States on August 6, 2010, followed by a wider release on September 10.

In 1957, when second-graders Bryce Loski and Julianna "Juli" Maryellen Baker first meet, Juli knows it's love, but Bryce isn't so sure, and tries to avoid Juli. By the sixth grade, Bryce tries to get rid of Juli by dating Sherry Stalls, whom Juli despises. Bryce's best friend, Garrett, takes an interest in Sherry and tells her the truth about Bryce asking her out, she doesn't take it well.

From Juli's perspective, Bryce returned her feelings, but was shy. After finding out Bryce and Sherry broke up, she thought she could have Bryce back.

In 1963, Bryce's grandfather Chet Duncan moves in with the family. Chet has different views about Juli. There's a large, old sycamore tree that Juli loves which no one understands. One day, it's cut down by a group of landscapers so a house can be built there, despite Juli's opposition. She becomes very depressed afterwards, as the tree let her see the world in a more enlightened way. Her father gives her a painting of the tree.

Chet gets to know Juli while helping her work on her lawn. Bryce begins to develop feelings for Juli, who begins to have mixed feelings about him. When Juli finds out that Bryce has been throwing away the eggs she offered his family right under her nose, out of fear of salmonella, she feels hurt and starts avoiding him.

After visiting her disabled uncle Daniel, Juli overhears Bryce supporting Garrett's badmouthing of him, which causes her to stop having any interest in him. When the Bakers are invited to the Loskis' for dinner, Juli confronts Bryce about what he said. During dinner, they sit opposite each other, she doesn't talk to Bryce or make eye contact with him. After dinner, she apologizes for her behavior. Bryce is upset, she apologizes, because it means she doesn't care enough to hold a grudge.

As the basket boy auction approaches, Juli hears that Sherry is planning to bid on Bryce against Melanie. Bryce thinks that Juli intends to bid on him because he hears that she has a wad of cash. Bryce worries about what will happen if she tries to bid on him, but she bids on Eddie Trulock.

During the basket boy lunch, Bryce and Sherry sit at a table across from Juli and Eddie. He sees she's having a good time with her date and gets jealous. He grabs her and attempts to kiss her, publicly humiliating her. He chases her after she dodges his kiss. Juli gets on her bike and cycles home. Garrett yells at Bryce, and they end their friendship after an argument.

Bryce tries to talk to Juli even though she wants to be left alone. Two days later, Bryce plants a baby sycamore tree in Juli's front yard to show her how he feels. When Juli sees the sycamore, she goes out to help him. As they plant the tree, Bryce puts his hand on Juli's, and they share loving smiles.

Watch a video clip from the movie *Flipped* (《怦然心动》), then work in groups discussing the following questions:

1. What are the main value differences between China and America from the

perspectives of individualism?

2. What kinds of values are reflected in the movie and how do you interpret them?

3. Do you think there are differences in the aspect of educating the next generation between China and America? What are the merits of each society?

Task 2 Extended reading

Two Casts of Mind

Perhaps the most difficult aspect of the Japanese for Westerners to comprehend is the strong orientation to collective values, particularly a collective sense of responsibility.

Let me illustrate with an anecdote about a visit to a new factory in Japan owned and operated by an American electronics company. The American electronics company, a particularly creative firm, frequently attracts attention within business community for its novel approaches to planning, organizational design, and management systems. As a consequence of this corporate style, the parent company was determined to make a thorough study of Japanese workers and to design a plant in Japan that would combine the best of East and West. In their study they discovered that Japanese firms almost never make use of individual work incentives, such as piece-work or even individual performance appraisal tied to salary increases. They concluded that rewarding individual achievement and individual ability is always a good thing.

In the final assembly area of their new plant long lines of young Japanese women wired together electronic products on a piece-rate system: the more you wired, the more you got paid. About two months after opening, the head foreladies approached the plant manager. "Honorable plant manager," they said humbly as they bowed, "we are embarrassed to be so forward, but we must speak to you because all of the girls have threatened to quit work this Friday." (To have this happen, of course, would be a great disaster for all concerned.) "Why," they wanted to know, "can't our plant have the same compensation system as other Japanese companies? When you hire a new girl, her starting wage should be fixed by her age." An eighteen-year-old should be paid more than a sixteen-year-old. Every year on her birthday, she should receive an automatic increase in pay. The idea that any one of us can be more productive than another must be wrong, because none of us in final assembly could make a thing unless all of the other people in the plant had done their jobs right first. To single one person out as being more productive is wrong and is also personally humiliating to us. The company changed its compensation system to the Japanese model.

Another American company in Japan had installed a suggestion system much as they have in the United States. Individual workers were encouraged to place suggestion to improve productivity into special boxes. For an accepted idea the individual received a bonus amounting to some fraction of the productivity savings realized from his or her suggestion. After a period of six months, not a single piece of suggestion had been submitted. The American managers were puzzled. They had heard many stories of the inventiveness, the commitment and the loyalty of Japanese workers, yet no suggestion to improve productivity had appeared.

The managers approached some of the workers and asked why the suggestion system had not been used. The answer: "No one can come up with a work improvement idea alone. We work together, and any ideas that one of us may have are actually developed by watching others and talking to others. If one of us was singled out for being responsible for such an idea, it would embarrass all of us." The company changed to a group suggestion system, in which workers collectively submitted suggestion. Bonuses were paid to groups which would save bonus money until the end of the year for a party at a restaurant or, if there was enough money, for family vacations together. The suggestion and productivity improvements rained down on the plant.

(Adapted from W. Ouchi, "Japanese workers and American workers: Two Casts of Mind")

Group work:

1. Discuss with your group members and analyze the reasons why individual values did not work out in Japan.

2. If you were given the choices between working in an American firm or in a Japanese firm, which one would you prefer and why?

3. If you are offered to further study abroad, which country would you like to choose, America, Japan or Britain?

4. Why do Japanese workers and American workers approach collective values differently?

Chapter 6 Value Differences in Intercultural Communication

Section II Belief and Culture

I Pre-tasks

Task 1 Moral kidnapping

Work in small groups, make a list of typical Chinese behaviors that relate to evil and good. How widespread are these behaviors within the culture? What is your opinion on "moral kidnapping"?

Task 2 Filiality

What are the similar values in China and Japan? Do you think the dominant values in a society affect people's behavior patterns? Or people behave in framed value systems?

II While-tasks

Perception, Belief and Culture

What you think and how you react to events is based in part on your perceptions of the world, as well as beliefs and values that have been instilled in you by your culture.

Perception

To steer your attention toward the topic of perception, we will begin with a few questions. The moon is a rocky, and physical sphere that orbits the earth; yet, when looking at this object, many Americans often visualize a human face; many American Indians as well as Japanese perceive a rabbit; Chinese claim to see a fairy lady and Samoans report a woman weaving. Why? In Japan and China, people fear the number four; in the United States, it is the number thirteen. For Americans, a "V" sign made with two fingers usually represents victory or peace. Japanese high school students see it as a sign of happiness or good luck. But when given with the palm facing inward, Australians and British equate the gesture with a rude American sign usually made with the middle finger. Why? Most Asians respond negatively to white flowers because white is associated with death. For Peruvians, Iranians and Mexicans, yellow flowers often invoke the same reaction. Why? In all these examples, the external object (moon, hands, flowers) were the same, yet the responses were different. The reason is perception—how diverse cultures have taught their members to look at the world in different ways. So we will discuss and define perception first and then briefly discuss beliefs and values.

What is perception?

Perception is the means by which you make sense of your physical and social world. As the German novelist Hermann Hesse wrote, "There is no reality except the one contained within us." The world inside you "include symbols, things, people, ideas, events, ideologies, and even faith". Your perception gives meaning to external forces by allowing you to interpret, categorize, and organize those stimuli that you choose to monitor. As Gamble and Gamble state, "Perception is the process of selecting, organizing, and interpreting sensory data in a way that enables us to make sense of our world." In other words, perception is the process whereby people convert external events and experiences into meaningful internal understanding. According to Singer, "We experience everything in the world not as it is—but only as the world comes to us through our sensory receptors," and this includes how you cognitively process the stimuli. Although the physical dimension is an important phase of perception, you must realize that the psychological aspects of perception are what help you understand intercultural communication.

Chapter 6 Value Differences in Intercultural Communication

Perception and culture

Whether you feel delighted or ill at the thought of eating the flesh of a cow, pig, fish, dog, or snake depends on what your culture has taught you about food. By exposing a large collection of people to similar experiences, culture generates similar meanings and similar behaviors. This does not mean, of course, that everyone in a particular culture will see something in exactly the same way.

An example of how culture affects perception and communication is found in a classic study. Mexican children from a rural area and children from the dominant culture in the United States viewed, for a second, a stereogram in which one eye was exposed to a baseball game while the other was exposed to a bullfight. Overall, the children reported seeing the scene that corresponded to their culture; Mexican children tended to report seeing the bullfight, and the American children tended to report the baseball game. What happened was that the children made selections based on their cultural backgrounds; they were inclined to see and to report what was most familiar.

Personal credibility is another perceptual trait shaped by culture that is subject to cultural variability. In Mexico, social status is a major indicator of credibility, but in the United States, it carries only modest importance. Even the perception of something as simple as the blink of an eye is affected by culture. Blinking while another person talks may be hardly noticeable to North Americans, but the same behavior is considered impolite in some countries.

In addition, the manner in which the elderly are perceived is also a product of culture. In the United States, culture teaches the value of youth and rejects growing old. According to one communication researcher, "Young people view elderly people as less desirable interaction partners than other young people or middle-aged people." This negative view of the elderly is not found in all cultures. For example, in Arab, Asian, Latin American, and American Indian cultures, older people are perceived in a very positive light.

It is clear from these examples that culture influences one's subjective reality that there are direct links among culture, perception and behavior.

Culture influences perception in two ways. Firstly, perception is selective. What is allowed in is, in part, determined by culture. Secondly, your perceptual patterns are learned. As we have pointed out that everyone is born into a world without meaning. Culture teaches you the meaning of most of your experiences. In other words, perception is culturally determined. We learn to see the world in a certain way based on our cultural background. Perceptions are stored within each human being in the form of beliefs and values. These two concepts, working in combination, form what are called cultural patterns.

Beliefs

What are your beliefs, how did you acquire them, and what function do they perform? Rogers and Steinfatt contend that, "Beliefs serve as the storage system for the content of our past experiences, including thoughts, memories and interpretations of events. Beliefs are shaped by the individual culture. Beliefs are important because they are accepted as truths. Beliefs are usually reflected in your action and communication behaviors." If, for instance, you believe that a good tan is a reflection of a healthy, active lifestyle and makes a person attractive, you will probably find time to lie out in the sun. On the other hand, if you believe that suntanned skin reflects a low social status, you will probably make an extra effort to avoid exposing yourself to the sun by wearing a hat, long-sleeved shirt and perhaps gloves and carrying an umbrella, on sunny days. If someone believes that his or her fate is preordained, you cannot declare that belief wrong just because it disagrees with your conviction that each person is the master of his or her own fate. You must be able to recognize that cultures have different realities and belief systems. People who grow up in cultures where Christianity is the predominant religion usually believe that salvation is attainable only through Christ. People who are Jewish, Islamic, Buddhist or Hindu do not subscribe to that conviction. They hold their own beliefs about salvation. What is powerful about beliefs is that they are so much a part of culture that in most instances you do not question them or even demand proof. You simply accept them because you know they are true and thus, they endure.

Exploring values

One of the most important functions of beliefs is that they form the basis of your values, which provide rules for making choices and for resolving conflicts. The significance of values is that they constitute a system that "represents what is expected or hoped for, required or forbidden. It is not a report of actual conduct but is the system of criteria by which conduct is judged and sanctions applied". To illustrate, Hofstede offers a short list of some topics that deal with values:

Chapter 6 Value Differences in Intercultural Communication

- Evil versus good
- Dangerrous versus safe
- Ugly versus beautiful
- Abnormal versus normal
- Irrational versus rational
- Dirty versus clean
- Decent versus indecent
- Unnatural versus natural
- Paradoxical versus logical
- Moral versus immoral

Your cognitive structure consists of many values. These values are highly organized. Values can be classified as primary, secondary and tertiary. Primary values are the most important; they specify those things worth dying for. In the United States, democracy and protection of oneself and close family members are primary values, secondary values are also quite important. Alleviation of the pain and suffering of others and securing material possessions are secondary values to most people in the United states. You care about such values, but do not hold the same intense feeling toward them as you do toward primary values. Tertiary values are at the bottom of our value hierarchy. Examples of tertiary values in the United States are hospitality to guests and cleanliness. Although you strive to carry out these values, they are not as profound as values from the first two categories.

Values, like all important aspects of culture, are transmitted by a variety of sources (family, proverbs, media, school, church, etc.) and therefore tend to be broad based, enduring, and relatively stable. Also, Hofstede reminds us that "values are programmed early in our lives" and therefore are often non-rational, especially when viewed by someone from another culture.

As you saw from Hofstede's list, values tell a member of a culture what is normal by identifying what things are good and bad, or right and wrong. Cultural values define what is worthwhile to die for, what is worth protecting, what frightens people, what subjects are worthy of study, and which topics deserve ridicule. As already indicated, values are learned within a cultural context. For example, the outlook of a culture toward the expression of affection is one of the many values that differ among cultures. In the United States, people are encouraged to express their feelings openly and outwardly and are taught not to be timid about letting people know they are upset. Think for a moment about what message is carried by the proverb, "The squeaky wheel gets the grease." This positive American attitude toward the public expression of emotion is very different from the one found in China. Chinese are socialized not to openly express their own personal emotions, especially strong negative ones. What is important about values is that they are translated into action. For instance, an awareness of the value the Japanese place on customer service in business transactions might prompt you to be more careful when dealing with a client from Japan.

(Adapted from Larry A. Samovar, Richard E. Porter, Edwin R. McDaniel. "Communication between Cultures", Chapter 5)

Word list:

1. instill [ɪnˈstɪl]
   vt. 徐徐滴入；逐渐灌输
2. steer [stɪə]
   vi. 驾驶；掌舵
   vt. 控制；引导
3. sphere [sfɪə]
   n. 范围；球体
4. stimuli [ˈstɪmjʊlaɪ]
   n. 刺激；刺激物；促进因素（stimulus 的复数）
5. cognitively [ˈkɑːgnətɪvli]
   adv. 认知地
6. credibility [kredɪˈbɪlɪtɪ]
   n. 可信性；确实性
7. Christianity [ˌkrɪstiˈænəti]
   n. 基督教
8. predominant [prɪˈdɒmɪnənt]
   adj. 主要的；卓越的；支配的；有力的；有影响的
9. salvation [sælˈveɪʃ(ə)n]
   n. 拯救；救助
10. paradoxical [ˌpærəˈdɒksɪk(ə)l]
    adj. 矛盾的；诡论的；似非而是的

Chapter 6 Value Differences in Intercultural Communication

Task 1 Reading comprehension

Exercise One: Work with your partners, decide whether the following statements are true (T) or false (F) according to what you have learned in the passage.

1. _____ In Japan and China, people fear the number four; in the United States, it is the number fourteen.
2. _____ Most Asians respond negatively to yellow flowers because yellow is associated with death.
3. _____ Perception is the means by which you make sense of your physical and social world.
4. _____ Although the psychological dimension is an important phase of perception, the physical aspects of perception are what help you understand intercultural communication.
5. _____ In Mexico, social status is a major indicator of credibility, but in the United States, it carries only modest importance.
6. _____ In Arab, Asian, American and American Indian cultures, older people are perceived in a very positive light.
7. _____ Culture teaches you the meaning of most of your experiences. In other words, perception is culturally determined.
8. _____ What is powerful about beliefs is that they are so much a part of culture that in most instances you do not question them, but occasionally you demand proof.

Exercise Two: Fill in the blanks with the words given below and change the form when necessary.

perception   primary   sphere   cognitive
category   stimuli   paradoxical   irrational

1. We'll talk about it much more next week of how we can _____ reframe what we were thinking.
2. The problems generally fall into two _____.
3. Human _____ is highly imperfect and by definition subjective.
4. He challenges every standard and method in his _____ of responsibility.
5. Sam had a very _____ personality; he was very shy, but often outgoing, too.
6. 95% of patients know their obsessions are _____.

7. The family continues to be the _____ source of care and comfort for people as they grow older.

8. Does the child respond to auditory _____?

Task 2　Case study

Case 1

George Hall was in Beijing attending a trade fair and looking for an opportunity to do business in China. He had been very successful in his business dealings in the US and prided himself on his ability "to get things moving". His first day was going well. He looked around at the displays of sporting equipment to get some idea of whom he might approach. He was sure that his products, tennis rackets with an unusual new design, would arouse some interest. On the second day he approached the company which he felt would be most responsive to his products. He introduced himself to the general, a Mr. Li. Since he had read that Chinese find getting down to business immediately too abrupt and rude, he began a casual conversation, eventually leading up to the topic of his products and suggesting how Mr. Li's company might benefit from using them. George then suggested that he could arrange to get together with Mr. Li and provide more specifics and documentation on his products.

Mr. Li responded in fairly good English, "That would be interesting."

Knowing that he had only a few days left in Beijing, George wanted to nail down a time, "When can we meet?" asked George.

"Ah. This week is very busy," replied Mr. Li.

"It sure is." said George, "How about 10 o'clock? Meet you here."

"Tomorrow at 10 o'clock?" asked Mr. Li thoughtfully.

"Right," said George, "I'll see you then?"

"Hmm, yes; why don't you come by tomorrow?" was the reply.

"OK," responded George, "It was nice meeting you."

The next day at 10 o'clock he approached Mr. Li's company's exhibit only to find that Mr. Li had some important business and was not able to meet with George. He called back later in the day and was told that Mr. Li was not available.

Questions for discussion:

1. What is the problem in this intercultural communication?

2. What are the respective approaches for Americans and Chinese toward punctuality?

Case 2

Charles was excited about his new promotion and transfer to China. He had done well in the marketing department of his company and had been promoted to assist the director of marketing at the company's recently established operations in Shanghai. He had studied a bit about Chinese, but so far had worked only in the United States and had little experience with Chinese individuals or culture. In the two months before relocating, Charles often went to the local university library to try to absorb all he could about China, its culture, and the ways of doing business. In addition, his company provided a week-long culture seminar just prior to his departure.

After arriving in Shanghai, Charles found that his work was exciting and that marketing to the Chinese was a new challenge. During his culture seminar he had learned several concepts that were important in Chinese business environment such as the concept of *guanxi*. He had also learned about individualism. He felt he understood these concepts and was sure he would learn more.

Because the marketing director had two assistants, Charles worked closely with Dashan, his Chinese counter part. Charles learned that Dashan came from a fairly influential family in the area. Dashan was quite motivated and worked very hard. To Charles it seemed that Dashan was quite "individualistic" as he worked hard for bonuses, was always going the extra mile, and had set a number of work related goals for himself.

After a few months, Dashan left the company to start a venture of his own. Charles kept in touch with him and noticed that Dashan's business was doing very well. One weekend, Dashan invited Charles for dinner. Many of Dashan's relatives were present as well as some friends whom Charles had not met. Charles found that Dashan's house was quite nice and equipped with many big-ticket consumer items, such as a first-class personal computer, air-conditioning, and modern kitchen appliances, Charles also learned that Dashan had recently bought a new car for his parents. It was clear that Dashan's business was very profitable and successful. Dashan was managing it himself and already had 40 or 50 employees. It seemed to Charles that Dashan was doing quite a good job of being "individualistic".

Pair work:

Work with your partner discussing whether Charles' interpretation is correct or not from the perspective of intercultural communication. What are the differences between child-parent relationships between China and America?

Case 3

Jack, an American student, was at the dinner table for the first time with his new host family in China. His hostess was a good cook, and there was plenty of delicious food on the table. Jack enjoyed the meal as well as the pleasant conversation. He ate so much that he felt absolutely stuffed. When he said, "It was delicious. Thank you for the meal." both the host and the hostess insisted that he eat more, saying, "There is still plenty, so please have more." Jack declined their offer very politely by saying that he had had enough, but the host and hostess insisted again and again. Jack was dismayed but he felt hesitant about resisting their offer. He put more food on his plate and somehow managed to finish it.

Group discussion:

Work in groups and try to explain the reasons for this kind of failure in cross-cultural communication.

III After-tasks

Task 1   Movie and culture discussion   *Everybody's Fine* Vs. *My Father and I*

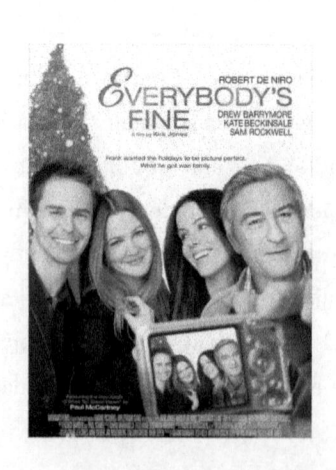

Chapter 6 Value Differences in Intercultural Communication

Everybody's Fine is a 2009 American drama film written and directed by Kirk Jones, and starring Robert De Niro, Drew Barrymore, Sam Rockwell, and Kate Beckinsale.

Frank Goode (Robert De Niro), a recently widowed retiree, is getting ready for his children, David (Austin Lysy), Rosie (Drew Barrymore), Amy (Kate Beckinsale) and Robert (Sam Rockwell) to come to visit him. One by one though, each of his children calls to cancel on him at the last minute. Feeling a bit down by the rejections, Frank decides to head out on a cross-country trip, visiting each of his kids, despite warnings against travel from his doctor. He is chronically ill with cardiac and respiratory problems from his life work making PVC-covered power lines. He deceives his children about his health, telling them that he is fine.

As Frank travels to each of his children's homes, beginning with his son David who is absent from his New York apartment, his other son and daughters divert his surprise visits and make excuses for not allowing him a lengthy visit. He begins to suspect that something is amiss.

Frank heads home to Elmira, New York, by plane and suffers a heart attack. The heart attack renders him in a dream-like state where he reflects on his visits to his children. While reflecting upon his visits, Frank realizes that each of his children is hiding a secret: Amy's husband is leaving her for another woman and Amy has found a new boyfriend; Robert is not a musical conductor nor is he going on tour to Europe; Rosie has mothered a child and is bisexual; David has gone missing. He awakes to find his children at the hospital to comfort him. His children finally tell him the big secret that David has died of a drug overdose. Upon his release from the hospital, Frank visits his wife's grave and talks to her. He tells her all about the kids and how they're all doing fine. The final scene depicts Frank as he loves and accepts his children (including their secrets).

My Father and I is a 2003 Chinese drama film directed by Xu Jinglei. This is also her debut works. The film depicts the relationship between a daughter and her father. The strong love between the daughter and her father is conveyed through the dribs and drabs in daily life.

Watch a video clip from the movie *Everybody's Fine* (《天伦之旅》), and another one from the movie *My Father and I* (《我和爸爸》), then work in groups to

discuss the following questions:

1. In terms of parent-child relationship, what are the similarities and differences between the two movies?

2. What is the ideal parent-child relationship in your opinion? Do you think it advisable to send the elderly parents to the nursing home?

Task 2 Extended reading

Cultural Patterns

Cultural patterns can be thought of as systems of integrated beliefs and values that work in combination to provide a coherent, if not always consistent, model for perceiving the world. These patterns contribute not only to the way you perceive and think about the world, but also to how you live in the world. Therefore, cultural patterns are useful in the study of intercultural communication because they are systematic and repetitive instead of random and irregular.

Cultural pattern are integrated

It is important to realize that cultural patterns do not operate in isolation, they are interrelated and integrated. In other words, they act in concert. If a culture values the elderly, that value gets attached to yet other values related to respect and decision making.

Cultural patterns are dynamic

Cultures change and therefore so do their values. The women's movement, for example, had greatly altered social organizations and some value systems in the United States. With more women than men now earning college degrees, we can see how the workplace and classrooms have changed in the United States during the last two decades. As globalization brings Western culture to nations throughout the world, it is common to see young people in some traditional countries now wearing Levis and dancing to American pop music.

Cultural patterns can be contradictory

In many instances, we find contradictory values in a particular culture. In the United States, we speak of "all people being created equal", yet we observe pervasive racial prejudice toward minorities and violence directed against gays. These sorts of contradictions are found in all cultures. *The Bible* advocates helping others and the Koran teaches brotherhood among all people. Yet, in both the Unites States and in many Arab cultures, some segments of the population are very rich and others are extremely poor.

Dominant United States cultural patterns

Regardless of the culture being studied, the dominant culture is that part of a population that controls and dominates the major economic and social institutions and determines the flow and content of information. In the United States, that group has been, and largely continues to be, while, male, and of European heritage.

Individualism

The single most important cultural pattern in the Unites States is individualism, often referred to as "freedom" by Americans. Broadly speaking, individualism, as developed in the works of the seventeenth-century English philosopher John Locke, holds that each person is unique, special, and completely different from all other individuals. The value of individualism is so commanding that many other American values spring from individualism. Gannon underscores the link between individualism and other values when he writes: "Equality of opportunity, independence, initiative and self-reliance are some of the values that have remained as basic American ideals throughout history. All of these values are expressive of a high degree of individualism." This emphasis on the individual has emerged as the cornerstone of American culture. So strong is this notion that some Americans consider that a person who fails to demonstrate individuality is out of step with society. Whether it is conveyed by literature, art, or American history, the message is the same: individual achievement, sovereignty, and freedom are the virtues most glorified.

American role models, be they the cowboys of the Old West or action heroes in today's movies or electronic games, are all portrayed as independent agents who accomplish their goals with little or no assistance. The individual is self-reliant; to depend on someone else implies weakness of loss of freedom. The result is that most Americans believe that all persons have a separate identity, which should be recognized and reinforced. As Kim points out, "In America, what counts is who you are, not who others around you are. A person tends to be judged on his or her own merit."

Equal opportunity

Closely related to individualism is the American value of equality. The Declaration of Independence states that "all men are created equal". Rather than focus on the literal meaning of "created equal", let us look at the ideals behind those words, which were best explained by Abraham Lincoln in 1860, when he said, "We do wish to allow the humblest man an equal chance to get rich with everybody else."

Thus, the value that pervades contemporary US society is best termed "equal opportunity". All people should have the same opportunity to succeed in life, and the state, through laws and educational opportunities, is expected to ensure that right.

The American value of equal opportunity translates into equality and informality in social relationships. For instance, most of the primary social relationships within a family tend to promote equality rather than hierarchy. Formality is not important and children are often treated as adults. In secondary relationships, most friendship and coworkers are also treated as equals, usually interacting on a first-name basis. People from cultures that adhere to formal social structures often find it disconcerting to work with Americans, whom they believe diminish the value of social status differences.

Material acquisition

Acquiring material possessions has always been an integral part of life for most Americans. As Stewart and Bennett note, "Americans consider it almost a right to be materially well off and physically comfortable." Americans have historically been willing to work hard to realize their dreams. Thus, the acquisition of material possessions, such as a large house, a variety of clothes for every occasion, convenient personal transportation, and a large selection of foods, is considered the just reward for hard work.

Progress and change

In the Unites States, change, newness, and progress are all highly valued. From altering their personal appearance through cosmetic surgery, to changing where they live at a faster rate than any other people in the world, Americans do not value the status quo. Nor have they ever. Ever since the country's earliest days, Americans have been passionate for progress. Various aspects of this orientation are optimism, receptivity to change, emphasis on the future rather than the past or present, faith in an ability to control all phases of life, and confidence in the perceptual ability of the common person. You can observe this passion for change and progress in the way that Americans have traditionally approached the environment—as something to be conquered, tamed, or harnessed for social or personal benefit.

Competitive nature

The football coach Vince Lombardi once said, "Winning isn't everything, it's the only thing." This attitude toward competition is an integral part of life in the United States and is taught from early childhood on. Whether it is through childhood games or being continually asked to answer questions in the classroom, a competitive nature is encouraged among children in the Unites States. People are ranked, graded, classified and evaluated so that everyone will know who the best is. The many "Top 10" lists of people, schools, hospitals and vacation locations provided by the media illustrate Americans' competitive nature. For competitive Americans, who hate losing, everything in life is a game to win.

Group work:

Discuss with your group members which cultural value in the United States impressed you the most.

Chapter 7

Contextual Differences in Intercultural Communication

民无信不立。

——孔子《论语 · 颜渊》

The purpose of a business is to create a customer.

——Peter Drucker

Section I Culture and Context

I Pre-tasks

Task 1 Different greetings

Look at the following two pictures. Then talk with your partner about the different ways of greeting between the East and the West.

Chapter 7 Contextual Differences in Intercultural Communication

Task 2 Of studies

君子曰：学不可以已。

青，取之于蓝而青于蓝；冰，水为之而寒于水。木直中绳，輮以为轮，其曲中规。虽有槁暴（pù），不复挺者，輮使之然也。故木受绳则直，金就砺则利，君子博学而日参省乎己，则知明而行无过矣。

故不登高山，不知天之高也；不临深溪，不知地之厚也；不闻先王之遗言，不知学问之大也。干、越、夷、貉之子，生而同声，长而异俗，教使之然也。诗曰："嗟尔君子，无恒安息。靖共尔位，好是正直。神之听之，介尔景福。"神莫大于化道，福莫长于无祸。

——荀子《劝学》

Studies serve for delight, for ornament, and for ability. Their chief use for delight, is in privateness and retiring; for ornament, is in discourse; and for ability, is in the judgment and disposition of business.

For expert men can excute, and perhaps judge of particulars, one by one; but the general counsels, and the plots and marshalling of affairs, come best from those that are learned. To spend too much time in studies is sloth; to use them too much for ornament, is affectation; to make judgment wholly by their rules, is the humor of a scholar.

They perfect nature, and are perfected by experience: for natural abilities are like natural plants, that need proyning (pruning) by study; and studies themselves do give forth directions too much at large, except they be bounded in by experience.

Crafty men contemn studies, simple men admire them, and wise men use them; for they teach not their own use; but that is a wisdom without them, and above them, won by observation.

Read not to contradict and confute; nor to believe and take for granted; nor to find talk and discourse; but to weigh and consider.

—*Of Studies by Francis Bacon*

Read the two extracts and discuss what the similarities and differences are in philosophies on education between China and America.

II While-tasks

Culture and Context

There is a well-known saying that everyone has to be somewhere. And while that expression might seem obvious and even inconsequential, it is not only true but also central to the study of human communication. We begin with the following truism: communication does not take place in a void. All human interaction is influenced to some degree by the cultural, social, and physical settings in which it occurs. These settings are called the communication context. What we are proposing is that your culture specifies the appropriate communicative behavior within a variety of social and physical contexts by prescribing certain rules. When communicating with members of your own culture, you rely on internalized cultural rules that stipulate the appropriate behaviors for the specific communication situation. These rules enable you to communicate effectively with each other, and since they are a product of your enculturation, you do not have to think consciously about which rules to use. But when engaging in intercultural communication, things can be different, because you and your communication partners may be operating under very different sets of rules. To be a competent intercultural communicator, you must be aware of how diverse cultural rules influence the communication context. Otherwise, you may encounter a variety of surprises—some of which could be embarrassing, detrimental, or both!

Communication is rule governed

Both consciously and unconsciously, people expect that their interactions will follow appropriate and culturally determined rules—rules that tell both parties what is suitable behavior for the specific situation. Rules can be thought of as guidelines for your action and the actions of others. These rules, as Wood points out, "…help define acceptable and unacceptable codes of thought, feeling, and behavior."

Context helps specify communication rules

Our assumption about communication is that the context specifies the appropriateness of the rules to be employed. Think for a moment how such diverse contexts as a classroom, bank, church, hospital, courtroom, wedding, funeral, or a day at the beach determines which communication rules you follow. In a job interview you might use formal or respectful words such as "sir" or "madam" when responding to your potential employer. Yet at a football or basketball game, your language would be far less formal, incorporating slang phrases and quite possibly derogatory remarks about the opposing team. For that job interview, you might wear what in the United States Americans call a "power suit" (i. e., a dark suit with white or blue shirt). For a sports event, jeans or shorts and a T-shirt could be appropriate. Your nonverbal behaviors would also be different. At the interview, you would probably shake hands with your prospective employer, but at the football game with friends, you might embrace them when you see them, slap them on the back, or hit a "high-five" (a hand gesture) as a form of greeting.

Communication rules are culturally diverse

Although cultures have many of the same social settings (schools, business meetings, hospitals, and the like), their members frequently abide by different rules when interacting within those environments. Consequently, concepts of dress, time, language, manners, and non-verbal behaviors can differ significantly among cultures. As we noted, when doing business in America, it was not uncommon for men and women to welcome each other to a meeting by shaking hands. However, in the Middle East, some deeply religious Muslim businessmen may choose to avoid shaking hands with a woman. This should not be perceived as rude or insulting, but as an indication of the man's religious devotion. Even the topics of conversation at an intercultural business meeting are influenced by cultural rules. American business executives are usually anxious to "get down to business" and often perceive small talk as a waste of time. They are, as Ferraro points out, anxious to get the "contracts signed and then move on to some new endeavor". Doing business in Argentina, you would witness a different set of contextual rules regarding "small talk" and the pace of the meeting. In Argentina, "Meetings begin and end with polite small talk. You may insult your Argentine counterparts if you rush off without chatting at the end of a meeting." You can even observe slight contextual differences when you compare business entertainment in Turkey and the United States. In Turkey, for example, your Turkish colleagues will insist on paying for all the entertainment. Turkish hospitality is legendary, and they will not permit you to pay for any part of the meal. In the United States, where the rules for business entertaining are very different, the cost of the meal or entertainment is often shared.

Communication rules regarding: (1) formality and informality, (2) assertiveness and interpersonal harmony, and (3) status relationships play a major role in how people respond to their interpersonal and organizational environments.

Formality and informality

Cultures can have views regarding events and people that range from extremely informal to very formal. The manifestations of informality and formality take many forms.

Informality

Grounded in a strong belief in individualism and equality, the United States has long been considered an informal culture. In North America people tend to treat others with informality and directness. They avoid the use of formal codes of conduct, titles, honorifics, and ritualistic manners in their interactions with others. In the United States, informality is manifested in a host of ways. For example, regardless of their social positions, most Americans will quickly move to using first names when meeting strangers. Even the simple greeting "Hi" can be seen as a reflection of American informality. Idiomatic speech and slang are liberally used on most occasions, with formal speech reserved for public events and fairly formal situations. People from almost any station in life can be seen in public wearing jeans, sandals, or other informal attire.

The informality and openness displayed by US Americans can be a source of confusion and misunderstanding for people from more formal cultures. Crouch, making the same point about North American business executives doing business in Mexico, notes, "Our disregard for formality sometimes makes international business more difficult."

Formality

In contrast to the high degree of informality found in the United States, there are many examples of cultures that place a high value on formality. In Egypt, Turkey, and Japan, for instance, the student-eacher relationship is very formal. This may be seen in the Egyptian proverb, "Whoever teaches me a letter I should become a slave to him forever." In these countries, when the teacher enters the room, students are expected to stand. When students meet their teachers on the street, they are expected to bow to them. Contrast this with the relaxed, informal student-teacher relationships found in the United States.

Chapter 7　Contextual Differences in Intercultural Communication

Formality is also evident in how cultures use forms of address. Not knowing these differences can cause problems. Germans, for example, address others and conduct themselves in a very formal manner, which many US Americans would consider extreme. Hall and Hall note, "American informality and the habit of calling others by their first names make Germans acutely uncomfortable, particularly when young people or people lower in the hierarchy address their elders or their superiors by their first names." Germany is not the only place where forms of address are directly linked to perception and values. Morrison, Conaway, and Borden report that titles play an important role in India, where first names are usually reserved for close friends.

Kim uses a peach and a coconut as metaphors to contrast US informality with Japanese formality. In the United States, one of the ways informality is manifested is that people tend to be friendly toward everyone and form relationships rather easily. Yet at the same time, highly personal feelings that would make an individual vulnerable are seldom on display to other people. This practice is likened to a peach, with a soft exterior and a hard center. The Japanese, in contrast, are characterized as being like a coconut, with a hard exterior that is difficult to penetrate. The Japanese use formality as a shell to keep people at a distance while deciding if a relationship is desired. Once the shell is penetrated, however, the Japanese are very affectionate and personal vulnerability is not a concern.

It is easy to imagine the outcome of a cross-cultural business venture if, at the initial meeting, the US Americans were offering personal information about themselves, speaking in an informal manner, and using their counterparts' first names, while the Japanese were doing the opposite.

Assertiveness and interpersonal harmony

The second important dimension of culture that affects the communication context is the manner in which people present themselves to others. While there are many aspects of communication styles, assertiveness and interpersonal harmony directly influence the intercultural setting—be it in a business meeting, classroom, or health care context.

Assertiveness

The United States culture is widely known for its assertive communication style. It is not uncommon for the US Americans to register for assertiveness training classes, where they are encouraged and taught to be frank, open, and direct. Think about the style of communication displayed on "talk radio" or the MSNBC or *Fox News* television political shows, where participants frequently end up shouting at each other in an effort to make a point and to increase the show's ratings. In the sports arena, "trash talk" is common place between members of opposing team. While the communication styles in these two settings tend to be exaggerations of the norm, they serve to illustrate the positive value that is placed on communicative assertiveness in the United States. The tradition of directness, assertiveness, and aggressive behaviors among Americans did not develop by chance. A culture that has a long history of valuing nonconformity, individualism, competition, freedom of expression, and even some select forms of rebellion is bound to encourage assertive behaviors. The reason Americans value assertive communication, according to Nadler and Broome, is obvious: "North American individuals are expected to stand up for their rights, and this often involves confrontation."

Interpersonal harmony

While the United States culture and some other cultures, such as Germany and Israel, see assertiveness as an asset, other cultures see it as threatening and detrimental to genial interpersonal relations. Among Northeast and Southeast Asian cultures, mutual agreement, loyalty, and reciprocal obligation underlie the importance placed on harmonious relations.

Maintaining harmonious relations and avoiding what appears to be aggressive behaviors is also a primary consideration among the Japanese. Japanese are very concerned about other people's feelings. So strong is that concern for the feelings of others that the Japanese are well-known for avoiding the word "no", which they find harsh. This Japanese desire for harmonious relations is more a product of adhering to accepted models of behavior than it is a compelling principle. Accordingly, to avoid disruption and maintain harmony within the organization, the market, or the nation, Japanese business executives will sometimes make corporate profit a subordinate consideration. Similarly, the Chinese tend to regard conflict and confrontation as unpleasant and undesirable. Chen and Xiao underscore this same point when they state, "It is without a doubt that harmony is one of the primordial values of Confucianism and of the Chinese culture."

Status relationships

The third communication variable that influences nearly all communication settings relates to a culture's perception of and response to status. Every culture and organization has specific culturally based protocols to guide interaction between people of varying social positions. Using a broad classification scale, a culture can generally be categorized as either egalitarian, with a low level of concern for social differences, or hierarchical, placing significant emphasis on status and rank.

Egalitarian

Egalitarianism facilitates and encourages openness among communication participants, stresses informal interaction between subordinates and seniors, and minimizes the expectation of deference and formality. A person's status is usually acquired through individual effort such as success in business or the achieving of an advanced degree—avenues that are open to everyone. This creates an environment of social mobility by encouraging the belief that everyone has the opportunity to improve his or her social status. However, individuals who enjoy positions of power often make it a habit to downplay appearances of their increased power and prestige. The United States, Australia, Israel, and New Zealand are considered highly egalitarian cultures. Most Americans are not very concerned with differences in social status and power. This is partly the result of the United States' frontier heritage, when early settlers were forced to rely on hard work to survive. The rigid social formality and protocol common in Europe at that time found little place in the harsh landscape of the colonies or along the western frontiers. As a result, equality, or the appearance of equality, became a cultural value that persists today. This value is easily illustrated by press reports on how American presidents spend their leisure time. Ronald Reagan was noted for chopping wood and horseback riding; Bill Clinton would often stop off at McDonald's while jogging in a T-shirt and running shorts; George W. Bush was frequently photographed clearing brush at his Texas ranch.

In nearly every setting, be it in the classroom or a staff meeting, manifestations of an egalitarian society can be seen. While egalitarianism can take a host of forms, the very common form is the use of names. In the United States, subordinates are often on a first name basis with their bosses. This same lack of linking names with "power" can be seen in many college and university classrooms where students call their professors by first name.

Hierarchical

Cultures that subscribe to a hierarchical view of social status are in marked contrast to egalitarian cultures. In these cultures, status is normally ascribed by birth, appointment, or age. In countries like Japan, China, most Latin American countries, and Spain, differences in status are made obvious through protocols that govern many interpersonal and organizational activities. Interactions between subordinates and seniors are conducted in a formal manner, and titles are always used. Seniors are often expected to assume a patriarchal role in response to the junior members' deference. In cultures that use status as a marker, teachers at all levels are accorded the utmost respect, even to the point where students are not expected to question their professors.

Confucian philosophy plays a major role in the hierarchical tradition of many Asian countries. Expressions of Confucian social hierarchy are clearly evident in China, Japan, Korea, Vietnam, and Singapore. Confucianism provides a specific, hierarchical social structure and contains well-defined guidelines for relations between seniors and juniors. Morrison and his associates offer some advice that illustrates how American business executives have to adapt to these social structures when dealing with the Chinese. They write, "When entering a business meeting the senior member of your group should lead the way. Often, senior executives in a delegation do the talking; junior members do not interrupt and only speak when spoken to."

One of the most vivid examples of a culture that places a value on established hierarchy is Japan. As McDaniel notes, "Hierarchy plays a much more prominent role in Japanese society than in Western nations. For the Japanese, hierarchy is a natural social division and normally permeates all aspects of their society." You can notice numerous expressions of this cultural value in the business setting. Even within a Japanese organization, hierarchy is reflected by the junior person always bowing lower than the senior does. In offices, desks are normally arranged in hierarchical order. In addition, the junior will use a formal, polite level of language, while the senior may elect to use an informal style. India also has a history of distinct hierarchical divisions derived from its caste system. Although the system was dissolved by law, the persistent "belief that there are qualitative differences between the castes" continues to influence relationships in India.

(Adapted from Larry A. Samovar, Richard E. Porter, Edwin R. McDaniel, "Communication between Cultures", Chapter 8)

Chapter 7 Contextual Differences in Intercultural Communication

Word list:

1. prescribe [prɪˈskraɪb]
   vt. 规定；开处方
2. stipulate [ˈstɪpjʊleɪt]
   vt. 规定；保证
3. competent [ˈkɒmpɪt(ə)nt]
   adj. 胜任的，有能力的，能干的
4. detrimental [detrɪˈment(ə)l]
   adj. 不利的；有害的
5. derogatory [dɪˈrɒgət(ə)rɪ]
   adj. 贬损的
6. endeavor [ɪnˈdevə]
   n. 努力；尽力
7. assertiveness [əˈsɜːtivnis]
   n. 肯定；果断，自信
8. attire [əˈtaɪə]
   n. 服装；打扮；盛装
9. vulnerability [ˌvʌlnərəˈbɪlətɪ]
   n. 易损性；弱点

Task 1 Reading comprehension

Exercise One: Work with your partners, decide whether the following statements are true (T) or false (F) according to what you have learned in the passage.

1. _____ In the Middle East, some deeply religious Muslim businessmen may choose to avoid shaking hands with a woman.
2. _____ The topics of conversation at an intercultural business meeting are not influenced by cultural rules.
3. _____ Even though American business executives are usually anxious to "get down to business", they will often take time to conduct small talks in order to get familiar with the counterparts.
4. _____ Turkish hospitality is legendary, and they will pay all the expenses for the meal and the entertainment.

5. _____ Grounded in a strong belief in individualism and equality, the United States has long been considered an informal culture.

6. _____ Germans, for example, address others and conduct themselves in a very informal manner, which is quite similar to that of the United States.

7. _____ While the United States culture and some other cultures, such as Germany and China, see assertiveness as an asset, other cultures see it as threatening and detrimental to genial interpersonal relations.

8. _____ In cultures that use status as a marker, teachers at all levels are accorded the utmost respect, only occasionally students can question their professors.

Exercise Two: Lack of cross-cultural awareness may result in failures in international marketing. Below are a few brand names which are quite popular in China, but failed in English-speaking countries. Can you figure out why they failed globally?

    While Elephant   Fang Fang   Golden Cock   Blue Moon

Exercise Three: Work with your partner and find out how the following brand names have been translated into Chinese and see if the translations have helped promote the sale of these products in China. Could you translate them in other ways?

1. Safeguard _____
2. Mercedes-Benz _____
3. Sprite _____
4. Chanel _____
5. Marlboro _____
6. Crest _____

Exercise Four: Fill in the blanks with the words given below and change the form when necessary.

    egalitarian   *hierarchical*   *stipulate*   *detrimental*
        prominent   *philosophy*   *protocol*   *harmony*

1. International rules _____ the number of foreign entrants.
2. One _____ symptom of the disease is progressive loss of memory.
3. People have long dreamt of a (n) _____ society.
4. The organizer was familiar with the _____ of royal visits.

Chapter 7　Contextual Differences in Intercultural Communication

5. Who wields power is not important, provided that the _____ structure remains always the same.

6. Annie's work reflects her _____ that life is full of mysteries.

7. As they smiled at each other, _____ was restored again.

8. Poor eating habits are _____ to health.

Task 2　Case study

Case 1

A US manufacturing firm bought a textile machine factory in Birmingham, England. In an attempt to make the workers in their new factory more productive, the US managers wanted to shorten the time-consuming tea break to which all workers were entitled. In England, a tea break can take half an hour per man, as each worker brews his own tea to his particular taste and sips out of a large, pint size vessel. The managers tried to speed up the "sipping time" to ten minutes. They went ahead and installed a tea-vending machine—just put a paper cup under the spigot and out pours a standard brew. The pint size vessel was replaced by a five-ounce cup printed—as they are in America—with morale-building messages imploring greater dedication to the job and loyalty to the company. Then one Monday morning the workers rioted. Windows were broken, and police had to be called to restore order. The factory never did get back into production. Even after the tea-brewing machine was hauled out, workers boycotted the company and it finally closed down.

Questions for discussion:

1. What made the workers riot and boycott the US company?

2. What mistakes do you think the US managers have made and what they should have done in order to make the workers more productive?

Case 2

What is "normal" business attire? In Indonesia, a businessman wears a loose cotton shirt over pants. A male proprietor of a small firm might not wear pants at all, but a skirt-like wrap. In Saudi Arabia a businessman wears a long robe over his trousers and shirt. In Japan, a businessman wears a dark suit with a white shirt. In each of these countries, expectations are that a serious, responsible businessman in that culture will dress like that.

Businessmen from the United States often dress informally, in sweaters and slacks, or in short-sleeved shirts without jackets. When they are in very warm countries they may wear shorts for leisure. This attire can be acceptable in certain situations, but it can also appear disrespectful in some countries.

Once a US automobile parts manufacturer was shown on television trying to make a sale to some Japanese automobile firms. He was dressed in a boldly patterned cardigan sweater; his hosts were all in dark suits and white shirts. The TV camera caught a few of the hosts repeatedly looking at his sweater with something like alarm in their eyes, and looking away again. Finally it was reported that he failed to make even a single sale.

Questions for discussion:

1. Do you think the sweater the US salesman wore was a factor in his failure?
2. What is wrong with the sweater?

Case 3

The marketing manager of a US knitwear firm was delighted with a multi-million-dollar order for men's underwear it received from a department store chain in Saudi Arabia. The jockey shorts were packaged in the usual way (three pairs to a package, with a picture of a male modeling the briefs) and sent off to the customer in Saudi Arabia.

However, Saudi customs officials were shocked to see a near totally nude man on packages that would be displayed in plain sight of Saudi women and children. Consequently, to satisfy Saudi customs officials, the entire shipment of men's briefs had to be sent back to the United States for repackaging, costing the firm thousands of dollars.

Questions for discussion:

1. What caused the loss for the American firm?
2. What do you think would be a proper way to package the underwear in order to be accepted by the Saudi Arabians?

III After-tasks

Task 1 Movie and culture discussion *Aliens in America*

Aliens in America (also known as *Raja*) is an American sitcom created by David Guarascio and Moses Port that aired on The CW for one season from 2007 to 2008. The show is about an American teenager in Wisconsin whose family takes in a Muslim foreign exchange student from Pakistan.

High schooler Justin Tolchuck (Dan Byrd) is a sensitive, 16-year-old just trying to fit in at his high school in Medora, Wisconsin. He lives with his well-meaning mom Franny (Amy Pietz) who just wants him to be "cool" and fit in, entrepreneur dad Gary (Scott Patterson) who is very laid back, and his newly popular younger sister Claire (Lindsey Shaw), who tries to raise her popularity in school. When the school guidance counselor, Mr. Matthews (Christopher B. Duncan) convinces the family to take in an international student, they accept him with the expectation that he will be a good-looking European or Latin American student that will make Justin popular. Although initially dismayed when Raja Musharraf (Adhir Kalyan), a 16-year-old Muslim boy from Pakistan turns up instead, they soon warm up to him and although their cultures are different, Justin and Raja form an unlikely friendship that might allow them to get past the social nightmare of high school. Justin especially feels compelled to stick by Raja when he starts to notice the blatant racist and xenophobic attitudes of his classmates and community.

Watch a video clip from the TV series *Aliens In America* (《他来自异乡》), then work in groups discussing the following questions:

1. Which of the misunderstandings occurred in the video clip is caused by cultural differences?

2. Do you agree that friendship is universal despite the color of the skin or cultural differences? Can you name a few examples to support your point of view? What about cross-cultural marriage? Do you think that the chances are slim for cross-cultural marriage to be successful?

Task 2 Extended reading

Intercultural Management and Negotiation

We begin our analysis of the influence of management styles with the following case study:

James has been a manager with Micro Tech, Inc., for eight years and is considered to be on a fast track to the executive ranks. Approximately six months ago, he was transferred from the home office in Seattle to take over as head of the Tokyo branch, his first international assignment. Soon after arrival in Japan, James began implementing some of the management programs that had made him a success in the United States. In one program, the top performer from each department was designed every month. Each of the departmental awards was presented with a desk plaque at a ceremony in front of his co-workers, given a gift certificate worth $100, and his picture placed in the lobby of the office building. Recently, James noticed a sharp drop in productivity and office morale seemed to be very low. Some of the workers even started complaining about having to attend the monthly award presentations where just one worker was selected as the "Top Performer".

As the above case study indicates, the tasks of a business manager are multifaceted. The ultimate objective is to motivate employees to work cooperatively and productively. For an international manager, the complexity of these tasks is compounded by the influence of culture. Even with experienced international companies, many well intended universal applications of management theory have turned out badly. This is because cultures have different views of what constitute good and bad management techniques. Consequently, the American style of management may not apply outside the borders of the United States. According to some scholars, "An understanding of these cultural differences will increase your ability to successfully meet the many demands placed on an international manager."

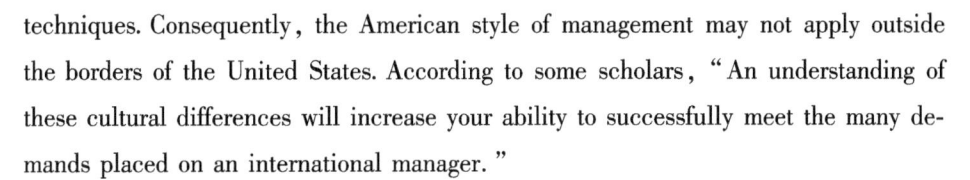

Leadership styles

Asian leadership style

Asian management style reflects the values of collectivism and harmony. Harmony is the ultimate goal of human interaction for the Chinese. Additionally, kinship, interpersonal connections, dignity and power are major factors dominating Chinese management practice. In Confucian-influenced cultures, seniority is the main source of power. In China, as well as most Asian nations, seniority derives from age and length of service in the organization. Seniority not only commands respect, it disarms criticism in Chinese society. Japanese management style also places a high value on harmony. To harmoniously integrating all employees into the organization, like an extended family, is the ultimate goal of Japanese management. Another important aspect of Japanese managerial style can be found in the expression, "Every person is either junior or senior." As mentioned before, a respect for one's superior is seen as your commitment to the organization and its mission. Therefore, while the manager stresses group achievement, he is concurrently afforded great respect.

United States leadership style

Managers in every culture reflect the key values of that culture. We noted that US managers act out a style that stresses "doing" over "being", individualism over collectivism, and low power distance instead of high power distance. Additionally, research on managers in the United States reveals that they reward individual achievement and initiative, action, and results, and seek to reduce status differences. Even the manner in which managers motivate their staff reflects cultural values. In doing oriented cultures, such as the United States, managers often inspire "employees with promises of promotions, raises, bonuses, and other forms of public recognition". While managers in other cultures may generate a very different set of values as they attempt to guide and direct their subordinates.

Different perception of negotiation

As you might suspect, culture plays a critical role when representatives from different cultural backgrounds set out to try to reach an accord acceptable to both sides. So demanding is the task that one experienced negotiator has characterized "cross-cultural and international settings as the most challenging". This challenge arises because cross-cultural negotiation participants are influenced by their respective national bargaining styles. These styles are often a product of contrasting historical legacies, diverse definitions of trust, different cultural values, a built-in level of ambiguity, different decision making processes, contrasting views toward protocol, varied attitudes toward risk taking and dissimilar perceptions of time. Even a culture's attitude toward formality and informality will find its way into a business meeting.

The outlook of the United States can easily create problems when American business people negotiate with members of collective based cultures. For example, Chinese and Japanese negotiators take a long-term view toward business ventures. Their first goals are to work on building a relationship, establishing a level of trust, and determining the desirability of entering into an extended association with the other organization. This personal approach is also the case in Mexico. "Mexican executives are not strongly competitive in the sense of wanting to surpass the performance of conflict and confrontation (which they try to avoid whenever possible). The non-confrontational philosophy in these cultures focuses on mutual interests, giving rise to a "win-win" perspective. This is quite in contrast to the more aggressive American view of "Business is business."

Negotiation

The place at which negotiations occur is culturally diverse and must be understood by anyone who is going to conduct business in an intercultural setting. In the United States, people grow up believing in the motto "He who hesitates is lost." Because of this, the US business people have been criticized for their short-term view of doing business. Some feel that they should not waste time; they should get in there and get the contract signed and get on to other business. In many cultures, this desire to hasten the proceedings will have negative consequences. Hence, the US notion of time is very likely to result in either frustration or the eventual alienation in an international negotiation.

The Western desire to move the negotiations along rapidly is not a popular approach for the Chinese and Japanese. There is even an Asian proverb that states, "With time and patience, the mulberry leaf becomes a silk gown." Business negotiations in China require patience and tenacity. In cultures who want a slow paced session, the first goal is to get to know the other party. The Chinese and Japanese see entering into a commercial arrangement as much like entering into a marriage: it is something that should last for a long time and be beneficial to both parties. Accordingly, they want to take time to ensure that relations with the other organization will be both compatible and productive. To achieve this, negotiations will move slowly. Early meetings will focus more on the general backgrounds of the other organizations and less on the specifics of the proposed business transaction.

In much of Latin American, business negotiations are also conducted at a much slower pace. There is even a proverb that states, "To hurried demand, a leisurely reply." In Argentina and Mexico, interpersonal relationships are so important that a great deal of time is spent in building rapport before actually beginning business. This same concern with relationships and its link to pace and patience is also found in India. As with everything in India, decisions are arrived at slowly. There is no point in trying to impose strict deadlines.

Developing intercultural negotiation skills

We conclude this section on the negotiation process across cultures with a bit of advice on how to sharpen your communication skills when sitting at the bargaining table with people from cultures that differ from your own.

1. Be prepared. The most important message embedded in our first suggestion asks to learn all you can about the host culture before negotiations begin. This means learning about the behaviors related to formality, status, non-verbal communication, the use of verbal language, and the like.

2. Be sensitive to the use of time. This admonition asks you to learn to adapt to a slower pace than you might be used to if you are from the US dominant culture. It also advises being patient when dealing with cultures that use a different tempo than the one found in your culture.

3. Listen carefully. Part of concentrating on the proceedings is learning to remain comfortable with silence and realize that a lack of words is also a form of communication.

4. Be flexible. Negotiation is a give-and-take process, so be prepared to be flexible. Know what concessions you are willing to make.

5. Get yourself in the mindset to create win-win outcomes. Effective negotiation skills allow you to see the possibilities for both parties to walk away from the table happy, instead of one party winning and one party losing. Keep an eye out for agreements that you could make that would add value for both parties instead of taking value from one.

6. Put yourself in your opponent's shoes. Before sitting at the negotiation table, effective negotiation skills would have you sit down by yourself or with a partner to practice running through a mock negotiation beforehand. Give serious consideration to the interests of your opponent and the pressures that he is facing. This will allow you to have confidence and be better at thinking on your feet during the actual negotiation. With a good warm up, you might even be able to come up with a great solution before the negotiations even begin, then you can use your negotiation time to gently walk your opponent through to your solution.

Group work:
1. What do you need if you want to be effective in cross-cultural negotiations?
2. Work with you group members and try to think of some important differences between the negotiation process in a mono-cultural environment and that in a cross-cultural environment.

Section II Business Context

I Pre-tasks

Task 1 Alternatives

If you have two options: One is to work as an associate engineer in China, the other is to work as an engineer in India, which one would you prefer and why?

Task 2 A reception dinner

Suppose you are going to hold a reception dinner for an international event and the guests are from China, America, Japan and Morocco, what factors need to be taken into consideration when preparing for the reception dinner?

II While-tasks

Intercultural Communication in Business Context
The International business setting

With the development of globalization, developed and developing nations are now tied directly to an international system of economic interdependence, and most countries have at least one asset within their borders that is needed by another country.

International interdependencies in this century are not restricted to trade and finished goods. Today, if you call about your phone bill, computer, or credit card application, you may talk to someone in India, Ireland, the Bahamas, or even the Philippines. If you use a US accounting firm to prepare your taxes, the forms may be completed in Bangalore, India. Communication technologies have allowed service industries to outsource tasks ranging from accounting to reading medical x-rays. Offshore service centers have become so extensive that sometimes local employees are given "accent neutralization" classes in an effort to suppress their native accents or are trained to affect a regional United States accent.

All of the intercultural changes in the business arena that we have been discussing create an environment where "doing business" requires people from different cultures to work together. For example, in 2007, the Coca-Cola Company operated in more than two hundred countries, but the North American market (the United States and Canada) produced less than 30 percent of its net operating revenues. McDonald's operates more than 31,000 outlets in 118 nations. Nearly one-third of Starbucks 15,000 stores are overseas, including over two hundred in mainland China. And the retail giant Wal-Mart has stores in Mexico, Germany, and China; it is even opening banks in Mexico.

American business people are also learning how to deal with people from other cultures, because many international corporations have a broad presence in the United States. For example, Chinese firms are involved in 3,500 investment projects in the United States. Tesco, a British company that owns a large chain of grocery stores named "Fresh & Easy", recently opened fifty-nine stores across Southern California and Arizona in five months, and two large suppliers form the United Kingdom established processing plants in California to help provide fresh foods to the new stores. A British firm has also purchased the Greyhound bus company. Anheuser Busch, maker of America's iconic Budweiser beer, was sold in 2008 to a Belgian company. In 2006, the American subsidiary of a Tokyo-based corporation gained control of Coco's and Carrows restaurants, which have a combined total of 210 outlets in the western United States.

The examples we have just cited are representative of the rise of multinational corporations and reflect the increasing international integration of business. The intercultural contact we have been discussing has created a need for knowledge and understanding of how to conduct business in a manner that accommodates different cultural rules. In this new marketplace, knowledge of cultural differences, cross-cultural teamwork, and multicultural collaboration are essential for an organization's success. It is obvious that globalization results in individuals from one culture working not only with, but also for, individuals from another culture. This situation often proves to be difficult because many problems can arise when one works or lives in a foreign environment. Communication across cultural boundaries is difficult. Differences in customs, behaviors, and values result in problems that can be managed only through effective cross-cultural communication and interaction.

The development of business communication skills in a multinational marketplace is a challenging endeavor. Such seemingly universal concepts as management, negotiation, decision making, and conflict management are frequently viewed differently in one culture than in another.

Business protocol

Since business protocol involves forms of ceremony, etiquette, and a correct code of conduct, it is important to understand these rules in any business transaction. However, business "rules" are also culture bound. You can see a differ-

Chapter 7 Contextual Differences in Intercultural Communication

ence in intercultural "regulations" in something as simple as a popular bumper sticker in the United States, which reads "Rules Are for Fools". While this sticker may express the high value Americans place on individualism and independence. In fact, in most parts of the world, culturally correct protocol is both expected and respected. To introduce you to some of the variations in protocol, we will examine (1) initial contacts, (2) greeting behavior and (3) gift giving.

Initial contacts

When engaging in international business, the ways in which you establish initial contact can range from making an E-mail, to placing a brief unsolicited telephone call, to writing a formal letter or using a "go-between" or emissary. Which of these procedures is best is directly related to the culture you wish to contact. If you fail to follow correct protocol and violate the rules of that culture, you will likely not gain access to the organization. A few examples should help clarify this point.

We begin with Japan. As Nishiyama points out, the typical American approach of a cold call or a letter of introduction will not work in Japan. Instead, the most effective means of establishing a business connection in Japan is through a formal, face-to-face meeting with the sole objective of making introductions. India has much the same attitude about initial contacts, because "India is a relationship-based culture" and therefore first exchanges are often "made through common business associates". While the "cold call" (contacting someone without an appointment) is common in the United States, we have already pointed out that the use of trusted intermediaries is common, and often required, in many other cultures. Egypt is another good example of this code of behavior. If you want an appointment in Egypt, you must send a letter of introduction to an Egyptian contact person who can facilitate arranging a meeting. In Africa, the use of an intermediary is also essential; this is exemplified by the Congolese proverb that states, "The friends of our friends are our friends." An intermediary is an absolute must in Africa when approaching someone of a higher status. Doing business in China also depends on go-betweens. The Chinese rely heavily on interpersonal relations, called *guanxi*, built and maintained through mutual obligations that begin with family and friends and extend to organizational acquaintances. An international business person coming to China will have to establish a *guanxi* network, which may take considerable time—even years.

Greeting behavior

United States. Once a meeting has been arranged, it is important that an effort be made to use the greeting practices of the host culture. Americans tend to be informal and friendly. In fact, persons from other cultures are surprised by the informality of the US Americans who often say "Hi" to complete strangers. In most countries of the world, saying "Hi" to strangers is uncommon. In the United States, both men and women shake hands on meeting and leaving. First names are generally used except when addressing very senior persons or in formal situations. Business cards are exchanged in business settings but seldom in strictly social gatherings.

China. The Chinese business community is more formal than that of the United States, and the Chinese always greet the most senior person first. They also use titles that clearly reflect the cultural emphasis on hierarchy. The use of titles by the Chinese is so pervasive that it often extends to work position such as Chief Engineer, Accountant, Department Manager, and even Foreman. In China, the order of personal names is reversed from that in the West. The Chinese place their family name (surname) first and their given name last. For example, in the name Wang Tao, Wang is the family name and Tao is the given name, so in English, the proper address would be "Mr. Wang". Many culturally uninformed Westerners have made the mistake of addressing their counter part by his or her first name, thinking it was his or her last name. The Chinese have widely adopted the Western handshake for initial and subsequent greetings. However, this does not extend to the common Western practice of placing a hand on the back or an arm around the shoulder. There are other non-verbal gestures in China that can carry different meanings from those assigned in the West. For instance, the head nod is used by the Chinese to acknowledge the speaker, not to signal agreement with what is being said. The hierarchical nature of Chinese society also dictates that direct eye contact should be avoided. Although in the West you are expected to maintain a high degree of eye contact during discussions, the Chinese consider this to be rude and disrespectful.

Japan. A common greeting ritual in Japan is the bow. As is the case with so many of Japanese behaviors, the bow is directly linked to status and rank. What is less well known about the bow is that, among the Japanese, the bow is a highly refined practice filled with many subtle nuances as to who bows first, how low, and how long. These distinctions, which the Japanese begin to learn as children, can be diffi-

Chapter 7 Contextual Differences in Intercultural Communication

cult for a foreigner to master. Yet some of the underlying meanings of bowing are important for Westerners to understand and appreciate. For foreign men and women, a respectful slight nod of the head and shoulders will be considered appropriate in most situations. Another important protocol in greeting the Japanese business person is the exchange of business cards. Like so much of human communication, the simple act of exchanging cards is deeply rooted in Japanese values. Business cards should be printed on one side in English and on the other in Japanese. They should also contain enough detailed information so that one's specific position within the company is clearly spelled out. When receiving a card, you should carefully read it before placing it in your pocket or purse. If you sit down to discuss business, the cards should be placed on the table in an order that corresponds to the seating positions of those across from you. This provides an easy way of remembering names, positions, and seniority.

Arab. Like the Japanese, Arabs have a very elaborate and complex structure of greeting behaviors. There are, by some estimates, thirty different blessings, both situational and relational, that can be part of the greeting. These various greetings involve numerous handshakes and, for the men, embraces and kisses on both cheeks. Titles are very important to Arabs, and are always used in the business context. Business cards, printed in both Arabic and English, are routinely exchanged. It is important to remember that Muslims never greet by shaking with the left hand, because it is used for personal hygiene.

Gift giving

An old adage says, "Beware of Greeks bearing gifts." However, among many cultures gift giving is a common practice and part of business protocol. The exchanging of gifts in the business context invokes a number of stated and unstated protocols. One problem is that individualistic Western cultures, especially that of the United States, often view extensive giving and the payment of money as a form of bribery. The United States anathema toward commercial bribery is so strong that it is prohibited by the Foreign Corrupt Practices Act, which "makes it unlawful to bribe foreign government officials to obtain or retain business". China has also enacted legislation to prohibit bribery in business transactions. In 2002, regulations were established that designated gifts in excess of $180 (US) as bribery. The international business representative must be able to distinguish between what is considered a gift and what is seen as a bribe. From the perspective of the United States, suitable gifts for exchange among employees from international organizations are small, relatively inexpensive mementos presented to commemorate an event or as an expression of appreciation and solidarity. Small gifts—such as pens, cups, and key rings engraved with your company logo—are not only acceptable, but virtually essential in global business. Home and office decorations and books and magazines are also popular.

For the business person going abroad, it is useful to know not only local views concerning gift giving, but also what gifts are appropriate in the culture where business will be conducted and when they should be given. Perhaps more so than in any other culture, gift giving in Japan is highly ritualistic. As part of the formality of the gift exchange in Japan, and as a means of showing respect, gifts are usually given and received with both hands. And, according to Nishiyama, gifts are exchanged at the beginning of any new business relationship. In Mexico and China, gifts are one part of a business relationship as well.

Understanding what constitutes an appropriate gift is as important as knowing when to give one. In Guatemala and Japan, white flowers should not be given as a gift; they are normally associated with funerals, as are chrysanthemums in Italy. Alcoholic beverages should not be given in Islamic countries or to a Muslim counterpart. Additionally, when giving a gift to a Muslim, you should not use your left hand, for as we mentioned elsewhere, this is considered the unclean hand. In Japan, to give a clock as a gift is equivalent to say I wish you were dead, because it reminds the recipient that time is running out. While thirteen is an inauspicious number in the United States, gift in numbers of four are inappropriate in China because four and death are pronounced quite similarly.

As the preceding examples indicate, the rules for gift giving vary considerably across cultures. Therefore, we recommend that prior to leaving for your international destination; you should need to know if a gift is expected, what type is appropriate, when to give a gift, and how it should be presented. While these seem like small, inconsequential considerations, without an understanding of what is proper and improper, you run the risk of destroying the international transaction before it even begins.

(Adapted from Larry A. Samovar, Richard E. Porter, Edwin R. McDaniel, "Communication between Cultures", Chapter 8)

Chapter 7 Contextual Differences in Intercultural Communication

Word list:

1. etiquette ['etɪket]
    n. 礼节，礼仪；规矩
2. bumper ['bʌmpə]
    n. 缓冲器，保险杆，减震物
3. initial [ɪ'nɪʃəl]
    adj. 最初的；字首的
4. emissary ['emɪs(ə)rɪ]
    n. 使者；密使
5. intermediary [ɪntə'miːdɪərɪ]
    n. 中间人；调解者；媒介物
6. distinction [dɪ'stɪŋ(k)ʃ(ə)n]
    n. 区别；差别；特性
7. hygiene ['haɪdʒiːn]
    n. 卫生；卫生学
8. chrysanthemum [krɪ'sænθɪməm]
    n. 菊花；菊属
9. inauspicious [ɪnɔː'spɪʃəs]
    adj. 不祥的，不吉的；恶运的
10. inconsequential [,ɪnkɒnsɪ'kwenʃ(ə)l]
    adj. 不重要的；不合理的；不合逻辑的

Task 1 Reading comprehension

Exercise One: Work with your partners, decide whether the following statements are true (T) or false (F) according to what you have learned in the passage.

1. _____ International interdependencies in this century are only restricted to trade and finished goods.
2. _____ Differences in customs, behaviors, and values result in problems that can be managed only through effective cross-cultural communication and interaction.
3. _____ The typical American approach of a cold call or a letter of introduction works effectively in Japan.

4. _____ In Egypt, you must send a letter of introduction to an Egyptian contact person who can facilitate a meeting.

5. _____ An international business person coming to China will have to establish a *guanxi* network, which is an easy to accomplish task since the Chinese are well-known for their hospitality.

6. _____ In most countries of the world, saying "Hi" to strangers is very common.

7. _____ The Chinese usually use titles to clearly reflect the cultural emphasis on hierarchy.

8. _____ In Western cultures, extensive giving and the payment of money is pervasive so as to establish good business relationship.

Exercise Two: Work with your partner and fill in the blanks with the words given below.

status   distributors   essential   ancestors
Israel   inappropriate   initial   facilitate

The ways in which you make 1. _____ contact and an appointment to conduct business can range from a brief telephone call to writing a formal letter of request or the use of a "go-between" or emissary. The manner in which the initial business contact is made and the amount of advance notice between the contact and appointment are key factors you must consider when doing business in another culture. If you want an appointment in Egypt, you must send a letter of introduction to a contact who can 2. _____ an appointment. In Africa, the use of an intermediary is also 3. _____. An intermediary is an absolute must in Africa when approaching someone of a higher 4. _____. When doing business in China, it is important to establish contacts before you invest in a trip. The United States Department of Commerce can assist in arranging appointments with local Chinese businesses and government officials, and can identify importers, buyers, agents, 5. _____, and joint venture partners. The date you plan your business trip is also of major importance when dealing with another culture. For example, in China, many businesses close the week before and the week after the Chinese New Year. In Japan, business is not conducted in Mid-August, because many people travel to the graves of their 6. _____. In 7. _____, their holy day begins at sunset on Friday and ends at sunset on Satur-

Chapter 7 Contextual Differences in Intercultural Communication

day. The business week, therefore runs from Sunday through Thursday. Attempting business on their holy day would be considered highly 8. _____ .

Task 2 Case study

Case 1

A Canadian sales representative in Venezuela goes to a shipping office to arrange for the ongoing shipment of an order in transit from Quebec to another country. She is on time for her appointment, but has to wait while the shipping agent serves a number of customers who are already in the office. When the Canadian's turn finally comes, she explains what she needs, and the agent begins filling out the documentation for the shipment and discussing prices. At the same time the agent takes a phone call, responds to a question from a co-worker about schedules, and directs the faxing of a message about something else—in effect working on three other projects besides the Canadian's, which makes the Canadian somewhat annoyed.

Questions for discussion:
1. What has the shipping agent done to make the Canadian annoyed?
2. What caused the problem in this business setting?

Case 2

Have you had your lunch?

When I first went to Hong Kong a number of years ago, I had no idea about the Chinese language or the Chinese culture. Shortly after my arrival, I went to the bank on my way to school. I was extremely surprised when the bank clerk asked me if I had had my lunch. In British culture, this question would be regarded as an indirect invitation to lunch, and between unmarried young people it indicates a young man's interest in dating a girl. Since he was a complete stranger, I was quite taken aback. I proceeded to school and was even more surprised when one of the teachers asked me the same question. By now I realized that it could not be an invitation, but I was puzzled as to why they kept asking it. In the following days, as I was asked the question again and again, I came to the conclusion that people must be concerned about my health. I was somewhat underweight, and I assumed they must be worried that I was not eating properly. Only later, did I find out that the question had no real significance at all, it was merely a greeting.

English people have a very strong sense of privacy. They are easily offended by comments which seem to invade their personal lives, so the Chinese greeting "Where are you going?" is uncomfortable to them. They regard it as a request for information and as an invasion of their privacy. In fact, many foreign teachers in China have complained that their room attendants are spies because the attendants have greeted them with "Where are you going?". (Helen Oatey, 1987)

Group work:

Discuss in groups the differences between the East and the West with regard to greetings and partings.

Case 3

Todd Davis was president of one of the largest international book publishing companies in the world. His company has just opened a new building complex in Boston, and they intended to centralize operations by bringing most of their employees, both domestic and international, to this central location. Since Mr. Davis wanted to make a good impression and have everyone feel welcome in the United States, he decided to present all the new senior international managers with a welcome gift. After the gift were presented, Mr. Davis had the strangest feeling that something had gone wrong. Here are some of the presents he gave to his staff:

A. The employee from Egypt was given a bottle of expensive rum.

B. The Japanese manager was given a clock and asked to open it in front of everyone.

C. The supervisor from India was given an expensive wallet made of cowhide.

D. The employee from France was given a bottle of American wine.

Questions for discussion:

1. What went wrong?
2. How to solve the problem?

Chapter 7　Contextual Differences in Intercultural Communication

Case 4

A problematic business meeting

A Chinese business delegation visited a British engineering company with whom they had recently signed a deal. The visit turned out to be highly problematic. What went wrong during the visit?

1. Seating arrangements for the welcome meeting

The welcome meeting took place in the company's conference room which had a large oblong table placed in the middle of the room. The British chairman sat at one end of the table, and the Chinese visitors sat round the rest of the table. Five other British staff either sat or stood behind the Chinese visitors because there was not enough room for them at the table. The British chairman was aware that the room was too small, and was embarrassed about this, but the company did not have a larger room on its premises as it was primarily a factory building. He sat at the "head" of the table for practical reasons- so that he could see and hear the guests more easily. However, in the follow-up interview, the Chinese delegation leader complained as follows:

It shouldn't have been that he sat in the chair position and we were seated along the sides of the table. With equal status, they should sit along this side and we should sit along that side, shouldn't we? That would have been the right way. You see, they were chairing, and we were audience, which naturally means that you do what you are told to. [His colleagues chorus agreement] They were, right from the start, they were commanding, in control, contemptuous. In actual fact we should have been given equal status...

2. Team introduction and a return speech

The British chairman started the meeting by welcoming the visitors, and then asked the British staff to introduce themselves in turn. When they had done this, he invited each of the Chinese visitors to introduce themselves, but this immediately caused confusion. The delegation leader turned to consult the others, and one of them requested in Chinese that he do it on their behalf. It was almost a minute before the delegation leader responded to the chairman's request, and at this point he began reading out a speech. Immediately the interpreter interrupted him saying, in Chinese, that they should first introduce themselves. This resulted in further worried faces and discussion in Chinese, before the visitors started introducing themselves individually. In the follow-up interview and video playback session, the Chinese visitors all argued that it was normal and polite for the head of the delegation to say "a few words of appreciation" and then introduce himself and each member of the delegation. They were clearly offended that he had not been given this opportunity. They discussed whether the interpreter was to blame for this, but concluded that he must have known British customs and that the British chairman cannot have wanted them to give a return speech. The head of the Chinese delegation argued as follows:

According to our home customs and protocol, speech is delivered on the basis of reciprocity. He has made his speech and I am expected to say something. But he had finished his speech, and he didn't give me the opportunity, and they each introduced themselves, wasn't this clearly implied that they do look down on us Chinese?

3. Business relationships

The sales manager for China was away on an overseas trip when the visitors arrived; he was due back during the middle of the visit. The Chinese visitors expected that, since he was their "old friend", he would made contact with them immediately after he returned, either officially in the office, or unofficially at the hotel, or at least telephone them. However, when he made no contact with them on the day of his return, they were annoyed. They repeatedly asked, and at one stage even demanded, the accompanying British staff to contact him, and then asked for his home telephone number. This continued for the next few days, including the weekend.

The sales manager eventually arranged a meeting with them the following Monday, one day before their departure. In the follow-up interview, he explained that he needed to spend time with his family, since he had been away on a long trip. However, from the Chinese visitors' point of view, he had failed to act as a genuine friend. (Adapted from Spencer Oatey and Xing, 2008)

Group work:

1. What is the problem in this intercultural communication? Work in groups and try to explain the reasons for this kind of failure in cross-cultural communication.

2. Role-play this problematic meeting in front of the whole class as the original version, or role-play this problematic meeting as an improved version and this time you are supposed to correct all the misunderstandings and problems occurred before and make the meeting a fruitful one.

III After-tasks

Task 1 Movie and culture discussion *Outsourced*

Outsourced is a romantic comedy film, directed by John Jeffcoat, released in 2006.

When Todd Anderson's job and entire department are outsourced, he reluctantly travels to India to train his replacement. Arriving in India, he experiences culture shock: he is confused by everything from catching a train to hiring a taxi.

Through his team of quirky Indian call center workers—including his friendly and motivated replacement Puro, and the charming, outspoken Asha—Todd soon realizes that he too has a lot to learn, not only about India and America but also about himself.

Todd's objective is to reduce the time needed to complete the average call from twelve minutes to six. If his team doesn't achieve this, his boss won't let him go home... In India, Todd experienced the farces(闹剧) about cultural shock and at last fell in love with Asha—the pretty and kind-hearted Indian girl.

In India, Todd experienced a great many of cultural differences in many aspects. In the aspect of daily life, Todd came to realize that the interaction with neighbors is very informal in India. The relations with the neighbors are just like family members who can come and go anytime, especially if you are living in a colony. While in America it is not like that. The people are so busy in America that they hardly find few minutes to talk to their neighbors. They leave for work on the mornings and return tired in the evenings. So the living styles between America and India are quite different. What's more, in India typically Sunday is the only holiday. However, in America Saturday and Sunday are holidays. During these two days they enjoy recreation, do household work, socialize with different people etc.

No two cultures are the same. One of the major differences that can be seen between American and Indian culture is in family relations. While the Indians are very much family oriented, the Americans are individual oriented. In Indian culture, the family values are given more prominence than the individual values. Indians respect family values. On the other hand, in American culture the individual values get prominence than the family values.

In the aspect of work, Todd found that the Indians love stability where as the Americans love mobility. Further more, Americans have great regard to time and its value compared with his Indian colleagues.

Watch a video clip from the movie *Outsourced* (《世界是平的》), and then work in groups to discuss the following questions:

1. What kind of cultural shocks did Todd Anderson experience in India?
2. What should we do to deal with the problems that arise from conflicting cultural norms?

Task 2　Extended reading

Intercultural Conflict Management

Conflict is an inescapable aspect of all relationships. If managed improperly, conflict can lead to irreparable breakdowns—separation or divorce at the interpersonal level, war on a national scale, or lost opportunities in commercial endeavors. Conflict involves people's thoughts (ideas), emotions (feelings and perceptions) and actions (behaviors). When conflict occurs, communication and culture come into play.

Conflict: An intercultural perspective

Conflict is an inevitable part of business settings, each culture's way of perceiving and dealing with conflict reflects its value system. In the United State, there is a belief that conflict is a part of competition and "self-expression" and therefore can be useful. This perception of conflict is also seen in other cultures. In the Middle East, people perceive conflict as a natural way of life. People are expected to have intense feelings on many issues and to express those feelings in an animated and confrontational manner. Greeks also have an expressive approach to conflict and are proud of their long tradition of argumentation and debate.

In general, as we noted elsewhere, collectivistic cultures dislike open and direct conflict, which is seen as a threat to organizational accord and stability and detrimental to the relationships among group members. For the Chinese, social harmony is of great significance. The attitude toward conflict is directly linked to the Confucian philosophy we discussed preciously. That is to say, the Chinese feel more comfortable using avoidance or compromise tactics when faced with a conflict situation. Similarly, for the Japanese, conflict is seen as embarrassing and distressing. They believe disputes should be resolved privately and prefer "reaching an agreement without confrontation, especially in the case of parties engaged in a long term relationship". Japanese companies incorporate small-group discussions and use trusted intermediaries to help prevent or resolve conflicts. Criticism, a potent source of disagreement and conflict, is expressed indirectly, in passive and accommodating styles. Since conflict carries the potential loss of face, the Japanese are likely to remain silent or use nonverbal behaviors to express disapproval—even at business meetings with members of other cultures.

Latino cultures also perceive and deal with conflict in a manner that reflects many of their cultural values. Because their culture values friendships in both business and social interactions, conflict is seen as something to be avoided in the business context. For example, protocol requires that people feel at ease with each other and interpersonal conflicts will disturb that comfort. Mexicans are another group that does not enjoy direct confrontation. Some European and Scandinavian cultures also deal with conflict in ways that are dissimilar to the conflict style found in the United States. German does not engage in direct face-to-face conflict. In Germany, conflict is generally avoided not by emphasizing harmony in personal relationships or by smoothing over differences of opinion, but rather by maintaining formality and social distance. For the French, losing control and engaging in social conflict is "a sign of weakness". Regardless of the motivation used to justify or avoid conflict, one thing should be clear by now—not all cultures deal with conflict in the same manner.

Managing intercultural conflict

As we just noted, perceiving and handling conflict is rooted in culture. However, some skills for responding to conflict can be employed regardless of the culture you are interacting with. Let us now examine some of those skills.

Identify the contentious issue

Whether the conflict is over personalities, specific points in a contract, or a verbal misunderstanding, you need to begin by discovering what is at the core of the disagreement. It does not make sense to argue over a particular point only to discover later that your counterpart did not even understand the central point of the controversy. This desire to isolate the disagreement shows your willingness to negotiate in "good faith". It also relieves some of the anxiety within the negotiation meeting. Once you have clarified the issues, all parties can begin to focus on solutions to the controversy.

Keep an open mind

Asking you to "keep an open mind" while engaged in a conflict is easier for us to suggest than for you to carry out. When we speak of trying to keep an open mind, we are not talking about giving blind allegiance to the other person's arguments and abandoning your principles. Rather, we are pointing out the advantages of trying to see things from another point of view and remaining open to the other person's position.

Do not rush

Since so many international business transactions are expensive (international air travel, hotels, etc), it is easy to feel that you must rush to accomplish your objective. We advise, however, that you not rush to resolve a conflict when interacting with members of a collective culture. In short, you must learn to slow down the entire negotiation process when conflict arises.

Keep the conflict centered on ideas, not people

Regardless of the culture, no one likes feeling threatened or being placed in an uncomfortable position. Hence, it is important to separate the propositions from the people. This keeps the negotiation focused on solving the problem that created the conflict instead of having the parties defend their egos. Therefore, to avoid having a person "lose face", you need to keep the focus on the content of the conflict and not on the individual.

Chapter 7 Contextual Differences in Intercultural Communication

Develop options

Develop options that benefit both sides. Negotiation partners should take time to search for a wide range of options before trying to come to an agreement. Insist on using some objective criteria for evaluating these options. The agreement should reflect fair standards that are shared by both parties.

Develop techniques for avoiding conflict

There are a number of techniques you can employ that might help resolve the conflict before it reaches the point of being irresolvable. Here are a few suggestions:

1. Learn to use collective pronouns that can help defuse conflict. Although at times you may have to refer to people by name. When you are with a group of people, try to develop the practice of using group pronouns. Group pronouns such as "we" and "our" are always a better choice compared with individual pronouns such as "I" and "you".

2. Repeat the other person's comments as objectively as possible so that you can determine if you actually heard what they meant to communicate. Often something is read into a comment that was not actually intended by the sender of the message.

3. Try to state as many points of agreement as possible. Often the areas of agreement can outweigh the differences, and therefore, conflict can be avoided. This can be done by using something as simple as a sentence that states, "We all can agree than this contract would be beneficial to both our companies."

Group activity:

Each group is supposed to role-play a conflict within the group by using one of the conflict styles (avoiding, competing, compromising, accommodating and collaborating). The conflict can focus on a business topic such as pricing, delivery, etc.

Chapter 8

Culture Barrier and Culture Shock

Diversity is the mix. Inclusion is making the mix work.

—Andres Tapia

Meanings are in people.

—David Berlo

It is not our differences that divide us. It is our inability to recognize, accept, and celebrate those differences.

—Lorde

Change your thoughts and you change your world.

—Peale

Section I Culture Barrier

I Pre-tasks

Task 1 Matching game

Please look at the following pictures. Each picture presents a type of communication barrier in our daily life. Try to find the correct type of the barrier from the box for each picture.

A. language barrier	B. cultural barrier
C. emotional barrier	D. perceptual barrier
E. interpersonal barrier	F. gender barrier

Chapter 8 Culture Barrier and Culture Shock

( ) ( ) ( )

( ) ( ) ( )

Task 2 Game playing

Have you ever played the game where you sit in a circle and one person whispers a story to the person on their left, who shares the story with the next person, and so on, until the story is retold to the one who started it. Let's play this game in group and finally see which group can present a story that most resembles the original story.

The story for your reference:

I lived in Taiwan for several years. My pay was six times higher than when I lived in Chinese mainland and don't let anyone fool you with the "cost of living" speech. Sure Chinese mainland had a lower cost of living but not six times lower. Maybe the cost of living is about half the cost of living of Taiwan. Even If your cost of living is twice as high and you only make twice as much you still come out ahead in the higher paying place because you save twice as much! Taiwan is a very comfortable little island which I have come to appreciate more in hindsight than at the time. The Taiwan students enjoyed hanging around Santa. I was not teaching English majors but non-English majors. Many of my students did not particularly like English and anything that made that class more fun was welcomed by the students.

II While -tasks

Culture Barriers to Communication

Culture is all socially transmitted behaviors, arts, architectures, languages, signs, symbols, ideas, beliefs, norms, traditions, rituals, etc. which is learnt and shared in a particular social group of the same nationality, ethnicity, religion, etc. Culture is handed down from one generation to another. It gives people their way of seeing the world and interpreting life. A single culture has many sub-cultures.

Cultural diversity makes communication difficult as the mindsets of people of different cultures are different, the languages, signs and symbols are also different. Different cultures have different meaning of words, behaviors and gestures. Culture also gives rise to prejudices, ethnocentrism, manners and opinions. It forms the way people think and behave. When people belonging to different cultures communicate, these factors can become barriers. The way you communicate is affected by the culture you were brought up in. The opposite is also true. Culture is, to a large extent, determined by the way we communicate. In America, people communicate freely and that is a part of their culture. In Germany, an Indian who is used to being very indirect with his communication might find their direct way of speaking rude. Being direct is part of the German culture and it is reflected in the way they communicate. Thus, communication shapes culture and culture shapes communication.

Language is a very complex thing, and communication between people speaking different languages is difficult. Language is a way of looking at the world, and even skilled translators can find it tricky to convey complex emotions and concepts, which can lead to misunderstandings. When you think about how often you misunderstand someone speaking your language, you can imagine how hard it is to get the full meaning from something a person with a different cultural background is saying to you. Therefore, language is widely considered as the prior barrier in intercultural communication. There are billions of people in the world who do not understand English or cannot communicate in English properly. Not speaking properly can cause various misunderstandings and be a barrier to communication. Different cultures have deve-loped their own language as a part of their heritage. People are comfortable communicating in their own language whereas have to work hard to learn new languages. For example, separation of East and West Germany for 40 years caused the language to differ a lot. The dialect became very different as people of East Germany had an influence of Russian language whereas West Germany had influence of English. They had a barrier in communicating with each other for decades. Even when people try to express in their own language, many misunderstandings arise. It becomes more profound in people speaking different languages.

Semantics including signs and symbols is also an important form of communication. Signs and symbols as a form of non-verbal communication cannot be relied upon in communication between people from different cultures as that is also different like language. Signs, symbols and gestures vary in different cultures. For example, the sign "thumbs up" is taken as a sign of approval and wishing luck in most of the cultures but is taken as an insult in Bangladesh. Similarly, the "V" hand gesture with palm faced outside or inside means victory and peace in US, but back of hand facing someone showing the sign is taken as insulting in many cultures. The culture sets some meanings of signs like the ones mentioned above, which might not be the same in other culture.

Another barrier is stereotyping. Stereotyping is the process of creating a picture of a whole culture, over generalizing all people belonging to the same culture as having similar characteristics and categorizing people accordingly. It is a belief about a certain group and is mostly negative. Stereotyping can be done on the basis of many things like nationality, gender, race, religion, ethnicity, age, etc. For example, Asian students are stereotyped to be good at Math which is a positive stereotype. But, there is also cultural stereotype of all people following a particular religion as being violent like Islam and is negative stereotyping. Moreover, inaccurate and hostile stereotypes of people from other places can be a barrier to communication. For example, a stereotypical American is thought to be impatient and arrogant as well as friendly and tolerant. The danger in entertaining stereotypes is that an individual is thought to possess characteristics that are ascribed to the group. Obviously, not all Americans are impatient and arrogant, nor are they all friendly and tolerant. Prejudging an individual can lead to misconceptions and barriers to communication. Therefore, negative stereotyping creates prejudices as it provokes judgmental attitudes. People look at those cultures as evil and treat the people following the religion wickedly. Media is a tool of mass communication which promotes stereotypes and prejudices and creates more communication barriers.

Cultural differences causes behavior and personality differences like body language, thinking, communication, manners, norms, etc. which lead to miscommunication. For example, in some cultures eye contact is important whereas in some it is rude and disrespectful. Culture also sets a specific norms which dictates behavior as they have guidelines for accepted behavior. It explains what is right and wrong. Every action is influenced by culture like ambitions, careers, interests, values, etc. Beliefs and emotions are also another cause for cultural barrier. For instance, mostly, people who believe in god can cope with their lows of life easily than atheists but atheists are more hardworking at all times which relates to their behavior and communication. Appropriate amount of emotion that must be displayed is also different in different cultures. Roles are defined by culture. Good communication only occurs between people with different cultures if both accept their differences with open mind. What is considered an appropriate display of emotion can differ from culture to culture. In some countries, displaying anger, fear or frustration in the workplace is considered inappropriate in a business setting. People from these cultures keep their emotions hidden and only discuss the factual aspects of the situation. In other cultures, participants in a discussion are expected to reveal their emotions. You can imagine what misunderstandings can arise if a business person displays strong emotion in the company of employees who feel that such behavior is out of place.

Ethnocentrism is the process of dividing cultures as "us" and "them". The people of someone's own culture are categorized as in-group and the other culture is out-group. There is always greater preference to in-group. There is an illusion of out-group as evil and inferior. This evaluation is mostly negative. If the culture is similar to us, then it is good and if is dissimilar, it is bad. Other's culture is evaluated and assessed with the standard being their own culture. Ethnocentrism affects the understanding of message, and encourages hostility. For example, the books in schools use reference of their own culture to describe other cultures by either showing common things or differences.

Similar to ethnocentrism and stereotyping, religion also disrupts communication as it creates a specific image of people who follow other religions. People find it difficult to talk to people who follow different religions. Religious views influence how people think about others. It creates differences in opinions. For example, in Pakistan, the Christians have to speak up for their rights as the majority is of Islam and the

Christians are discriminated. There is also a lack of communication between these religious groups.

There are other cultural barriers like frames of reference, political opinions, priorities of life, age, etc. Cross-cultural communication is not only a barrier but also an opportunity for creativity, new perspectives, and openness to new ideas and unity in the world. To make communication effective, the causes of cultural communication barriers must be eliminated as many as possible. Cross-cultural understanding must be increased as it decreases communication barrier caused by culture difference. (1306 words)

(Adapted from Sneha Mishra, "Cultural Barriers to Communication")

Word list:

1. transmit [trænsˈmɪt]
    vt. 传输；发射；传送，传递；传染
    vi. 发送信号
2. ethnicity [eθˈnɪsɪtɪ]
    n. 种族地位，种族特点，种族渊源
3. ethnocentrism [ˌeθnəʊˈsentrɪzəm]
    n. 民族优越感
4. heritage [ˈherɪtɪdʒ]
    n. 遗产；传统；文化遗产；继承物
5. semantics [sɪˈmæntɪks]
    n. 语义学；词义学
6. arrogant [ˈærəgənt]
    adj. 傲慢的，自大的；带有傲慢，出自傲慢
7. ascribe [əˈskraɪb]
    vt. 把……归于，认为……是由于；认为……具有
8. atheist [ˈeɪθɪɪst]
    n. 无神论者
9. illusion [ɪˈluːʒn]
    n. 错觉；幻想；假象；错误观念
10. hostility [hɑˈstɪləti]
    n. 敌意，敌对状态；战争行动；愤怒反对，愤怒反抗

Task 1 Reading comprehension

Exercise One: Work with your partners, decide whether the following statements are true (T) or false (F) according to what you have learned in the passage.

1. _____ Culture diversity mainly refers to the different minds or thinking of different people in different cultures.
2. _____ Culture can affect people's way of communication and the way of communication can also reflect the features of culture.
3. _____ Different cultures make communication difficult. So if there is a good translator, there will be no barriers any more.
4. _____ The example of the barrier in language communicating between East and West Germany shows the culture influence may overweigh the language influence.
5. _____ Semantics only refers to signs and symbols as an important form of communication.
6. _____ The culture sets some meanings of signs, which might not be the same in other culture.
7. _____ Stereotyping is the process of creating a picture of a whole culture, over generalizing all people belonging to the same culture as having similar characteristics and categorizing people accordingly. Therefore, it helps the newcomer to understand and get used to the new culture quickly.
8. _____ Stereotypes are thought to possess characteristics that are ascribed to the group, so it is dangerous to apply the stereotypes to an individual.
9. _____ Ambitions, careers, interests, values, etc. are very related to personal orientations and can hardly be influenced by culture.
10. _____ Business is very serious and formal issue, so people from different cultures should keep their emotions hidden and only discuss the factual aspects of the situation in order to ensure smooth business cooperation.

Exercise Two: Fill in the blanks with the words given below and change the form when necessary.

complex   ethnocentrism   stereotype   mindset   dissimilar
perspective   disrupt   norm   non-verbal   display

Chapter 8 Culture Barrier and Culture Shock

1. The different _____ of people in different cultures not only creates the cultural diversity in communication, but also makes it difficult.

2. _____ is regarded dangerous because it affects the understanding of message, and encourages hostility.

3. Asian students would react positively if they are _____ to be good at Math.

4. Cultural barriers may frame certain unbiased opinion toward certain culture, but a barrier can also be converted into an opportunity for creativity, new _____, and openness to new ideas and unity in the world.

5. Signs, symbols and gestures as a form of _____ communication cannot be relied upon in communication between people from different cultures as that is also different like language.

6. Culture also sets a specific _____ which dictates behavior as they have guidelines for accepted behavior.

7. If a business person _____ strong emotion in the company of employees who feel that such behavior is out of place, misunderstandings can arise unsurprisingly.

8. To make communication effective, the causes of cultural communication barriers, which are various and _____, must be eliminated as many as possible.

9. Similar to ethnocentrism and stereotyping, religion also _____ communication as it creates a specific image of people who follow other religions.

10. In different cultures, people tend to evaluate the culture which is similar to them is good, while the culture which is _____ to them is evil or inferior.

Task 2 Case study

Case 1

A student from Japan was visited by her sister, and when they went to a department store, a clerk came over to them. "Hi!" she said, "How are you today?" Surprised, the sister asked, "Do you know her?" The Japanese student said, "No, I don't." The sister said, "The American people are wonderful. They are so nice and polite, friendly and helpful to people that they do not know well, much beyond my expectations. I am very relieved now. You must have made many friends in America now." The student said bitterly, "Not really. I haven't made any real friends yet since I came here 5 months ago. It is very difficult to make friends with Americans. They are not so friendly as they seem to be. Sometimes I even feel they are cold."

Questions for discussion:

1. Why do the Japanese student and his sister had totally different impressions of Americans?

2. What do you think of the American friendship from a cultural perspective?

Case 2

In an official meeting between Virginia government and the representatives of 6 Indian nations, the commissioner told the Indians that one of the colleges offered a fund for educating Indian youth; and that if the chiefs would send down their sons to that college. It is one of the Indian rules of politeness not to answer a public proposition the same day that it is made. So they delayed their answer till the following day. The Indian Speaker said:

"For we know that you highly esteem the kind of learning taught in those colleges, and that the maintenance of our young men would be expensive to you. We are very grateful for your good proposal and thank you heartily.

But, you, who are wise, must know that different nations have different conceptions of things, and you will not therefore take it a miss. If our ideas of this kind of education happen not to be the same with yours. Several of our young people were formerly brought up at the colleges. They were instructed in all your sciences, but when they came back to us, they were bad runners, ignorant of every means of living in the woods, unable to bear either cold or hunger, knew neither how to build a cabin, take a deer, neither fit for hunters, warriors, nor counselor. They were totally good for nothing.

We are however not the less obligated by your kind offer, though we decline accepting it. If the gentlemen of Virginia will send us a dozen of their sons, we will take care of their education, instruct them in all we know and make men of them."

Questions for discussion:

1. Why did the Indians decline the offer made by the Virginia government?

2. If you were the Virginia official, what would your reaction be?
3. What kind of cultural conflicts can be observed in this case?

III After-tasks

Task 1 Movie and culture discussion *Lost in Translation*

Bob Harris (Bill Murray), an aging American movie star, arrives in Tokyo to film an advertisement for Suntory whisky, for which he will receive $2 million. Charlotte (Scarlett Johansson), a young recent Yale graduate, is left behind in her hotel room by her husband, John (Giovanni Ribisi), a celebrity photographer on assignment in Tokyo. Charlotte is unsure of her present and her future and about the man she has married as she believes he takes more interest in his celebrity models, most notably a young and popular American actress named Kelly (Anna Faris), than he does in her. At the same time, Bob's own 25-year marriage is tired and lacking in romance as he goes through a midlife crisis.

One night, after a long photo shoot, Bob retreats to the hotel bar. Charlotte, sitting at a table with John and friends, notices Bob and has a waiter bring him a bowl of peanuts from her table. Later, Bob and Charlotte have brief encounters each night at the hotel bar, until Charlotte invites Bob to meet up with some local friends of hers. Bob accepts and arrives later at her hotel room dressed in an outfit for a young appeal style. Meanwhile, the two begin a friendship bond through their adventures in Tokyo together while experiencing the differences between Japanese and American cultures, and between their own generations.

On the penultimate night of his stay, Bob attracts the attention of the resident vocalist. The next morning, Bob awakens to find this woman in his room, having apparently slept with her. Charlotte arrives at his room to go out for breakfast only to find the woman in his room, leading to conflict and tension over a subsequent lunch. Later that night, during a fire alarm at the hotel, Bob and Charlotte reconcile and express how they will miss each other as they make one more trip back to the hotel bar.

On the following morning, Bob is set for his departure back to the United States. He tells Charlotte goodbye at the hotel lobby shortly before checking out and sadly watches her retreat back to an elevator. While riding in a taxi to the airport, Bob sees Charlotte on a crowded street and he gets out and goes to her. Bob embraces Charlotte and whispers something (substantially inaudible to the audience) in the tearful Charlotte's ear. The two share a kiss, say goodbye and Bob departs.

Questions:
1. What culture shock symptoms do the characters in this movie display?
2. How do the characters deal with their culture shock?
3. What do you think of their solutions to the problems? Do you have any better suggestions?

Task 2 Extended reading

Reflections on Multiculturalism

Multiculturalism is an attractive and persuasive notion. It suggests a human being whose identifications and loyalties transcend the boundaries of a nationalism and whose commitments are pinned to a larger vision of the global community. To be a citizen of the world, an international person, has long been an ideal toward which many strive. Unfortunately, history is also rich with examples of totalitarian societies and individuals who took it upon themselves to shape everyone else to the mold of their planetary vision.

Less common are examples of men and women who have striven to sustain a self-process that is inclusively international in attitude and behavior. For good reason, nation, culture, and society exert tremendous influence on each of our lives, structuring our values, engineering our view of the world, and patterning our responses to experience. Human beings cannot hold themselves apart from some form of culture influence. No one is culture free. Yet, the conditions of contemporary history are such that we may now be on the threshold of a new kind of person, a person who is socially and psychologically a product of the interweaving of cultures in the 20th century.

We are reminded daily of this phenomenon, in the corner of a traditional Japanese home sits a television set tuned to a baseball game in which the visitors, an American team, are losing. A Canadian family, meanwhile, decorates their home with sculptures and paintings imported from Pakistan, India, and Ceylon. Teenagers in Singapore and Hong Kong pay unheard-of prices for used American blue jeans while high school students in England and France take courses on the making of traditional Indonesian batik. A team of Malaysian physicians inoculates a remote village against typhus while their Western counterparts study Ayurvedic medicine and acupuncture. Around the planer the streams of the world's cultures merge together to form new currents of human interaction. Though superficial and only a manifestation of the shrinking of the globe, each such vignette is a symbol of the mingling and melding of human cultures. Communication and cultural exchange are the preeminent conditions of the twentieth century.

For the first time in history of the world, a patchwork of technology and organization has made possible simultaneous interpersonal and intercultural communication. Innovations and refinements of innovations, including modems, electronic mail, facsimile machines, digital recording, cable television, satellite dishes and desktop publishing have brought people everywhere into potential contact. Barely a city or village exists that is more than a day or two from any place else, railroads, highways, and airports has created linkages within and between local, regional, national and international levels of human organization.

The impact is enormous. Human connection through communication has made possible the interchange of goods, products, and services as well as the more significant exchange of thoughts and ideas. Accompanying the growth of human communication has been the erosion of barriers that have, throughout history, geographically, linguistically, and culturally separated people. As Harold Lasswell once suggested, "The technological revolution as it affects mass media has reached a limit that is subject only to innovations that would substantially modify our basic perspective of one another and of man's place in the cosmos." It is possible that the emergence of the multicultural person is just such an innovation.

A new kind of person

A new type of person whose orientation and view of the world profoundly transcends his or her indigenous culture is developing from the complex of social, political, economic, and educational interactions of our time. The various conceptions of and international, transcultural, multicultural, or intercultural individual have each been used with varying degrees of explanatory or descriptive utility. Essentially, they all attempt to define someone whose horizons extend significantly beyond his or her own culture. An internationalist, for example, has been defined as a person who trusts other nations, is willing to cooperate with other countries, perceives international agencies as potential deterrents to war and who considers international orientation of groups by measuring their attitudes toward international issues, that is, the role of the United Nations, economic versus military aid, international alliances and so on. And at least several attempts have been made to measure the world-mindedness of individuals by exploring the degree to which persons have a broad international frame of reference rather than specific knowledge or interest in some narrower aspects of global affairs.

Whatever the terminology, the definitions and metaphors allude to a person whose essential identity is inclusive of different life patterns and who has psychologically and socially come to grips with a multiplicity of realities. We can call this new type of person multicultural because he or she embodies a core process of self-verification that is grounded in both the universality of the human condition and the diversity of cultural forms. We are speaking, then, of a social-psychological style of self-process that is different from others. The multicultural person is intellectually and emotionally committed to the basic unity of all human beings while at the same time recognizing, legitimizing, accepting and appreciating the differences that exist between people of different cultures. This new kind of person cannot be defined by the language he or she speaks, the number of countries visited, or the number of personal international contacts made. Nor is he or she defined by profession, place of residence, or cognitive sophistication. Instead, the multicultural person is recognized by a configuration of outlooks and worldviews, by how the universe as a dynamically moving process is incorporated, by the way the interconnectedness of life is reflected in thought and action, and by the way this woman or man remains open to the imminence of experience.

The multicultural person is, at once, both old and new. On the one hand, this involves being the timeless "universal" person described again and again by philosophers through the ages. He or she approaches, at least in the attributions we make, the classical ideal of a person whose lifestyle is one of knowledge and wisdom, integrity and direction, principle and fulfillment, balance and proportion. To be a universal man means not how much a man knows but what intellectual depth and breadth he has and how he relates it to other central and universally important problems. What is universal about the multicultural person is an abiding commitment to the essential similarities among people everywhere, while paradoxically maintaining an equally strong commitment to differences. The universal person, does not at all eliminate culture differences, but seeks to preserve whatever is most valid, significant and valuable in each culture as a way of enriching and helping to form the whole. In this embodiment of the universal and the particular, the multicultural person is a descendant of the great philosophers of both the East and the West.

On the other hand, what is new about this type of person, and unique to our time, is a fundamental change in the structure and process of identity. The identity of the multicultural person, far from being frozen in a social character, is more fluid and mobile, more susceptible to change, more open to variation. It is an identity based not on a "belongingness", but on a style of self-consciousness that is capable of negotiating ever new formations of reality. In this sense, the multicultural person is radical departure from the kinds of identities found in both traditional and mass societies. He or she is neither totally a part of nor totally apart from his or her culture; instead, he or she lives on the boundary. To live on the edge of one's thinking, one's culture, or one's ego, is to live with tension and movement. It is in truth not standing still, but rather a crossing and return, a repetition of return and crossing, back and forth—the aim of which is to create a third area beyond the bounded territories, an area where one can stand for a time without being enclosed in something tightly bounded. Multiculturalism, then, is an outgrowth of the complexities of the twentieth century. As unique as this kind of person may be, the style of identity that is embodied arises from the myriad of forms that are present in this day and age. An understanding of this new kind of person must be predicated on a clear understanding of cultural identity. (1378 words)

(Adapted from Peter Adler, "Beyond Cultural Identity: Reflections on Multiculturalism")

Section II   Culture Shock

I   Pre-tasks

Task 1   The same world, different map?

Please look at the following world maps and read the captions carefully. Can you try to explain the difference from a cultural perspective?

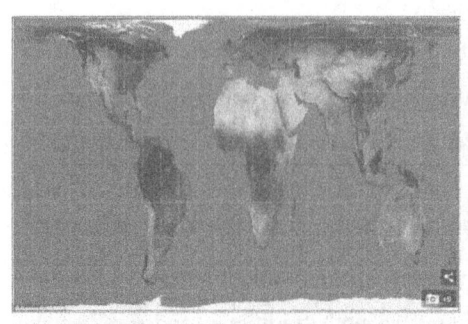

The Peter's projection (pictured) accurately shows different countries relative sizes. Although it distorts countries' shapes, this way of drawing a world map avoids exaggerating the size of developed nations in Europe and South America. Boston public schools recently announced that they will shift to using world map based on Peters projection, reportedly the first time a US public school district has done so.

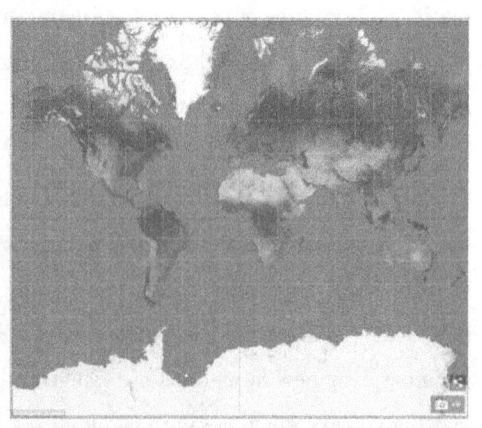

The more commonly used Mercator projection (pictured) exaggerates the size of the Earth around the poles and shrinks it around the equator. It's especially problematic given that the first world maps based on the Mercator projection were produced by European colonialists. Imagine drawing a world map on an orange, peeling the skin to leave a single piece and then flattening it. It would, of course, rip. But imagine you could stretch it. As you did so, the map drawn on its surface would distort. The distortions this introduces are massive, and this is why the Mercator projection is inaccurate.

Task 2   Elsa's diary

Read the following comments in Elsa's diary and discuss with your neighbors about what might have happened to her.

Chapter 8 Culture Barrier and Culture Shock

Elsa, a student sojourner, traveled from Asia to England. She wrote in her diary:

During the fight, the images, or I should say, my imagination about what England is like and how British people look like, kept lingering in my mind. In my opinion, Britain is quite a traditional, old-fashioned country. People there are all with perfect propriety. Gentlemen and ladies in nice suits and gowns are the most outstanding images that first come to my mind whenever I think of England.

A few weeks later she was much less enthusiastic when she wrote:

I used to think that all English were polite and gentle. Some are gentlemen but a lot are not... From reading books, I thought that all the British people are very cultured, going to the theater and reading literature but I was too naive. That makes me a little bit disappointed as I expected that the whole country was very cultured...

II While-tasks

Culture Shock

People move from one country to another for different reasons. Studying or working opportunities abroad, intercultural marriages, as well as unstable political situations can make people leave their own country. These different situations can be viewed in terms of short-term or long-term, and voluntary or involuntary migration. Someone who is just attending a three-week language course in a foreign country will probably have different experiences than someone who is going to work abroad for three years. The situation is different as well between those who actively choose a foreign country to work or study there, and those who go there as refugees.

It's common to experience culture shock when you're transplanted into a foreign setting. This is a normal reaction to a new environment where you are no longer in control as you have been at home. You may experience a range of emotions when adapting to a foreign culture, from excitement and interest to frustration, depression and fear of the unknown. Culture shock is a term used to describe what happens to people when they encounter unfamiliar surroundings and conditions. In the beginning, there are many practical matters that require attention. For example, moving to a new apartment, taking care of administrative matters, and even buying food at a grocery store can be very challenging issues in a new environment. At the same time, finding new social contacts and facing situations where your own behavioral patterns don't seem to work at all may create a feeling of confusion.

The term "culture shock", like that of jet lag, is now part of the popular vocabulary. It is often used to cover all these different dimensions of encountering a new cultural environment. It was initially introduced in 1960, and referred to the distress experienced by the sojourner as a result of losing all the familiar signs and symbols of social interaction. These signs or cues include the thousand and one ways in which we orient ourselves to the situations of daily life: when to shake hands and what to say when we meet people, when and how to give tips, how to give orders to servants, how to make purchases, when to accept and when to refuse invitations, when to take statements seriously and when not. Now these cues which may be words, gestures, facial expressions, customs, or norms are acquired by all of us in the course of growing up and are as much a part of our culture as the language we speak or the beliefs we accept. All of us depend for our peace of mind and our efficiency on hundreds of these cues, most of which we do not carry on the level of conscious awareness.

Normally there are six aspects of culture shock:

(1) strain due to the effort required to make necessary psychological adaptations;

(2) a sense of loss and feelings of deprivation in regard to friends, status, profession and possessions;

(3) being rejected by and/or rejecting members of the new culture;

(4) confusion in role, role expectations, values, feelings and self-identity;

(5) surprise, anxiety, even disgust and indignation after becoming aware of culture differences;

(6) feelings of impotence due to not being able to cope with the new environment.

Therefore, the symptoms of a culture shock can be very different in different people. Some experience only a little discomfort for a few weeks, while others may be struggling for several months or even years. Previous international experience, personality, expectations, motivation, and cultural distance all play an important role in the process. Symptoms can be both physical and mental, since people react differently to changes. Eating and sleeping problems are an example of physical symptoms, while mental symptoms have more to do with feelings of anxiety and personal loss. People differ greatly in the degree to which culture shock affects them, but almost everyone is affected by it in one way or another. Symptoms vary, but can include: boredom; withdrawal (e. g. spending excessive amounts of time reading; avoiding contact with host nationals); feeling isolated or helpless; sleeping a lot or tiring easily; irritation over delays and other minor frustrations; suffering from body pains and aches; longing to be back home; unduly criticizing local customs or ways of doing things etc. The symptoms of culture shock can appear at different times. Although, one can experience real pain from culture shock; it is also an opportunity for redefining one's life objectives. It is a great opportunity for leaning and acquiring new perspectives. In many cases, culture shock is presented as the removal or distortion of many of the familiar cues of one's environment, and their substitution by other cues which are strange.

Culture shock has many stages. Each stage can be ongoing or appear only at certain times. The first stage is the incubation stage. In this first stage, the new arrival may feel euphoric and be pleased by all of the new things encountered. This time is called the "honeymoon" stage, as everything encountered is new and exciting.

Afterwards, the second stage presents itself. A person may encounter some difficult times and crises in daily life. For example, communication difficulties may occur such as not being understood. In this stage, there may be feelings of discontent, impatience, anger, sadness, and feeling incompetence. This happens when a person is trying to adapt to a new culture that is very different from the culture of origin. Transition between the old methods and those of the new country is a difficult process and takes time to complete. During the transition, there can be strong feelings of dissatisfaction.

The third stage is characterized by gaining some understanding of the new culture. A new feeling of pleasure and sense of humor may be experienced. One may start to feel a certain psychological balance. The new arrival may not feel as lost and starts to have a feeling of direction. The individual is more familiar with the environment and wants to belong. This initiates an evaluation of the old ways versus those of the new.

In the fourth stage, the person realizes that the new culture has good and bad things to offer. This stage can be one of double integration or triple integration depending on the number of cultures that the person has to process. This integration is accompanied by a more solid feeling of belonging. The person starts to define him/herself and establish goals for living.

The fifth stage is the stage that is called the "re-entry shock". This occurs when a return to the country of origin is made. One may find that things are no longer the same. For example, some of the newly acquired customs are not in use in the old culture.

These stages are present at different times and each person has their own way of reacting in the stages of culture shock. As a consequence, some stages will be longer and more difficult than others. Many factors contribute to the duration and effects of culture shock. For example, the individual's state of mental health, type of personality, previous experiences, socio-economic conditions, familiarity with the language, family and/or social support systems, and level of education.

Culture shock can be a very painful experience for many sojourners, but it can make one develop a better understanding of oneself and stimulate personal creativity. An individual can gain important understanding about cultural relativism and become better prepared for a next sojourning experience. (1233 words)

(Adapted from Stephen Bochner, "Cultures in Contact: Studies in Cross-Cultural Interaction")

Word list:

1. refugee [ˌrefjuʊˈdʒiː]
   n. 避难者，难民
2. dimension [daɪˈmenʃn]
   n. 尺寸；[复] 面积，范围；[物] 量纲；[数] 次元，度，维
   adj. （石料，木材）切成特定尺寸的
   vt. 把……刨成（或削成）所需尺寸；标出尺寸
3. sojourner [ˈsʌdʒɜːnə]
   n. 旅居者，寄居者
4. impotence [ˈɪmpətəns]
   n. 无能为力
5. withdrawal [wɪðˈdrɔːəl]
   n. 移开；撤回，撤退，撤开；收回，取回
6. distortion [dɪˈstɔːʃn]
   n. 扭曲，变形；失真，畸变；[心理学] 扭转
7. substitution [ˌsʌbstɪˈtjuːʃn]
   n. 替换；代替；代用；<化>取代（作用）

Chapter 8 Culture Barrier and Culture Shock

8. incubation [ˌɪŋkjʊˈbeɪʃn]

   n. 孵化；孵卵；<医，生>（传染病的）潜伏期；<生>（细菌等的）繁殖

9. initiate [ɪˈnɪʃɪeɪt]

   vt. 开始，发起；传授；创始，开辟；接纳新成员

   n. 新加入某组织（或机构、宗教）的人，新入会的人；被传授初步知识的人

   adj. 被传授初步知识的；新入会的

10. integration [ˌɪntɪˈgreɪʃn]

    n. 整合；一体化；结合；（不同肤色、种族、宗教信仰等的人的）混合

11. duration [djʊˈreɪʃn]

    n. 持续，持续的时间，期间；（时间的）持续，持久，连续；[语音学] 音长，音延

12. relativism [ˈrelətɪvɪzəm]

    n. 相对论，相对主义

13. indignation [ˌɪndɪgˈneɪʃn]

    n. 愤怒，愤慨，气愤

14. euphoric [juːˈfɒrɪk]

    adj. 欣快症的，欣快的；精神愉快的

Task 1 Reading comprehension

Exercise One：Work with your partners, decide whether the following statements are true (T) or false (F) according to what you have learned in the passage.

1. _____ Immigration refers to the studying or working opportunities abroad, or situation of leaving their own country because of intercultural marriages, as well as unstable political situations etc.

2. _____ For those people who move to a foreign country in terms of short-term or long-term, and voluntary or involuntary, they will experience similar situations.

3. _____ A range of emotions from excitement and interest to frustration, depression and fear of the unknown is normal for anyone is transplanted into a foreign setting, it is the process of adapting to a foreign culture.

4. _____ Culture shock is a term used to describe what happens to people when they encounter unfamiliar surroundings and conditions. It may be presented as many practical matters as well as behavioral patterns.

5. _____ Culture shock refers to the distress experienced by the sojourner as a result of losing all the familiar signs and symbols of social interaction which include words, gestures, facial expressions, customs, or norms etc.

6. _____ People depend for our peace of mind and our efficiency on hundreds of these cues with conscious awareness. Therefore culture shock can be overcome.

7. _____ It is normal if you have feelings of impotence due to not being able to cope with the new environment, so it is not due to culture shock.

8. _____ Different people may have different symptoms of culture shock, but the discomfort of culture shock only last for a few weeks for everyone.

9. _____ Symptoms of culture shock can be both physical and mental, and always occur at the initial stage of moving into a new environment.

10. _____ Transition between the old methods and those of the new country is a difficult process and takes time to complete. During the transition, there can be strong feelings of dissatisfaction. And this transition always occur at the last stage of culture shock.

Exercise Two: Fill in the blanks with the words given below and change the form when necessary.

involuntary   familiar   isolate   dimension   content
deprivation   indignation   strain   initiate   distortion

1. Compared with voluntary migration, people from _____ migration may expose to greater cultural shock.

2. Culture shock is very complex and unconscious, because it may cover all kinds of different _____ of encountering a new cultural environment.

3. In a new environment, the effort required to make necessary psychological adaptations can be presented as a symptom of _____.

4. A sense of loss and feelings of _____ in regard to friends, status, profession and possessions can arise psychological discomfort for a newcomer.

Chapter 8 Culture Barrier and Culture Shock

5. Feeling of being _____ or helpless, sleeping a lot or tiring easily, suffering from body pains and aches, longing to be back home are commonly happened symptoms of culture shock.

6. In many cases, culture shock is presented as the removal or _____ of many of the familiar cues of one's environment, and their substitution by other cues which are strange.

7. One aspect of culture shock contains surprise, axiety, ever disgust and _____ after becoming aware of cultural differences.

8. The feelings of _____ , impatience, anger, sadness, and feeling incompetence happen when a person is trying to adapt to a new culture that is very different from the culture of origin.

9. In the third stage, characterized by gaining some understanding of the new culture, people will _____ an evaluation of the old ways versus those of the new.

10. The individual's state of mental health, type of personality, previous experiences, socio-economic conditions, _____ with the language, family and/or social support systems, and level of education will all contribute to the duration and effects of culture shock.

Task 2 Case study

Case 1

A highly experienced CNN newsperson who traveled to Lagos, Nigeria, in order to report an important news event. He had worked previously in Nigeria. Other news people warned the CNN employee that he should arrange for a security service in Lagos International Airport at 10:00 P. M. The CNN reporter encountered few difficulties, other than a demand for a bribe from customs officials for allowing him to bring his television camera into this country. He took a taxi from the airport and settled down for the 30-mile trip into the city. A few miles from the airport, the taxi driver turned into a side road and stopped the vehicle. The diver then put a revolver to the sojourner's temple and politely invited him to step outside the car, to strip naked and to toss his clothes inside the taxi. Then the diver step off in the night, laughing.

Questions for discussion:

1. What had the CNN reporter experienced in Lagos, Nigeria?

2. Do you think it was just a bad luck that the CNN reporter encountered this accident? Why or why not?

Case 2

Jenny Smith, an American girl, who has been living in Philippines since she was 8. She finally went back to her motherland America when she was in high school. But her life back in the US was really difficult for her. Here is her story:

"I only went back to live in the USA before I graduated from high school and flew back over to live in my 'home country' long-term. It was disorienting enough being a college student for the first time, but I had to also face American culture simultaneously. I remember feeling depressed that people weren't friendlier, and that I felt like I was in a completely new world when I should have been 'at home'. Fortunately, I had wanted to return to the States, unlike some of my classmates. Knowing that I would eventually move back made my experience at boarding school in Manila often feel more like a holding tank- I knew I would leave it all behind eventually, and as graduation drew closer, I had to loosen my grip on just about everything and everyone in my life.

But in California, I felt like I didn't know how to do anything, or how to be me in a completely new context. I couldn't figure out how to dress—I never seemed to be able to look like everyone else. There were no answering machines in the Philippines, and whenever I got one when I was making a call in the States, I would freeze up. I didn't know how to pump gas because, even though I had a Philippines driver's license, we never had to pump our own there. Also, I failed my California driver's license test three times! (Undoubtedly in part due to learning to drive in the Philippines!) Using a debit card kind of freaked me out, as did many other automated situations. I could go on and on about the things that I just didn't know how to do. It didn't matter that I knew how to wash my own laundry skillfully by hand in a plastic basin, or that I knew how to care for pigs, goats, chickens and turkeys. (OK, monkeys, parrots, geese, and owls too!) That I could kill and gut a chicken myself, and cook it for dinner. That I knew how to check someone's blood pressure, and that I had cleaned and dressed a hundred wounds in poor areas throughout my adolescence. No one in my new life knew that I spoke another language like a native, and that I could also get around pretty well in Tagalog. Or that I was skillful at squatting for long periods of time and eating neatly with my fingers. It wasn't relevant that I was frankly pretty amazing at climbing trees. I felt completely inept in the skill set I needed for my new American life. Plus, I basically looked the same as everyone else, so no one treated me like a foreigner that needed help.

Questions for discussion:
1. What kind symptoms can be observed from Jenny's story?
2. Which stage was she experiencing according to culture shock theory?
3. Can you give her some suggestions to help her out?

III After-tasks

Task 1 Movie and culture discussion *Fresh off the Boat*

Like many pioneering TV series, ABC's *Fresh off the Boat*, a sitcom about a Taiwanese-American family running a Western-themed chophouse in Orlando, Florida. The story follows the course of Eddie Huang's Taiwanese family as they make their way from Chinatown of Washington, D. C. to Orlando, Floridato open up a cowboy-themed steak restaurant. His mother struggles with the culture clash between her upbringing and a Florida community that doesn't have a large Asian population, his father embraces the "American Dream", and Eddie struggles with assimilating into school.

The show has a radical quality, simply because it arrives in a television landscape with few Asian characters, almost none of them protagonists. The show emphasizes family warmth, that theme is complicated by sharp sociological details: the only black kid in the school calls Eddie a "Chink" and smirks at his hip-hop T-shirt; Jessica grabs every free sample at the supermarket, then gives the employee a hilariously dismissive wave; Louis hires a white host to attract customers ("A nice happy white face, like Bill Pullman," he explains firmly). There's no violence, but there are specific immigrant perspectives, shown through multiple lenses.

From the beginning, we see Eddie through his mother's eyes as often as we see her through his. Jessica is a brazen, mysterious goad to her son; on the show, she's a full character, Eddie's equal in cultural alienation. In one of the most interesting early episodes, mother and son are both drawn to Honey, a trophy wife who lives next door. Eddie sees a hot milf he can show off to the boys; Jessica sees a kindred spirit who will eat her "stinky tofu" and bond over "Dolores Claiborne" —then pulls away when she realizes that Honey is the town home-wrecker. The show hits every awkward angle of this triangle, including a surreal fantasy sequence in which Eddie, inspired by his hero Ol' Dirty Bastard, sprays Capri Sun on gyrating video vixens. (His mom intrudes, complaining that he's wasting juice, while his father offers the women free samples from the restaurant: "Come on, Fly Girls. Try a rib! Tell a friend.")

In the final scene, at a block party, everyone's loneliness collides, as Eddie gropes Honey, and Jessica sees her neighbor's humiliation. Opening her heart to a fellow-outsider, Jessica seizes the karaoke mike to serenade Honey with an awkward, earnest rendition of "I Will Always Love You". The sequence doesn't "go hard"; it goes soft, quite deliberately. But somehow it still manages to find strangeness within its sentimentality. *Fresh off the Boat* is unlikely to dismantle the master's house. But it opens a door.

Even though the season-two finale of *Fresh off the Boat* made it almost certain that the Huangs would be traveling to their native Taiwan, China, the journey still feels like a big deal. For one, the season-three premiere marks the first time that any American network television show—sitcom or otherwise—has been filmed in the capital city of Taipei. And even if one were to ignore this geographical distinction (which, with a show like *Fresh off the Boat* where the characters' backgrounds are so important, you really can't), there's the pure visual thrill of a trip overseas. It's rare that any family sitcom gets to travel somewhere so far and so different from its regular location, especially when so many of them are shot on sound stages.

From a cultural standpoint, they go to great lengths to showcase various aspects of Taiwanese culture, from the bustling night market to the swooping architecture of its Taoist temples. And because Gene's fiancée is an actress, the Huangs even get a glimpse into the world of Taiwanese commercials, obviously very different from the ones they have in America. Those sorts of differences have always been at the heart of *Fresh off the Boat*, and it works well for the series to flip them, to have the Huangs—both the adults and the kids—suddenly feel as out of place in Taipei as they once did in Orlando. The weather, education system, names, and just about everything else in their new surroundings simply isn't what they're used to anymore. Does this means that they've fully and comfortably been absorbed into American culture? Of course not. They still find much to like and connect to in Taiwan, China, and their Chinese heritage will always be a huge part of their identity.

Questions:

1. What kind of cultural elements are specifically portrayed in each series or each episode?

2. How to define the cultural identity of this immigrant family?

3. Who is the most successful model of cultural assimilation in this series?

Task 2　Extended reading

Understanding Cultural Transition

If you have ever found yourself unpacking suitcases with your belongings somewhere far from home, you are probably familiar with a peculiar feeling that often accompanies change. It dwells on the continuum of excitement and anxiety, elation and dread, and depending on the hour, can leap from one extreme to the other. Then, as the fog of jet lag wears off, you meet your new neighbors and figure out where to buy food, this feeling settles deeper in your stomach as lingering low-gradestress.

A widely used framework for demystifying the stress of cultural transitions is Kate Gerardo's 5Rs of Culture Change. According to the 5R model, the main areas that are affected when we move across cultures are Routines, Reactions, Roles, Relationships, and Reflections about ourselves. The strength of the model lies in helping individuals understand the causes of transition stress and as a result, adapt their coping strategies accordingly. Berardo (2012) explores the significance of each of the areas affected by change, outlines a list of potential impacts on individuals, and offers suggestions for their management. Given the psychological significance of routines, reactions, roles, relationships and reflections for our wellbeing, the 5Rs can also be a valuable tool during change in general, guiding us towards a better understanding of ourselves and our responses to stress in times of transitions. Below is a review of the 5Rs model, together with some practical tips on how to manage each aspect of change.

1. Routines

Routines guide behaviors through predictable structures. Their significance has been established at various stages of life—from contributing to the cognitive development of preschoolers, to facilitating wellbeing among older populations. In family settings, routines and rituals promote adjustment, foster a sense of belonging and are vital for the psychological wellbeing of family members. During cross-cultural moves routines are usually among the first to get disrupted, as everything from the foods we eat to our weekend activities undergoes change. As a result, feelings of being not grounded or anchored may arise. Since routines and rituals can have protective qualities and can act as buffers against stress, their maintenance during vulnerable conditions such as transitions can ensure better adaptation. The first choice is to keep old routines where possible and work on creating new ones. And then incorporate hobbies that help you relax into your daily activities. At the same time, you should realize that establishing new routines takes time. Cultivating non-place-based routines that can be practiced anywhere is another wise move (e.g., music; deep breathing).

2. Reactions

The way others react to us can be impactful on our emotions and behaviors. Moreover, the feedback we receive from social interactions influences how we see ourselves (our self-concept). In new cultural environments, interactions can result in unexpected reactions from the people around us, even for everyday conducts that we are accustomed to at home. Various social scenarios, from how much we tip at restaurants to how we address our colleagues at work, can provide numerous opportunities for linguistic and cultural differences to manifest as unpredictable reactions during our communications. The discrepancy between expected and actual feedback may reduce confidence and lead to high levels of uncertainty. As a result, some may withdraw from social situations to minimize the occurrence of negative feedback, while others may adopt an overly critical attitude towards the new culture. The concrete measures include: Gain an understanding of others' reactions by learning about the new culture; Identify people (e. g., local acquaintances; other expatriates) who can help you make sense of the unexpected reactions; Learn skills (e. g., language; sociocultural rules) for effective communication; Give yourself time to understand the new cultural ways; Remind yourself of your strengths.

3. Roles

Our roles are part of our identities. They give us meaning and purpose, while enhancing our resources, social connections and sense of gratification. Having multiple roles is associated with greater psychological wellbeing, as well as with mental and physical health benefits, including lower levels of distress, anxiety and depression. A greater involvement in our roles leads to greater wellbeing. Moving across cultures can result in changes in our roles and responsibilities. For some, it may include expanded professional responsibilities, while for others it may mean giving up a career to become a stay-at-home parent. The meaning individuals attach to their roles is important for understanding their psychological impact and how they may react to rule changes. For example, excitement and anticipation may result from newly acquired roles and responsibilities, while unwanted roles may trigger feelings of pressure and defensiveness. Roles that had to be given up may bring forth sadness and a sense of loss. The following points should be focused: Gain clarity on your new roles and responsibilities as quickly as possible; Manage expectations on how to live out the new roles and reflect on the roles that you are no longer fulfilling; Strategize how to keep the same roles in the new culture.

4. Relationships

As part of our basic psychological needs, relationships are crucial to our wellbeing. Positive, stable and satisfying relations with others promote human flourishing and increase resilience. In stressful situations, relationships serve as a function of support and have a detrimental role in adaptive functioning. Moving affects our relationships in various ways. For instance, our relations with those who move with us may deepen from shared experiences, while at the same time may require additional efforts as we adjust to transitions together. Some relationships may drift apart, while others may thrive from the distance. New relationships can produce positive feelings such as enrichment and satisfaction, while changes in existing relationships can result in worry, guilt and a sense of loss. The useful tips are: Determine the most important relationships for you and find ways to maintain them (e. g. , through social media; regular communications); Keep an open dialogue about hopes, needs, concerns within existing relationships; Be proactive in making new connections and building a new support network.

5. Reflections about yourself

Reflection is a higher-order mental process referring to the cognitive and affective exploration of one's experiences, in order to categorize and make sense of them. As a key to adult learning, reflection provides a framework for new interpretations while reinforcing established frames of reference. Cultural transitions can instigate changes in the way we think about ourselves. Our values may become more pronounced as we discover what is important for our own wellbeing and what stress-management strategies work best for us. With prolonged stays in other cultures, we may recognize changes in our own behaviors, including a collection of new habits, gestures, and even ways of thinking. Moving fosters self-reflection-as individuals and as members of our cultures. As we confront questions of self-identity, such as where we feel at home and where we belong, we may experience a range of emotions towards the new culture and the way it is affecting us. The following ways can facilitate better self-reflection: Acknowledging that these changes are a natural step of cultural transitions; Self-reflecting about the changes you are experiencing (e. g. , keep a diary); Seeking support from other expatriates who may have shared similar experiences.

The process of transitioning through cultures is very complex, with numerous factors influencing our adaptive outcomes. In novel cultural contexts, often times the predictability of our action—reaction patterns is broken, routines are disrupted, relationships evolve, roles shift, and we begin acquiring a new sense of identity. Such changes can be overwhelming. A good place to start with the management of transition stress is to identify its causes, understand its roots and start making small adjustments to our ways of thinking and behaving. In the end, one of the biggest insights that the uncertainties of transitions can offer is finding the balance of accepting the changes we cannot control while remaining a "psychological activist" for the maintenance of our own wellbeing. (1302 words)

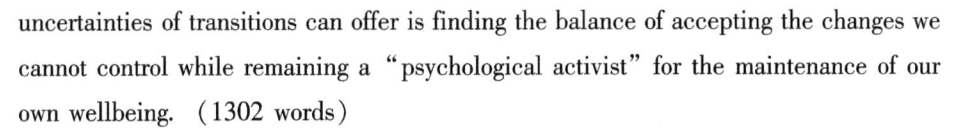

(Adapted from Marianna Pogosyan, "Understanding Transition Stress")

Critical thinking questions:

1. Do you still remember your first experience of being exposed to a totally strange culture either in your homeland or in a foreign country? How would you like to describe it?

2. What do you think of this 5Rs model of cultural transitions? Which one may work most effectively and which may not?

3. What is the difference between cultural transition and cultural assimilation?

Chapter 9

Cultural Identity in Intercultural Communication

A nation's culture resides in the hearts and in the soul of its people.

—Mahatma Gandhi

The crucial differences which distinguish human societies and human beings are not biological. They are cultural.

—Ruth Benedict

Section I Cultural Identity

I Pre-tasks

Task 1 Cultural markers

Please read the following examples of the markers of cultural identity and answer the questions.

Identity is often signaled by involvement in commemorative events. The Fourth of July in the United States, Bastille Day in France, and Independence Day in Mexico are celebrations of national identity. The annual Saint Patrick's Day parade in New York City is an opportunity for people of Irish heritage to take pride in their ethnic identity. Oktoberfest celebrations allow people to rekindle their German identity, and the Lunar New Year is a time for the Chinese and many other Asian cultures to observe traditions that reaffirm their identities. Every summer, villages and cities all across Japan hold matsuri festivals, which are based on ancient Shinto traditions. These celebrations serve as a symbol of unity within the community and offer an opportunity for the participants to evince their regional identity.

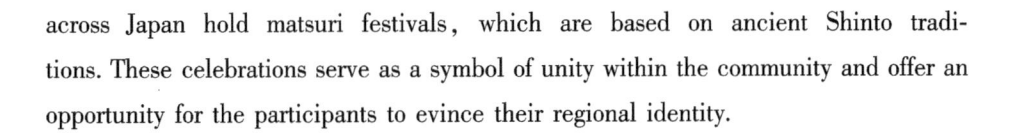

Questions:
1. What do you think are the important markers of cultural identity?
2. What are the functions of these cultural markers in establishing and enacting identity?

Task 2 Who is more beautiful?

Look at the following picture and think about cultural influences on what constitutes gender beauty and how it is displayed vary between cultures.

Questions:
1. What do you think is the implication of this picture?
2. What do you learn from their attitude towards exposure to the sun?

II While-tasks

Understanding Cultural Identity

In today's world, increasing globalization raises more awareness of cultural diversity. With issues such as terrorism, politics and religious differences overwhelming the media these days, the need for cultural awareness has become more important. Cultural identity is becoming more relational and contextual, as well as constantly evolving. They are complex, ambiguous and multifaceted.

Cultural identity refers to a person's sense of belonging to a particular culture or group. This process involves learning about and accepting traditions, heritage, language, religion, ancestry, aesthetics, thinking patterns, and social structures of a culture. Normally, people internalize the beliefs, values, norms, and social practices of their culture and identify themselves with that culture. The culture becomes a part of their self-concept. However, some studies have noted that existing cultural identity theory may not account for the fact that different individuals and groups may not react to or interpret events, happenings, attitudes, etc. in the same ways as other individuals or groups.

Individuals undergo self and cultural identity transformation in order to achieve understanding, harmony and balance within themselves and their environment, and in their connection with others. Cultures also change in this process, because social, political, economic and historical influences affect cultural and intercultural interactions. Cultural groups reflect, re-create, unify, and maintain their ethnic and cultural identities.

Cultural identities are negotiated, co-created, and reinforced in communication with others. They reflect our unique, personal life histories and experiences. They may also be seen as manifestations of social reality.

Definition of Cultural Identity

The definition of cultural identity, in its most basic form, is a sense of belonging. This includes a shared sense of companionship, beliefs, interests and basic principles of living. When a person identifies with their culture, they often embrace traditions that have been passed down through the years. The cultural identity links a person to their heritage can help them to identify with others who have the same traditions and basic belief systems. Some people claim that a person's cultural identity is the foundation or groundwork on which every other aspect of their being is built. It is the cornerstone of what makes them who they are. Embracing one's culture often means practicing a specific religion, wearing a certain type of clothing or something else that represents their culture. It creates an outward, visible means of identifying that person as a part of a particular culture or nationality.

Elements of Cultural Identity

Cultural identity is not just defined by a group or culture with which you identify. Cultural identity also consists of racial, religious, class, gender, sexuality and familial identities. Additionally, national, social and personal identities also contribute to one's cultural identity, as these properties envelope the entire person, making him/her who he/she is.

Gender identities

Our gender identity is influenced by the way we are treated by our parents, other relatives, neighbors and friends. Boys and girls are dressed in different colors and they are introduced to different types of toys. In every culture there are communications and interactions which are considered feminine, masculine or androgynous.

Age identities

Age is also one aspect of our identity. Cultures view and treat people of different ages in different ways. For example, in Asian cultures, getting old is seen as positive. Elderly people are respected and they are cared for by their children. In some European cultures, however, not all elderly people are highly respected. In many cases they may live separated from the younger generation and feel lonely.

Spiritual identity

Depending of the culture and context spiritual identity can be more or less apparent. In some countries people might even be ready to die for their beliefs. People's spiritual identity may even lead to conflicts or, in worst cases, war.

Class identity

Our social class identity influences how we behave and communicate towards other people. A person's class identity is not necessarily noticed until he or she encounters another person representing another social class.

National identity

A person's citizenship of a nation is referred to as national identity. But national identity can also be acquired by immigration and naturalization and usually becomes more pronounced when persons are away from home country.

Regional identity

With the exception of very small nations like Monaco or the Holy See (Vatican City), every country can be divided into a number of different geographical regions, and often these regions reflect varying cultural traits. In some countries regional identities are stronger than the national identity. Regional identities may also carry positive, negative, real or not real generalizations about people living there.

Personal identity

Personal identity consists of the characteristics that set one apart from others in his or her in-group, make one unique. People in different cultures have strikingly different construal of the self, of others, and of the interdependence between the two. People from individualistic cultures like the United States work to exemplify their differences from others, but members of collectivistic cultures tend to emphasize their group membership or connection to others.

Cultural Stereotypes

The term stereotype is a bit of industry jargon that originated in the world of printing. A stereotype is an inflexible mold used to print the same image over and over again. In intercultural communication, the term stereotype refers to some inflexible statements about a category of people, and these stereotypical statements are applied to all members of the group without regard for individual differences. It assumes that everyone from a group has certain characteristics and allows no room for individual differences, so it is by no means the same as information about another culture.

Cultural stereotypes can be positive or negative. Stereotypes that refer to a large group of people as lazy, coarse, vicious, or moronic are obviously negative. There are, of course, positive stereotypes, such as the assumption that Asian students are hardworking, well mannered, and intelligent. However, because stereotypes narrow our perceptions, they usually jeopardize intercultural communication and take on a negative tone. This is because stereotypes tend to over-generalize the characteristics of a group of people. For example, we know that not all Asian students are hardworking and intelligent, and that there is no large group of people in which everyone is lazy.

Cultural Superiority

It may very well be a natural world-wide phenomenon that people tend to have a more positive image of their own culture than they do of other cultures. They feel that their culture has achieved more, or has made more material progress, or they are more attractive or bigger or cleaner, or they have a longer, richer tradition.

This feeling of superiority may be accompanied by a wide range of emotion—indifference to other cultures, feeling sorry for other cultures, having a rather patronizing concern to "help" them, to outright dislike and contempt for them; superiority with the recognition of the principle of cultural equality. Here there is a desire to reduce or eliminate any feeling of superiority, even if there is actually no informed recognition of the worth and validity of the other country; genuine exploration in which people seek to see the other cultures from its own perspectives and not judge it by external values. Its internal logic, its validity, its strengths are slowly uncovered and genuine respect emerges.

Problems with Cultural Identity

Throughout history, there have been clashes as far as cultural identity is concerned. For example, in early America, Caucasians and Africans co-existed in owner-slave relationships where Africans were viewed as uncivilized. World War II involved the Holocaust where Nazi troupes killed over 6 million Jewish people because the Germans felt they were "racially superior". Both instances involved racial identities, an issue that exists in many communities and nations today. Other issues involve religious and cultural identity, for example, the conflicts between Catholics and Protestants in Ireland and, as of 2010 in France, the fight to prevent females who follow Muslim beliefs from wearing burkas.

Acquiring and Developing Cultural Identities

Individuals acquire and develop their identities through interaction with others in their cultural group. Identity development, then, becomes a process of familial and cultural socialization, exposure to other cultures, and personal development. The initial exposure to your identity came from your family, where you began to learn culturally appropriate beliefs, values, and social roles. The media also played a considerable role in your identity development. The near-constant exposure to media stereotypes creates a sense of how we should look, dress, and act in order to present age- and gender-appropriate identities.

The model for majority identity development follows the first stage, unexamined identity, where identity is not a concern. Acceptance, the second stage, is characterized by acquiescence to existing social inequities, even though such acceptance may be at an unconscious level. At the next stage, resistance, members of the dominant culture become more aware of existing social inequities, begin to question their own culture, and increase association with minority culture members. Achievement of the fourth and final stage, redefinition and reintegration, brings an increased understanding of one's dominant culture identity and an appreciation of minority cultures.

(Adapted from Samovar, Larry, Porter, Richard and McDaniel, Edwin,

"Cross-cultural Communication", Chapter 3)

Word list：

1. relational ［rɪˈleɪʃənəl］
    adj. 有关的；相关的
2. contextual ［kɒnˈtekstjʊəl］
    adj. 上下文的；取决于上下文的；与上下文一致的
3. ambiguous ［æmˈbɪgjʊəs］
    adj. 模棱两可的；模糊的；不明确的
4. multifaceted ［mʌltɪˈfæsɪtɪd］
    adj. （宝石等）多刻面的；多方面的；多才多艺的
5. ancestry ［ˈænsestrɪ］
    n. （家族）血统；名门出身；（总称）祖先，祖宗
6. aesthetics ［esˈθetɪks］
    n. 美学；美术理论
7. androgynous ［ænˈdrɒdʒɪnəs］
    adj. 雌雄同体的；中性的，不区分男女的
8. generalization ［ˌdʒenərəlaɪˈzeɪʃən］
    n. 一般化，普遍化；概括，归纳；一般规律，普遍原理
9. construal ［kənˈstruːəl］
    n. 解释，说明；解读
10. jargon ［ˈdʒɑːgən］
    n. 莫名其妙的话；语无伦次的话，胡言乱语
    vi. 讲难懂的话；喋喋不休
11. coarse ［kɔːs］
    adj. 质量粗劣的，粗制滥造的；粗粒的；粗糙的
12. moronic ［mɔˈrɒnɪk］
    adj. 痴呆者的；智力迟钝的
13. jeopardize ［ˈdʒepədaɪz］
    vt. 使处于危险境地；危及，危害
14. acquiescence ［ˌækwɪˈesəns］
    n. 默然（或勉强）同意；默认；默许

Chapter 9 Cultural Identity in Intercultural Communication

Task 1 Reading comprehension

Exercise One: Work with your partners, decide whether the following statements are true (T) or false (F) according to what you have learned in the passage.

1. _____ The definition of cultural identity, in its most basic form, is a sense of belonging.
2. _____ In some countries regional identities are stronger than the national identity.
3. _____ In most European cultures, getting old is seen as positive. Elderly people are highly respected and they are cared for by their children.
4. _____ Cultural stereotype assumes that everyone from a group has certain characteristics and allows no room for individual differences.
5. _____ Cultural identity is an abstract, complex and static concept that has been defined in many different ways.
6. _____ The fourth and final stage of identity development, redefinition and reintegration, brings an increased understanding of one's dominant culture identity and an appreciation of minority cultures.
7. _____ The near-constant exposure to media creates a sense of how we should look, dress, and act in order to present age-and gender-appropriate identities.
8. _____ It may very well be a natural world-wide phenomenon that people tend to have a more negative image of their own culture than they do of other cultures.
9. _____ The conflicts between Catholics and Protestants in Ireland do not involve cultural identity.
10. _____ Culture has very little influence on determining one's personal identity.

Exercise Two: Fill in the blanks with the words given below and change the form when necessary.

> over-generalize   superior   androgynous   jeopardize   construal
> internalize   contextual   familial   cornerstone   reinforce

1. Cultural identity is the _____ of what makes people who they are.

2. In every culture there are communications and interactions which are considered feminine, masculine or _____ .

3. Cultural stereotypes tend to _____ the characteristics of a group of people.

4. Normally, people _____ the beliefs, values, norms, and social practices of their culture and identify themselves with that culture.

5. World War II involved the Holocaust where Nazi troupes killed over 6 million Jewish people because the Germans felt they were "racially _____".

6. Cultural identities are negotiated, co-created, and _____ in communication with others.

7. People in different cultures have strikingly different _____ of the self, of others, and of the interdependence between the two.

8. Because stereotypes narrow ourperceptions, they usually _____ intercultural communication and take on a negative tone.

9. Identity development, then, becomes a process of _____ and cultural socialization, exposure to other cultures, and personal development.

10. Cultural identities is becoming more relational and _____, as well as constantly evolving.

Task 2 Case study

Case 1

The city of Kenai, Alaska was planning a celebration of 200 years since the first Russian fur traders came to the region. A Native Indian tribe which lived in Alaska for a thousand years was offended by the implication that before the Russians came to the region there was no civilization there. As a result the celebration turned to a year-long event and Native Indian culture became its basis. By the end of the celebration, the Kenai Bicentennial Visitors and Cultural Center was completed. Thus, accommodation of different cultural interests helped the region to recognize its historical past.

(Adopted from "Resolving Conflict in a Multicultural Environment" by Andrea Williams, MCS Conciliation Quarterly. Summer, 1994. P 2—6)

Questions for discussion:

1. What does this case exemplify?

2. What do you learn about identifying and avoiding cultural conflicts from this case?

3. How was this cultural conflict resolved in this case?

Case 2

The differences in nationality within the American pattern may be illustrated by the fact that it is not uncommon for one American to say to another, "What nationality are you?" meaning, "What country did your ancestors come from?" Application blanks for jobs and registration forms for schools often contain a space labeled "Nationality _____." An American may fill the blank with "German", "Polish", "Italian", or "English", although he was born in the United States and neither he nor perhaps even his parents or grandparents may have ever gone outside the country, unless for a summer vacation trip to the Canadian side of Niagara Falls. That these people write down the national origin of their ancestors rather than the name of the land in which they were born does not mean that they are not patriotic Americans. It merely means that they are still conscious of their differences in ancestry. This feeling of identity with the cultural background of one's ancestors along with a pride in being an American has long been a characteristic of the American people. American culture is the product of many different cultures blended together to form something new.

Questions for discussion:
1. What characteristic of the American people is manifested in this case?
2. What challenges do people from other cultures experience in American society?
3. Is American society the disillusionment of the melting pot?

III After-tasks

Task 1   Movie and culture discussion   Exploring Emigration: Cultural Identity

https://www.teachingchannel.org/videos/teaching-cultural-identity

Lesson Objective: Learn about another culture through film

Length: 8 mins

Description: Karen Daley teaches 7th grade social studies in Elkridge, Maryland. Today she's using video clips to generate discussion among her students. She's trying to help them create mediate self and peer to self connections.

The topic for discussion is "Understanding Cultural Identity through Media".

The first thing they do is to define culture, American culture in particular. She asks them what comes to their mind when it comes to American culture, and students come up with McDonald's, obesity, melting pot, salad bowl. Then she gives students a context for viewing media, a 3-minute clip from a documentary *God Grew Tired of Us*. It's about Sudanese immigrants coming to America for the first time. She wants the students to watch and see the challenges that the boys are facing with respect to keeping cultural identity alive. Then she reviews the media with her students to establish comprehension, which is an interesting way to learn from each other. And then she analyses media to improve critical thinking skills. Students are actually from different parts of the world, and they are willing to share their personal experiences and feelings with the class.

Questions:

1. How does this lesson help students develop empathy?

2. What do the students' reflections tell you about the impact of this lesson?

3. How would this lesson have been different if students had read about Sudanese immigrants instead of watching the documentary?

Task 2 Extended reading

Identity in Intercultural Communication

Your identity is established, maintained, and modified through communicative interaction with others. It also influences interaction through shaping expectations and motivating behaviors. You are constantly moving in and out of different identities as you interact with other people, and with each identity, you employ a set of communicative behaviors appropriate for that identity and setting. Your culture has shaped your understanding and expectations as to what are the correct communication practice for various social settings, for example, a classroom, hospital, or sales meeting. However, these understandings and expectations are culture bound, and what is appropriate in one culture may be inappropriate in another.

Understanding Communication

Generally speaking, communication with another involves predicting or anticipating their responses. When communicating with someone familiar we are usually confident in our anticipation, and may not even notice that we are making such predictions. In contrast, when we communicate with strangers we are more aware of the range of their possible responses, and of the uncertainty of our predictions.

Intercultural communication is a discipline that studies communication across different cultures and social groups, or how culture affects communication. It is used to describe the wide range of communication processes and problems that naturally appear within an organization or social context made up of individuals from different religious, social, ethnic, and educational backgrounds. Intercultural communication is sometimes used synonymously with cross-cultural communication. In this sense it seeks to understand how people from different countries and cultures act, communicate and perceive the world around them. Many people in intercultural business communication argue that culture determines how individuals encode messages, what medium they choose for transmitting them, and the way messages are interpreted.

Identity in Intercultural Interactions

In an intercultural meeting, the varying expectations for identity display and communication style carry considerable potential for creating anxiety, misunderstandings, and even conflict. Imagine how students from a culture that does not value communicative assertiveness would feel in a typical US classroom. Being unaccustomed to having the instructor query students, they would probably be reluctant to raise their hands and would likely consider US students who challenged the teacher to be rude or even arrogant. To avoid potential problems during intercultural interaction, you need to develop intercultural competence. Intercultural competence occurs when the avowed identity matches the identity ascribed.

In order to communicate effectively in an intercultural situation, an individual's avowed cultural identity and communication style should match the identity and style ascribed to him or her by the other party. But since the communication styles are likely to be different, the participants will have to search for a middle ground, and this search will require flexibility and adaptation. As a simple illustration, the Japanese traditionally greet and say goodbye to each other by bowing. However, in Japanese/ US business meetings, the Japanese have learned to bow only slightly while shaking hands. In doing this, they are adjusting their normal greeting practice to accommodate those individuals from the United States. Longtime US business representatives to Japan have learned to emulate this behavior. Thus, a mutually satisfying social protocol has evolved. In achieving this, the participants have demonstrated the principle components of intercultural communication competence: motivation, knowledge, and skills.

There is no denying that forces such as globalization, immigration, and intercultural marriages are bringing about an increased mixing of cultures, and this mixing is producing people who possess multiple cultural identities. Cultural identity becomes blurry in the midst of cultural integration, bicultural interactions, interracial marriages, and the mutual adaptation process. Increasing numbers of people are living "in between" cultural identities now, that is, they identify with more than one ethnicity, race, or religion.

In the past, it was not uncommon for children of international adoption to be raised by their United States families with little or no appreciation of the culture of their native land. This was evident in the 2002 Academy Award—nominated documentary *Daughter from Danang*, which related the trials of a mixed Vietnamese and American woman who returned to Vietnam in search of her identity after twenty-two years in the United States. She was driven by a desire to find out more about her birth family and herself, but because she had never been exposed to the Vietnamese culture, the reunion ended in disaster. The potential for such unfortunate meetings should be reduced in the future, because a greater awareness of the importance of cultural identity is moving many parents to recognize and promote the cultural traditions of their adopted children.

Immigration, intercultural marriages, and multiracial births are creating a social environment where many United States youths consider cultural diversity as a normal part of social life. The Internet has afforded people an opportunity to conduct in-depth genealogical research, and one result is a growing number of US Americans who now consider themselves American Indians. The blurring of racial and ethnic boundaries has also been promoted by US corporations. This can be seen in many entertainment genres, such as hip-hop, country and western, and alternative music, which enjoy fans from every ethnic category. Products, especially clothes, endorsed by prominent sports figures are worn by numbers of all cultural groups. United States sports fans identify with team members from China, Cuba, the Caribbean, Latin America, Japan, Korea, Lithuania, and many other nations, as well as those from a variety of US ethnic groups.

The global marketplace is giving rise to "intercultural transients". These are travelers who regularly alternate residence between their homeland and a host foreign country, and must manage frequent cultural changes and identify renegotiations. Over the past decade, a growing number of nations have made dual citizenship available, which has added to the number of intercultural transients. Carlos Ghosn serves as a model example of an intercultural transient. Ghosn was born in Brazil, attended schools in Lebanon and France, and speaks five languages. A citizen of Lebanon, he is the CEO of both Nissan (a Japan-based company) and CEO of Renault (a French firm), positions he holds concurrently. To fulfill his responsibilities, Ghosn has to divide his time between Japan, France, and the United States, and must adjust to the intricacies of each culture. As transportation technology continues to make access to distant lands easier, the ranks of intercultural transients will expand.

Issues of identity can be expected to remain complex—and perhaps become more so—as multiculturalism increasingly characterizes contemporary society. It is clear, however, that the old understanding of a fixed cultural identity or ethnicity is outdated, and identity is rapidly becoming more of an "articulated negotiation between what you call yourself and what other people are willing to call you". But regardless of what form they may take or how they are achieved, your identities will remain a consequence of culture.

Fundamentally, identity is about similarities and differences. In other words, we identify with something as a result of preference, understanding, familiarity, or socialization. You may prefer hip-hop style instead of cowboy boots and jeans. You may understand American football better than cricket, and you may be more familiar with hamburgers and French fries than with bratwurst and sauerkraut. You will likely have greater tolerance toward those people and things you prefer, understand, and find familiar.

Similarities and differences also play a critical role in social relations. Psychologists conducting research in the area of interpersonal attraction have established an important principle: the more similar two people are to each other, the more likely they are to like one another. But by definition, intercultural communication involves people from dissimilar cultures, and this makes differences a normative condition. Thus our reaction to, and ability to manage those differences is key to successful intercultural interactions. Our preference for things we understand and are familiar with can adversely influence our perception of and attitude toward new and different people and things.

Problems in Intercultural Communication

The problems in intercultural communication usually come from problems in message transmission. In communication between people of the same culture, the person who receives the message interprets it based on values, beliefs, and expectations for behavior similar to those of the person who sends the message. When this happens, the way the message is interpreted by the receiver is likely to be fairly similar to what the speaker intends. However, when the receiver of the message is a person from a different culture, the receiver uses information from his or her culture to interpret the message. The message that the receiver interprets may be very different from what the speaker intends.

Attribution is the process in which people look for an explanation of another person's behavior. When someone does not understand another, he/she usually blames the confusion on the other's "stupidity, deceit, or craziness".

Effective communication depends on the informal understandings among the parties involved that are based on the trust developed between them. When trust exists, there is implicit understanding within communication, cultural differences may be overlooked, and problems can be dealt with more easily. The meaning of trust and how it is developed and communicated vary across societies. Similarly, some cultures have a greater propensity to be trusting than others.

(Adapted from Samovar, Larry, Porter, Richard and McDaniel, Edwin, "Cross-cultural Communication", Chapter 3)

Chapter 9 Cultural Identity in Intercultural Communication

Critical thinking questions:

1. What determines how individuals encode messages, what medium they choose for transmitting them, and the way messages are interpreted in intercultural communication?

2. What are "intercultural transients"? Why is there an increasing number of them?

3. What does it mean to say "identity is rapidly becoming more of an articulated negotiation between what you call yourself and what other people are willing to call you"?

Section II Intercultural Communication

I Pre-tasks

Task 1 Impacts of Brexit

Look at these pictures and explain the impacts of Brexit on people: What happens to EU citizens living in the UK? What happens to UK citizens working in the EU? Will Brexit hurt the UK's cultural future?

Task 2 Trump's Great Wall

Throughout his presidential campaign, Donald Trump was adamant that he would fortify the southern border with a wall ("a wall is better than fencing and it's much more powerful"). Now President Trump has set in motion his plan to build an "impenetrable, physical, tall, powerful, beautiful, southern border wall" between the US and Mexico. What do you think of "Trump's Great Wall"?

II While-tasks

Improving Cultural Self-awareness in Intercultural Communication

A major obstacle to effective intercultural communication is not that we find it difficult to understand others, but because we don't understand ourselves and our own cultural characteristics.

Attaining cultural competence and developing our intercultural communication skills require us to change the relevant elements of our own approach to ensure synergy with the other party. This is necessary in order to overcome the cultural barriers (differences). If we don't know what our approach is, or the reasons we take this approach, then we can't really change it.

If we don't know why we think the way that we do, why we have a particular attitude toward something, why we value some things and not others, or why we behave or react in a particular way, then we don't know what influences our perceptions towards others. And if we don't know what our assumptions about others are based on, then we can't question or challenge these assumptions.

What is known least well, and is therefore in the poorest position to be studied, is what is closest to oneself.

Edward Hall

What's right or wrong, good or bad, or normal or abnormal is subjective and based on a comparison of what we observe against what our cultural conditioning tells us it should be. If we fail to understand that these are our perceptions only and not necessarily universal, and if we fail to understand that these perceptions are no better (or worse) than those of other cultures, then we will fail to see the need to adapt. This is the first hurdle, and arguably the biggest, in attaining cross-cultural competence.

Understanding Ourselves

Cultural awareness starts with cultural self-awareness. Only once we are culturally self-aware can we begin to predict the effect that our behaviors will have on others. Therefore, understanding ourselves is the first step in attaining higher levels of cultural competence. This starts with a thorough understanding of our own culture and how this affects our own values, norms, attitudes and behaviors, as we cannot understand and adapt to other cultures unless we have attained a degree of cultural self-awareness.

Years of study have convinced me that the real job is not to understand foreign culture but to understand our own.

Edward Hall

Cultural self-awareness also involves examining and questioning our own attitudes toward other cultures. Before trying to understand the attitudes of others, we should have a thorough understanding of our own and explore the assumptions upon which these attitudes are based. By challenging these assumptions, we can determine whether the attitudes we hold are those that will allow us to see situations objectively rather than having a distorted point of view. Unhelpful attitudes toward other cultures are a major intercultural communication barrier, and unless we are aware of these attitudes and are willing to change them, we will not overcome this barrier.

Ethnocentric Attitudes

An ethnocentric attitude is one based on the belief that our culture is superior, and the "right one", and that all cultures should be the same as ours. Consequently, it is determined that there is no need for us to adapt, and if any adaption is required it should be the other party who does so. We need to adopt the attitude that one culture is no better or worse than another—they are just different. Effective communication requires empathy, and an ethnocentric attitude prevents an empathetic approach.

Perception

Perception has been defined as "the internal process by which we select, organize and interpret information from the outside world" (Klopf & Park, 1982: 26). In other words, it's the process individuals go through to acquire and make sense of information from the environment. The process is affected by our backgrounds, needs, experiences, influences, education, upbringing, etc., that is, the things that are learned and are a reflection of our cultural experiences. In short, we tend to perceive what we expect to perceive.

What we know already determines how we see the world around us. For example, our society has taught us that a red light means stop and a green light means go. We now know what these signals mean and how we are expected to react when we see them. We take this as fact and also assume that they mean the same thing to everyone else. If, however, we belonged to a different society where we learnt that green means stop and red means go, then this is fact and we would react according to this belief. What is right or wrong depends on what we have learned. We don't see things as they are; we see things as we are.

Improving Our Cultural Self-awareness

Intercultural communication challenges our perceptions, our interpretations, and our evaluations of other people and other circumstances. These are culturally relative, and our natural tendency is to fall back to the comfortable familiarity of our own culture. This prevents, or at best limits, our accurate understanding of the culture of others.

In order to improve our cultural self-awareness we need to be able to analyze ourselves, our attitudes and the assumptions we are using when making judgments of other cultural characteristics. We need to be aware that in many cases we are guessing or using misguided assumptions when evaluating others and their cultures. We need to stand back and consider that we do not know everything, that our way is not the only way, and that it is not necessarily the best way. We can learn to see, understand, and control our own cultural conditioning. Looking at ourselves through the eyes of people from other cultures and acknowledging that there are alternative realities will greatly assist in recognizing the accuracy of our perceptions and the validity of our attitudes.

An effective way to create a greater level of awareness of our own cultural characteristics is by writing down a description of our own culture as we see it and then a description of our culture as we believe that others see it. We can then identify examples or evidence to support each of the characteristics we have identified. This activity encourages us to examine our culture carefully and helps in determining the validity of our analysis. It is usually the case that, if you have had limited experience with other cultures, then you will have difficulty in describing your own, whereas those that have had more exposure to other cultures will not find this as challenging. This demonstrates the point that experience with other cultures helps us to understand our own.

Chapter 9 Cultural Identity in Intercultural Communication

From the example in Table 9.1 we can see that we were able to validate our view by providing evidence to support it. We can then question the validity of the view of others when we compare it to ours. By completing this activity, we are forced to analyze and gain a greater understanding of ourselves.

Table 9.1 Providing evidence to validate a viewpoint

My culture as I see it (characteristics)	Examples	My culture as I believe others see it (characteristics)
Hard working	80% of my acquaintances work more than 60 hours per week	Unwilling to work hard and take a lot of time off

This exercise could be varied by substituting "my culture as I believe others see it" with "my culture as others actually see it" and enlisting someone from another culture to complete this and add examples to support their view. For characteristics identified by either party where evidence cannot be provided, these should be discussed and a consensus reached about their relevance.

We can then list the relevant characteristics of both sides (see Table 9.2), and examine the results to identify these four variables:

Table 9.2 Providing evidence to validate two perspectives

My culture as I see it (characteristics)	Examples (evidence)	My culture as I believe others see it (characteristics)	Examples (evidence)
Hard working	80% of my acquaintances work more than 60 hours per week	Unwilling to work hard and take a lot of time off	Assumption only no examples

1. what I see about my culture that they also see;
2. what I see about my culture that they don't see;
3. what they see about my culture that I don't see;
4. what I don't see about my culture that they don't see either (identified by research).

The "Johari Window" model in Figure 9.1 can be used to plot our findings, and to assist in visualizing and understanding our results.

Intercultural awareness starts with self-awareness. Only after we understand our own behavior, can we control it and the effect that it will have on others. Only after we understand ourselves can we attempt to understand the culture of others and make the necessary adjustments in order to improve the effectiveness of our interactions.

Figure 9.1　The Johari Window

	what I see	what I do not see
	Agreement	My blind spot
	Their blind spot	Shared blind spot

Source: Adapted from S. Jourard (1964), *The Transparent Self*, Van Nostrand Reinhold, Princeton, NJ, USA.

The trouble with this world is not that people know too little, but they know too much that ain't so.

Mark Twain

(Adapted from Ioppolo, Sebastian, "Intercultural Communication Connecting with Cultural Diversity", Chapter 3)

Word list:

1. synergy ['sɪnədʒɪ]
   n. 协同；协同作用；增效
2. perception [pə'sepʃən]
   n. 知觉；看法；洞察力
3. hurdle ['hɜːdl]
   n. 障碍；栏
4. distort [dɪ'stɔːt]
   vt. 扭曲；使失真；曲解
5. ethnocentric [ˌeθnə'sentrɪk]
   adj. 种族优越感的；民族中心主义的
6. empathy ['empəθɪ]
   n. 同情；同感；共鸣
7. upbringing ['ʌpbrɪŋɪŋ]
   n. 教养；养育；抚育
8. validity [və'lɪdɪtɪ]
   n. 有效性；正确；正确性
9. substitute ['sʌbstɪtjuːt]
   v. 替代

10. consensus [kənˈsensəs]
    n. 一致看法；共识

Task 1 Reading comprehension

Exercise One: Work with your partners, decide whether the following statements are true (T) or false (F) according to what you have learned in the passage.

1. _____ Understanding ourselves is the first step in attaining higher levels of cultural competence.
2. _____ What's right or wrong, good or bad, or normal or abnormal is unquestionably universal, and there is no need for adaption.
3. _____ Before trying to ander stund the attitudes of others, we should have a thorough understanding of our own.
4. _____ An ethnocentric attitude is based on the belief that all cultures are equally good, and effective communication requires empathy.
5. _____ What we know already determines how we see the world around us.
6. _____ Cultural awareness refers to our natural tendency in intercultural communication to fall back to the comfortable familiarity of our own culture.
7. _____ We need to be aware that we don't know everything, that our way is not the only way, and that it is not necessarily the best way.
8. _____ If you have had limited experience with other cultures, you may find it hard to describe your own culture.
9. _____ The "Johari Window" is a technique used to help people better understand their strength and limits.
10. _____ A major barrier to effective intercultural communication is not that we find it difficult to understand others, but because we don't understand ourselves and our own culture.

Exercise Two: Fill in the blanks with the words given below and change the form when necessary.

exposure	*ethnocentric*	*validity*	*visualizing*	*hurdle*
upbringing	*distorted*	*synergy*	*description*	*perception*

1. Failure to understand cultures that are different and equal is a big _____ in attaining intercultural competence.

2. Attaining cultural competence requires us to change the relevant elements of our own approach to ensure _____ with the other party.

3. The perceptual process is affected by our backgrounds, needs, experiences, education, _____, etc., that is, the things that are learned and are a reflection of our cultural experiences.

4. Effective communication requires empathy, and a(n) _____ attitude prevents an empathetic approach.

5. _____ has been defined as the internal process by which we select, organize and interpret information from the outside world.

6. Looking at ourselves through the eyes of people from other cultures and acknowledging that there are alternative realities will greatly assist in recognizing the accuracy of our perceptions and the _____ of our attitudes.

7. Those that have had more _____ to other cultures will find it less challenging to understand and describe their own culture.

8. The "Johari Window" model can be used to plot our findings, and to assist in _____ and understanding our results.

9. An effective way to create a greater level of awareness of our own cultural characteristics is by writing down a(n) _____ of our own culture both as we see it and as we believe that others see it.

10. We need to determine whether the attitudes we hold are those that will allow us to see situations objectively rather than having a(n) _____ point of view.

Task 2 Case study

Case 1

Please read the following news item from *Chicago Tribune* (Aug. 23, 2017) on the kidnap of Yingying Zhang, a Chinese visiting scholar at the University of Illinois at Urbana-Champaign, and answer the questions.

Family of Missing Chinese Scholar at U. of I. Speaks of Pain and Uncertainty

When Yingying Zhang's mother learned that her daughter had gone missing from the University of Illinois at Urbana-Champaign on June 9, she fainted. She could not eat or sleep, and became too weak to work.

Chapter 9 Cultural Identity in Intercultural Communication

The time since only has become more agonizing for the Zhang family. Their hopes have been dashed at every turn: First, the hope Zhang was merely missing, not kidnapped; then, the hope that she would be found safe and unharmed. Then, the hope that her body would be found quickly.

More than two months later, Zhang, a visiting scholar from China, remains missing. Federal authorities say the 26-year-old is presumed dead. Brendt Christensen, a former U. of I. doctoral candidate living in Champaign, has been charged with kidnapping and pleaded not guilty in federal court last month.

Zhang's family members gave their most extensive comments on her disappearance in an emotional news conference and interview Tuesday. As students and parents on campus lugged around suitcases and duffel bags in preparation for the start of fall classes next week, Zhang's father and her longtime boyfriend, Xiaolin Hou, talked of their ordeal.

"This is a very painful process. Our dreams have been shattered," Hou said afterward in an interview through an interpreter. "We just keep on telling ourselves this is the worst and we cannot really lose any more."

This month, Zhang's father sent a letter to President Donald Trump, asking the president to ensure that all efforts were being devoted to finding her. Hou said the family has vowed not to leave the US until they can bring Zhang's remains home to China for a proper burial, in accordance with Chinese culture. "Consistent with our deeply-held Chinese cultural values, we cannot imagine returning to China without her."

Suspect to plead not guilty in kidnapping of University of Illinois scholar from China

Questions for discussion:

1. Why is it important for the family to "bring Zhang's remains home to China for a proper burial, in accordance with Chinese culture"?

2. What is "our deeply-held Chinese cultural values" in the letter?

Case 2

(CNN) A Swiss hotel has been accused of anti-Semitism after a manager reportedly posted signs instructing Jewish guests to shower before using its pool.

"To our Jewish guests, women, men and children, please take a shower before you go swimming," one sign said. "If you break the rules I'm forced to close the swimming pool for you."

Another sign in the kitchen addressed to "our Jewish guests" said the hotel's freezer would only be available from 10 to 11 a.m. and from 4:30 to 5:30 p.m. "I hope you understand that our team does not like being disturbed all the time," it read.

Guests spotted the placards at the Paradies hotel in the Swiss resort village of Arosa. The news of the signs spread quickly after an outraged guest posted a picture to Facebook.

Israeli Deputy Foreign Minister Tzipi Hotovely called the incident "an anti-Semitic act of the worst and ugliest kind" and demanded the person who posted the signs "be brought to justice".

Read More

Former Israeli Foreign Minister Tzipi Livni strongly condemned the placards—while also alluding to last weekend's white supremacist rally in Virginia. "There is no place in the free world for Nazi flags, Ku Klux Klan masks, or disgusting notices in hotels that are aimed at Jews alone."

An Israeli guest told CNN affiliate Channel 2 that the hotel manager was nice to his family upon their arrival, and so they were shocked to find the posted signs. "No one addressed her because we didn't want to start a confrontation," he said, noting the hotel had many Jewish guests, mostly from the United States, the UK and Belgium.

"It was very strange and the sort of anti-Semitic incident we have not been exposed to before," he said.

Paradies hotel manager Ruth Thomann did not respond to CNN's calls for comment. However, Thomann defended herself to Swiss media, saying she is not anti-Semitic.

Thomann told the Swiss newspaper Blick she was trying to address the issue of guests not showering before they used the pool during a period where many Jewish guests were staying at the hotel.

"I made the sign without sensitivity and now I am paying for it dearly," she told Blick.

She also said the sign limiting the use of the freezer was misunderstood, and that she was only trying to help hotel staff. "As a service we offer to our Jewish guests, they can store their kosher food in our (staff) freezer," she said.

Thomann said she posted the sign to limit guests' use of the freezer and to allow staff more privacy, according to Blick.

The signs have since been removed, a representative with the Israeli Embassy in Switzerland said in a statement.

CNN's Oren Liebermann and Michael Schwartz contributed to this report.

(http://edition.cnn.com/2017/08/16/europe/swiss-hotel-outrage-trnd/)

> To our Jewish Guests
> Women, Men and Children
> Please take a shower before you go swimming and although after swimming.
> If you break the rules, I'm forced to cloes the swimming pool for you.

Questions for discussion:

1. What do you think of the posted signs at the Paradies hotel? Are they anti-semitic?

2. What could people learn from this case?

III After-tasks

Task 1　Movie and culture discussion　*My Big Fat Greek Wedding* 2 (2016)

The film starts with Toula (Nia Vardalos) and her dad Gus (Michael Constantine) driving her daughter Paris (Elena Kampouris) to school. They stop to pick up

Nick's (Louis Mandylor) kids, and then Nikki's (Gia Carides) kids. Gus bugs Paris about finding a Greek boyfriend and to get married soon and have sons. This goes all the way to school when Paris gets out of the car. Toula, trying to comfort her daughter, only embarrasses her in front of everyone.

Introduction to the movie *My Big Fat Greek Wedding* 2 (2016)

Toula narrates that she has been trying to stay close to Paris, even going as far as to volunteer at her school, but all it does embarrass both of them. On top of that, Toula and Ian (John Corbett) haven't had much of a romantic spark to their relationship since getting married.

Paris is at a college fair at school. Toula and Ian want her to pick Northwestern University so she can stay close to home. The whole Portokalos clan shows up for support, including Maria (Lainie Kazan), Angelo (Joey Fatone), Aunt Voula (Andrea Martin), and Mana-Yiayia (Bess Meisler). Paris talks to the rep from Northwestern (Rob Riggle), which prompts the Portokalos men to confront him and ensure that she gets accepted. However, Paris is set on going to school far from Chicago, to Toula's dismay.

Gus has taken it upon himself to prove that he is a direct descendant from Alexander The Great. He gets Toula to teach him how to use a computer so he can trace his ancestry. It proves to be such a struggle that Ian and Nick must help as well. Gus finds his marriage certificate and sees that it was never signed by a minister, meaning he and Maria are technically not legally married. Gus breaks the news to Maria and insists they must set up a wedding immediately. Maria refuses, as she wants Gus to propose properly, which he didn't do 50 years earlier. Gus doesn't see the point in do-

Chapter 9   Cultural Identity in Intercultural Communication

ing so, so Maria turns against him.

Following this, Voula tells Toula that she and Ian need to go on a date to retain the romance in their marriage, but to avoid arguments, they must not talk about Paris. Toula and Ian go out for dinner that night, and they do talk about Paris and how concerned they are that she might pick a school away from Chicago. When they get home, they start to fool around in the car until Maria, Voula, and Nikki catch them. After they leave, they continue.

The family meets a famous TV personality named George (John Stamos) and his wife Anna (Rita Wilson). Knowing George is Greek, Gus invites him and Anna to their restaurant and to bring their son so he can meet Paris. When they arrive at the restaurant, the family is stunned (and disappointed) to see that George and Anna's son is 7 years old.

One evening, Maria calls Toula's home to tell her and Ian that Gus got stuck in the bathtub since his bad hip locked. Toula, Ian, Nick, and Angelo rush over to help, but they're afraid to do so because Gus is nude. They try to turn him over, but they eventually resort to calling an ambulance. As he is being carried away, Gus then proposes to Maria properly, and she accepts (begrudgingly).

The Portokalos women help Maria plan her wedding, but her demands become so hectic that their wedding planner quits on them. Meanwhile, Paris receives acceptance letters from both Northwester and NYU. She tells her parents that she wants to go to Northwestern just to make them happy, even though that's not what she wants. Toula, being tasked to fix everything, assembles the family together so that Maria can have the wedding she really wants. With everybody having a job to do, the time has come to plan another big fat Greek wedding.

At school, Paris witnesses her crush Bennett (Alex Wolff) approaching his own crush to ask her to the prom. Unfortunately, the girl's new boyfriend asks her as well. Paris saves Bennett and asks him herself to go to prom. He accepts.

Prom night arrives, which is the same day as the wedding. Paris tells Toula and Ian that she wants to go to NYU, and while it hurts them to send her away, Toula and Paris share a tender moment before Bennett shows up. On the way to prom, Paris bonds with Bennett after learning that he comes from a Greek family.

Gus receives a surprise visit from his older brother Panos (Mark Margolis). He is there to support his brother, and they have a drink with Ian and Nick. Ian gets his buddy Mike (Ian Gomez) to get his police buddies to get them all to the church on time.

At the church, Maria is walked down the aisle by Nick. Problem is, Gus has gotten pretty drunk and he can't stop giggling. Maria walks away since he won't take this seriously, prompting the women to run and convince her to go on with it. Panos enters and tells Maria that Gus has loved her for the last 50 years since she agreed to go with him to America. Maria knows she loves Gus too, and they proceed with the wedding. As it goes on, Toula and Ian rekindle their spark, while Paris and Bennett share their first kiss at prom.

The family gathers at home for the reception. Paris and Bennett join them, and Bennett is jumped by Paris's cousins. Toula gives Gus a letter from the ancestry site confirming that he is a direct descendant of Alexander The Great. He proudly goes up to announce it. Toula lets Ian know that she really wrote it.

The film concludes with the whole family dropping Paris off at her dorm in NYC.

Questions:

1. What's the gradual change of Toula's attitude toward the issue of being a Greek?

2. What is missing in Toula and Ian's life in raising Paris?

Task 2   Extended reading

Tourism and Intercultural Communication

In 2014, 1.1 billion people traveled abroad generating over $1.4 trillion through the global travel industry. Recovering from the economic crisis, the tourism industry projects an increase of 3.3% annually from 2010 to 2030 with an estimated 1.8 billion people trave ling abroad by 2030. One out of every eleven jobs worldwide is associated with the tourist industry (United Nations World Tourism Organization [UNWTO], 2014). Yet, mass travel and tourism often exploit unequal relationships of wealth and power as people from richer, more economically advantaged countries travel to poorer, more economically disadvantaged countries. Frequently, colonial patterns of exploitation and displacement, as well as notions of authenticity and exoticization are re-inscribed in contemporary intercultural encounters in tourist context.

Young people, predominantly students, from the age of 15 to 30, account for approximately 20% of annual travel, which represents a huge market for governments and

Chapter 9　Cultural Identity in Intercultural Communication

tourist industries to target their appeals. A study released by the World Youth Student and Educational Travel Confederation surveying over 34,000 young travelers from 137 countries found that youth travel is increasingly complex appealing to larger and more diverse populations than ever before. Motivations for and orientations to travel for youth have changed in recent years as youth travelers aim to immerse themselves in local cultures, learn new languages, and see traveling as a way of life. With rising youth unemployment in many advanced capitalist countries, young people with some access to resources travel for work, education, and cultural experiences. Less focused than in the past on traditional leisure destinations, 22% of young people travel to learn languages, 15% to acquire work experience, and 1% to study abroad. Youth travelers are also spending money at higher rates than ever before; flashbackers, or backpackers who travel with laptops, tablets, smart-phones, and other electronic devices, are changing youth tourism as travelers develop friendship networks and travel plans through the Internet and social media.

Travel can provide opportunities for intercultural engagement, learning about the unknown, and appreciation of the different ways human beings around the world live and make sense of their lives. Yet today, the majority of tourists choose options that limit their exposure and access to the very places they pay to visit. Pat Thomas (2009), British editor of the *Ecologist*, observed the following:

Most of us are not travelers at all—as vulnerable to processes of commodification as places we visit…The smaller the world gets, the more we seem to want it to be as much like home as possible (but with cleaner sheets and towels and without the washing up).

According to surveys administered by Halifax Travel Insurance, British touristson international vacations spent less than 8 hours a week outside of the hotel; three quarters of the 2,000 surveyed made no effort to learn the local language, and 70% never visited a local attraction (Thomas, 2009). Similar to tourists to New Mexico in the early 1900s, package tours to Spain for Britain, and to Jamaica or Mexico for US tourists offer exotic yet often limited and sanitized experiences of cultural other. In addition to questioning the goal of looking for "home" when one travels, which often precludes intercultural exchange, it is important to note finding "home" when traveling (in the sense of finding what is familiar from your culture around the world) is not even an option for much of the world. Today, the cultural and economic hegemony of the West is experienced in contradictory ways by Western tourists. On the other hand, Western tourists desire and often demand the familiarity of "home", yet simultaneously, complaints abound that other cultures are too "Americanized", too "Westernized", or too much like home.

Tourism is one of the world's largest industries employing more than 266 million people worldwide (World Travel & Tourism Council, 2013). TV, magazine, and Internet ads; billboards; and travelogues present tourism as good for local economies. The travel industry purports that tourism brings in foreign capital, provides jobs, and preserves local cultures. Undoubtedly, international tourism is a source of foreign capital for many economies around the world; in cases like Mexico, tourism is a significant economic resource. Yet, slick advertisements that display cultural and natural resources in alluring and desirable ways gloss over the economic, environmental, and social conditions just below the surface. Vying for the attention of consumers, city, state, and national governments collaborate with the tourist industry to offer ever-growing enticements, which frequently draw on natural and cultural resources as different, authentic, exotic, titillating, and romantic. Culture, within the equation of tourism and profit, is most often seen as an unimportant backdrop or as a commodity for capitalization. Either way, the impact of tourism on local cultures and people is transformative. The framing of cultural practices, forms and spaces as well as cultural histories as commodities to be "preserved" and "marketed" trades on colonial and postcolonial stereotypes that fix and essentialize local cultures. Presented as "pure" or "authentic", local cultures are constructed as if they exist or once existed as homogenous entities suspended outside of time and history, completely erasing pre-colonial, colonial, and postcolonial intercultural encounters. This framing in tourist literature and at cultural sites and performances for tourist masks the decimation, hybridization, and adaptation local cultures have engaged in and survived for centuries and continue to negotiate today.

(Adapted from Sorrells, Kathryn, "Intercultural Communication-Globalization and Social Justice", Chapter 8)

Critical thinking questions:

1. In what way has motivations for and orientations to travel for youth have changed in recent years?

2. What's the point of finding "home" when traveling (in the sense of finding what is familiar from your culture around the world)?

3. What's the impact of tourism on local cultures and people?

Chapter 10

Being an Effective Intercultural Communicator

By nature people are nearly alike; by practice they get to be wide apart.
—Confucius

The whole purpose of education is to turn mirrors into windows.
—Sydney J. Harris

Section I Effective Intercultural Communication

I Pre-tasks

Task 1 Quote discussion

Please read following quote about intercultural communication and answer the questions.

Culture makes people understand each other better. And if they understand each other better in their soul, it is easier to overcome the economic and political barriers. But first they have to understand that their neighbor is, in the end, just like them, with the same problems, the same questions. (Paulo Coelho)

Questions:

1. What does it mean to say "culture makes people understand each other better"?
2. Do you agree that humanity is fundamental for intercultural communication?

Task 2   Differences and connections

Look at the following picture of the Thinker and the Terra-Cotta Warrior. Think about the connection between them.

Questions:

1. What have you learned from this picture?

2. What are the effective ways for people from different cultural backgrounds to communicates with each other?

II   While-tasks

Becoming a Competent Intercultural Communicator

Intercultural communication is now taking place all over the world, especially in many large cities. We are encountering people with different ways of communicating in every area of our lives including our careers and the business world, our social lives and in our academic courses. It sounds exciting but at the same time, communication with the culturally different is frequently associated with adverse emotional responses leading to feelings of awkwardness and anxiety. We must be prepared to meet the challenges of language differences, unfamiliar and perhaps strange customs and behaviors, and cultural variability in both verbal and non-verbal communication styles, to achieve success.

Defining Intercultural Communication Competence

Intercultural communication competence in its most unadorned form is simply behavior that is appropriate and effective in a given context. It is the overall internal capability of an individual to manage key challenging features of intercultural communication: namely, cultural differences and unfamiliarity, inter-group posture, and the accompanying experience of stress. That is to say, being a competent communicator means having the ability to interact effectively and appropriately with members of another linguistic-cultural background on their terms.

Barriers to Intercultural Communication

The complex nature of human behavior produces many communication problems, which is the reason why we should explore how diverse cultural orientations influence the way we perceive and interact with an increasingly culturally diverse world.

Anxiety

When we are anxious because of not knowing what we are expected to do, it is only natural to focus on that feeling and not be totally present in the communication transaction. For example, you may have experienced anxiety on your very first day on a new college campus or in a new job. You may be so conscious of being new—and out of place—and focus so much of your attention on that feeling that you make common mistakes and appear awkward to others.

Assuming Similarity Instead of Difference

When we assume similarity between cultures, we can be caught unaware of important differences and behave as we would in our home culture. The inverse can be a barrier as well. Assuming differences instead of similarity can lead to our not recognizing important things that cultures share in common. It's better to assume nothing. Ask "What are the customs?" rather than assuming they are the same or different everywhere.

Ethnocentrism

To be ethnocentric is to believe in the superiority of one's own culture. Another name for ethnocentrism is the anthropological concept of cultural relativism. It does mean that we must try to understand other people's behaviors in the context of their cultures before we judge it. It also means that we recognize the arbitrary nature of our own cultural behaviors and be willing to reexamine them by learning about behaviors in other cultures.

Stereotypes

Stereotypes are perceptions and beliefs we hold about groups or individuals based on our previously formed opinions or attitudes. Stereotypes do not develop suddenly but are formed over a period of time by our culture. They are made up of bits and pieces of information that we store and use to make sense of what goes on around us.

While stereotyping may reduce the threat of the unknown, it interferes with our perceptions and understanding of the world. When applied to individuals or groups, often stereotypes are problematic because they are over simplified, over generalized and/or exaggerated, their content are beliefs based on half-truths or distortions.

Prejudice

Prejudice is generally referred to as the unfair, biased or intolerant attitudes or opinions toward another person or group simply because they belong to a specific religion, race, nationality or another group. Like stereotypes, prejudice involves the preconceptions of individuals or groups based on unfounded opinions, attitudes or beliefs.

Prejudice can take many forms, ranging from those that are almost impossible to detect to those that are clearly intentional. As an extreme and intentional form of prejudice, discrimination impedes intercultural communication as it involves the unfavorable treatment and/or denial of equal treatment of individuals or groups because of race, gender, religion, ethnicity or disability.

Language

Language is one of the most obvious barriers to intercultural communication but perhaps not the most fundamental. People who do not share a language or who feel that they have imperfect command of another person's language may have some difficulties communicating. There is also the possibility of misunderstanding occurring between people when they do not share a common language.

Improving Your Intercultural Communication Skills

Knowing yourself and your personal biases is a crucial element in becoming a competent intercultural communicator. You need to be self-reflexive and know from where you are coming when you enter into an intercultural interaction.

Be Aware of Your Culture

Your first step toward knowing yourself should begin with your own culture. It provides you with valuable insights for understanding your beliefs and attitudes, your values and assumptions. Think about the way you communicate. Are you direct or indirect? Do you use non-verbal gestures frequently or rarely and in what contexts? Do you seek agreement from the people who are listening to you when you make a statement? What aspects of your culture shape the way you interact with others?

Chapter 10 Being an Effective Intercultural Communicator

Examine Your Personal Attitudes

Not only do you need to know the values, attitudes, and perceptions of your culture, but you also need to be aware of your own belief system. If you hold a certain attitude toward gay men, and a man who is gay talks to you, your pre-communication attitude will affect your response to what he says. Knowing your likes, dislikes, and degrees of personal ethnocentrism enables you to place them out in the open so you can detect the ways in which these attitudes influence communication.

Understand Your Communication Style

This involves discovering the kind of image you portray to the rest of the world, the manner in which you present yourself to others. If you perceive yourself in one way, and the people with whom you interact perceive you in another way, serious problems can arise.

Monitor Yourself

The process of self-observation and analysis is often called "self-monitoring". The advantages include discovering the appropriate behaviors in each situation, having control of your emotional reactions, creating good impressions, and modifying your behavior as you move from situation to situation.

Tips for Intercultural Communication

Mind your mindset.

Mindset matters. The best starting point for any intercultural encounter is a mindset that is tolerant, mindful, and that truly desires effective communication to take place.

Be a code-breaker

Be aware of the degree to which we are all "coded" by our culture. We typically don't think of the way we do things as being culturally coded. We think of that as being normative. An important lesson on the path to becoming an intercultural communicator is to realize that much of what we just assume to be "True" is a function of our own cultural coding, just like much of what other people assume to be "True" is a function of theirs. When we realize that, we can begin to see that there isn't necessarily a "Right" or "Wrong" to many of the things we do or say or think. Rather, it's a matter of cultural coding.

Differences can make a difference

There are some culturally-based differences that do matter, particularly when it comes to studying and working together. Culture can shape how willing we are to take risks, what our attitudes are toward collaboration, what our preferences are in terms of personal space or punctuality. Competent intercultural communicators need to be aware of cultural differences and turn them into assets, rather than seeing them as barriers or hurdles to effective communication.

See similarities

Although there are culturally-based differences that are real, there are many ways in which humans are humans, no matter what their cultural identity is. As the American musician, Melissa Etheridge, puts it, "There are differences we cannot hide, but we are all one spirit inside." Recognizing that "one spirit inside" and looking for ways in which we are similar to people from different cultural backgrounds can help us become more effective communicators.

Listening up

In any communication encounter, listening is key, and that is particularly true for intercultural exchanges. Listening well involves filtering out distractions, focusing your attention on what another person is saying, making sure you really understand the message, interpreting the message, and responding appropriately. Indeed, listening well is essential to effective intercultural communication.

Meta-communicate

Meta-communication, or communication about communication, can be a useful ally when it comes to intercultural communication. Competent communicators will recognize when it's time to move their talk to a meta-level and discuss communication problems that may be getting in the way of effective interaction.

Take perspective

Perspective taking is important. You may be familiar with the Native American proverb that says, "Don't judge a man until you have walked a mile in his moccasins." That's what perspective taking is all about. Try to put yourself into the shoes of the people you encounter from other cultures. You'll likely discover that the others' perspectives and behaviors are logical from their standpoints. Understanding the "logic" of the other's cultural coding can help make us more effective communicators.

Space out

"Spacing out" means that all of the participants in the interaction will move out of their cultural comfort zones into a space that they create together—a space that makes the best use of the skills and viewpoints that all of the individuals bring to the table. This space that brings together diverse perspectives and ensures that all of them will be heard is the power of intercultural communication.

Developing Communication Flexibility

Many experts in communication competence believe that one definition of competence is having the ability to adjust and fashion your communication behavior to fit the setting, the other person, and yourself.

An obvious component of being flexible is having a tolerance for ambiguity. It starts with being nonjudgmental, practicing patience, expecting the unexpected, and being adaptive.

(Adapted from Samovar, Larry, Porter, Richard and McDaniel, Edwin, "Crosscultural Communication", Chapter 8)

Word list:

1. adverse [ˈædvɜːs]
    adj. 敌对的；对立的；不友好的；不利的
2. unadorned [ˌʌnəˈdɔːnd]
    adj. 不加装饰的，简朴的
3. relativism [ˈrelətɪvɪzəm]
    n. 相对主义（认为不存在绝对正确，只能通过比较来判断事物的一种哲学思想）
4. arbitrary [ˈɑːrbɪtəri]
    adj. 任意的；专横的；武断的；反复无常的；变幻莫测的
5. preconception [ˌpriːkənˈsepʃən]
    n. 事先形成的看法；先入之见，成见
6. impede [ɪmˈpiːd]
    vt. 妨碍；阻碍，阻止
7. reflexive [rɪˈfleksɪv]
    adj. （动词或代词）反身的
8. normative [ˈnɔːmətɪv]
    adj. 合乎规范的；按规定准则的

9. collaboration [kəˌlæbəˈrɪʃən]
    n. 合作；协作
10. punctuality [ˌpʌŋktjʊˈælɪtɪ]
    n. 严守时间；正确；规矩
11. meta-communication [ˈmetəkəmjuːnɪˈkeɪʃən]
    n. 元信息传递学；元信息传递（指用比较直观的方式传递信息）
12. moccasin [ˈmɒkəsɪn]
    n. 莫卡辛鞋；软帮平底鞋
13. ambiguity [ˌæmbɪˈgjuːətɪ]
    n. 模棱两可；不明确（的事物）

Task 1 Reading comprehension

Exercise One: Work with your partners, decide whether the following statements are true (T) or false (F) according to what you have learned in the passage.

1. _____ Intercultural communication competence in its most unadorhed form is simply behavior that is approprion and effective in a given contest.
2. _____ When we are anxious because of not knowing what we are expected to do, it is only natural to try to escape from any communication transaction.
3. _____ It's better to assume there are different customs everywhere rather than assuming they are the same.
4. _____ When applied to individuals or groups, stereotypes are often helpful because they are based on truths and universal experiences.
5. _____ An important lesson on the path to becoming an intercultural communicator is to realize that much of what we just assume to be "True" is just a matter of cultural coding.
6. _____ Competent intercultural communicators need to be aware of cultural differences and treat them as barriers or hurdles to effective communication.
7. _____ Speaking is key in intercultural exchanges.
8. _____ Try to put yourself into the shoes of the people you encounter from other cultures, and you'll likely discover that the others' perspectives and behaviors are logical from their standpoints.

Chapter 10　Being an Effective Intercultural Communicator

9. _____ When we communicate with those from another culture we should move out of our cultural comfort zones into a space that makes the best use of the skills and viewpoints that all of the individuals bring to the table.

10. _____ An obvious component of being flexible is having a tolerance for ambiguity.

Exercise Two: Fill in the blanks with the words given below and change the form when necessary.

adverse　　appropriate　　tolerant　　normative　　punctuality
essential　　favorable　　nonjudgmental　　problematic　　ethnocentric

1. When applied to individuals or groups, often stereotypes are _____ because they are over simplified, over generalized and/or exaggerated, their content are beliefs based on half-truths or distortions.

2. As an extreme and intentional form of prejudice, discrimination impedes intercultural communication as it involves the _____ treatment and/or denial of equal treatment of individuals or groups because of race, gender, religion, ethnicity or disability.

3. The best starting point for any intercultural encounter is a mindset that is _____, mindful, and that truly desires effective communication to take place.

4. Being a competent communicator means having the ability to interact effectively and _____ with members of another linguistic-cultural background on their terms.

5. Communication with the culturally different is frequently associated with _____ emotional responses leading to feelings of awkwardness and anxiety.

6. To be _____ is to believe in the superiority of one's own culture.

7. We typically don't think of the way we do things as being culturally coded. We think of that as being _____.

8. Culture can shape how willing we are to take risks, what our attitudes are towards collaboration, what our preferences are in terms of personal space or _____.

9. Listening well is _____ to effective intercultural communication.

10. Intercultural communication competence starts with being _____, practicing patience, expecting the unexpected, and being adaptive.

Task 2 Case study

Case 1

Sugawara (1993) surveyed 168 Japanese employers of Japanese companies working in the United States and 135 of their US coworkers. Only 8% of the US coworkers felt impatient with Japanese coworkers' English. While 19% of the Japanese employees felt their spoken English was poor or very poor and 20% reported feeling nervous when speaking English with the US coworkers, 30% of the Japanese employees felt the US coworkers were impatient with their accent, and almost 60% believed that language was the problem in communicating with the US coworkers. For some, anxiety over speaking English properly contributed to avoiding interactions with the US coworkers and limiting interactions both on and off the job to other Japanese only.

Questions for discussion:

1. In this case, what barrier did the Japanese employees encounter working in the United States?

2. What made the Japanese employees feel frustrated and tent to avoid interactions with their US coworkers?

3. What is your suggestion on breaking this barrier?

Case 2

In 1997, a Danish woman left her 14-month-old baby girl in a stroller outside a Manhattan restaurant while she was inside. Other dinners at the restaurant became concerned and called New York City Police. The woman was charged with endangering a child and was jailed for two nights. Her child was placed in foster care. The woman and the Danish consulate explained that leaving children unattended outside cafés is common in Denmark. Pictures were wired to the police showing numerous strollers parked outside cafés while parents were eating inside. The Danish woman had assumed that Copenhagen is similar to New York, that what is commonly done in Copenhagen is also commonly done in New York.

Questions for discussion:

1. What do you think is the main reason for the intercultural communication problem in this case?

2. What could be done to interact more effectively and appropriately in a different culture?

3. Have you ever been in a similar intercultural communication which ended up in misunderstanding or conflict?

III After-tasks

Task 1　Movie and cultural discussion *A United Kingdom*

Introduction to the movie *A United Kingdom* (2016)

A United Kingdom tells the inspiring true story of Seretse Khama (David Oyelowo, *Queen of Katwe*), the King of Bechuanaland (modern Botswana), and Ruth Williams (Rosamund Pike, *Gone Girl*), the London office worker he married in 1948 in the face of fierce opposition from their families and the British and South African governments. The film charts the journey of Seretse and Ruth from initially meeting and falling in love in London, through their struggle to be accepted by both Seretse's people in Bechuanaland and the British government. Why are the British government interested in a private marriage, you may ask? Because of the close ties between the British government and that of South Africa, which, at the time, had just instituted the policy of apartheid that segregated white and black people throughout the country. Seretse's neighboring Bechuanaland is a British protectorate, and to maintain good relations with South Africa, Britain, in the form of officials Alistair Canning (Jack Davenport, *Kingsman: The Secret Service*) and Rufus Lancaster (Tom Felton, *Risen*), opposes the marriage of Ruth and Seretse. Once the marriage goes ahead, the British position as well as that of Seretse's uncle and regent, Tshekedi Khama (Vusi Kunene, *Eye in the Sky*), moves to blocking Seretse's ascension to the throne.

All this politicking might put some viewers off, but director Amma Asante and writer Guy Hibbert brilliantly balance official meetings and issuing of reports and edicts with personal dramas and a genuinely moving love story. Ruth and Seretse make an adorable and believable screen couple, the chemistry between the two leads creating a palatable sense of companionship, respect and affection. Oyelowo is excellent as the man who loves his country, people and wife equally, and is determined to embrace all of these without placing any of them second. Pike is equally impressive as a woman assailed from all sides, but never wavering in her decision to stick with her husband and hold to an egalitarian and, let's face it, accurate belief that skin color is no indication of character or human value. Nor does the filmtip into mawkish sentimentality, as this marriage in the public eye is one of resolve and mutual support rather than gooey-eyed sentiment, despite attacks from both Ruth and Seretse's family, his tribal elders, her government and British people in the street who taunt this inter-racial couple.

Seretse and Ruth defied family, apartheid and empire—their love triumphed over every obstacle flung in their path and in so doing they transformed their nation and inspired the world.

Task 2 Extended reading

Managing Intercultural Conflicts

The pace and volume of global transactions, the ease of global communication using technology, the abundance of cheaper transportation costs, and the frequency of businesses using cross-border talent is fostering millions of interactions a day between people of different cultures. Yet the process of intercultural communication can be

Chapter 10 Being an Effective Intercultural Communicator

more complicated than we realize. When people bring with them different sets of culturally constructed perspectives toward appropriate behaviors, it is no surprise that conflicts and disputes arise. Further, it should be no surprise that people have different sets of perceptions about appropriate ways to handle conflicts.

Cultural Assumptions

Our attitudes, expectations and behaviors are generally influenced by and result from our cultural value patterns, such as individualistic or collectivistic. These different patterns of values can be the first thing that engenders intercultural frustration. Intercultural conflicts arise because of the differences in values and norms of behaviors of people from different cultures. A person acts according to the values and norms of his or her culture; another person holding a different worldview might interpret his or her behavior from an opposite standpoint. This situation creates misunderstanding and can lead to conflict. Often people of the mainstream America, the Anglo culture, perceive their own cultural distinctiveness.

Identifying intercultural conflicts

The definition of conflict is an expressed struggle between interdependent parties with incompatible goals or unmet emotional needs. In an intercultural context, conflict is the explicit or implicit emotional struggle or frustrations between people from different cultures over perceived incompatible goals, norms, values, face concerns, scarce resources, and/or communication outcomes. Intercultural conflict occurs when different cultural values and beliefs clash. It has been used to explain violence and crime.

Intercultural conflict can be identified by the following signs: (1) It usually has complicated dynamics. Cultural differences mentioned above tend to create complex combinations of expectations about one's own and others' behaviors. (2) If addressing content and relational issues do not resolve the conflict, it can be rooted in cultural differences. (3) Conflict reoccurs or arises strong emotions even though the issue of disagreement is insignificant.

Resolving intercultural conflicts

How we manage conflict matters much more than whether or not we engage in it in the first place. It is the management of conflict that shapes the outcome, and it always begins with identifying whether cultural issues are involved.

Take the lead

In a multicultural environment, the prevalent question to ask is: Who is adapting to whom? Not everyone is immediately enthusiastic about improving their intercultural communication skills. There are many resistances to learning something new. One of the biggest is that we wait for someone else to take the lead. We hear people ask all the time, in a challenging tone, "Why should I make the extra effort to adapt my way of communicating? Why don't others make that effort for me?"

It is not always true that people resist changing, but more typically they do not know how to change. It is hard to change what you cannot see. Since most people cannot see how they communicate, they do not know what to do differently or how. Unfortunately, everyone is paying a high price for this lack of awareness.

What are the consequences of waiting for others to change? Obviously this results not only in wasted time and effort but also creates negative emotions and lack of trust, due to delays and misunderstandings. Communication turns out to be more significant than most of us realize, so why not take the lead? You have nothing to lose and lots to gain in terms of more harmonious working relationships and intercultural trust, as well as efficiency.

Be aware

The resolution process should start from the parties' acknowledgment that their conflict contains a cultural dimension. Next, there should be willingness on both sides to deal with all conflict dimensions including the cultural one. Third, systematic phased work on the conflict is needed. For instance, the parties describe what they find offensive in each other's behavior, so that they understand the other party's cultural perceptions, and they both learn how the problem would be handled in the culture of the opponent, finally they develop conflict solutions. Resolution of the conflict is particularly complicated if the conflict arose not just out of misunderstanding of the other's behavior, but because of incompatible values.

Learn about other cultures

People can prevent intercultural conflicts by learning about cultures that they come in contact with. This knowledge can be obtained through training programs, general reading, talking to people from different cultures, and learning from past experiences. Important aspects of cultural education are understanding your own culture and developing cultural awareness by acquiring a broad knowledge of values and beliefs of other cultures, rather than looking at them through the prism of cultural stereotypes. So be a learner: when you are trying to solve a problem with people from all different parts of the world, you know that you have a rich opportunity for learning. Try to focus less on asserting your own opinion or ideas and instead, try to find out what other people's ideas are, how those ideas might reflect their own culture and how various points of view could create a stronger solution to your problem.

Respect cultural differences

People are both alike and different, as President Shimon Peres of the State of Israel once said, "All people have the right to be equal and the equal right to be different." A complete and honest intercultural ethical perspective both grants similarities and recognizes differences. By accepting and appreciating both, you are better able to assess the potential consequences of your communicative acts and to be more tolerant of those of others.

Be empathic

Empathy, broadly defined, is a part of interpersonal sensitivity and social competence, the ability to sense, perceive accurately, and respond appropriately to one's personal, interpersonal, and social environment. Empathy has been recognized as important to both general communication competence and as a central characteristic of competent and effective intercultural communication.

While knowledge about another's culture can be used to make predictions, empathy also demands that the point of analysis be the individual's personality. It is best to view empathy as a complex activity composed of many variables. It involves a cognitive component, an affective dimension, and a communication element.

Practice effective listening

In today's high-tech, high-speed, high-stress world, communication is more important than ever, yet we seem to devote less and less time to really listening to one another. Genuine listening has become a rare gift—the gift of time. It helps build relationships, solve problems, ensure understanding, resolve conflicts, and improve accuracy.

When a person decides to communicate with another person, he/she does so to fulfill a need. The person wants something, feels discomfort, and/or has feelings or thoughts about something. In deciding to communicate, the person selects the method or code which he/she believes will effectively deliver the message to the other person. The code used to send the message can be either verbal or non-verbal. When the other person receives the coded message, they go through the process of decoding or interpreting it into understanding and meaning. Effective communication exists between two people when the receiver interprets and understands the sender's message in the same way the sender intended it.

There is a real distinction between merely hearing the words and really listening for the message. When we listen effectively we understand what the person is thinking and/or feeling from the other person's own perspective. It is as if we were standing in the other person's shoes, seeing through his/her eyes and listening through the person's ears. Our own viewpoint may be different and we may not necessarily agree with the person, but as we listen, we understand from the other's perspective. To listen effectively, we must be actively involved in the communication process, and not just listening passively.

Intercultural conflict competence refers to a process of integrating knowledge, mindfulness, and constructive conflict skills in managing group membership differences on a cultural level. To engage in optimal conflict competence, we have to acquire in-depth knowledge, heightened mindfulness, and constructive conflict skills—and apply them ethically in a diverse range of intercultural situations.

(Adapted from Samovar, Larry, Porter, Richard and McDaniel, Edwin, "Cross-cultural Communication", Chapter 8)

Critical thinking questions:

1. In what way could intercultural conflict be identified?

2. Why do some people feel reluctant to adapt their way of communicating when intercultural conflicts arise?

3. Some say that "empathy is the bedrock of intercultural communication". What do you think? Is it in any way overstated?

Chapter 10 Being an Effective Intercultural Communicator

Section II Intercultural Competence

I Pre-tasks

Task 1 Intercultural marriages

Look at the pictures of Facebook CEO Mark Zuckberg and his wife Priscilla Chan and answer the questions.

Questions:

1. What do you know about this couple?

2. What do you think of intercultural marriages? What are some of the common issues with intercultural marriages?

Task 2 Road and belt

Look at the following picture and think about the connection between them.

Questions:

1. What do you think this picture is about?

2. The Silk Road Economic Belt and the 21st-century Maritime Silk Road, better known as The Belt and Road (B&R), is a development strategy that focuses on con-

nectivity and cooperation. In what way do you think it's going to promote intercultural communication?

II While-tasks

Removing Barriers to Effective Communication

Both the original message and the feedback can be affected by various sorts of interference (also known as "barriers" or "noise"). Interference can be caused by things such as perception, gender, age, language differences, power differences, cultural differences, etc. Problems with communication can occur at every stage of communication process. At each stage there is the potential for misunderstanding and confusion creating barriers to effective communication. The goal should be to lessen the frequency of problems at each stage of this process with clear, concise, accurate and well-planned communications.

Unclear language can create a hindrance in understanding, as can delivering in a tone or manner that is counterproductive to the meaning of the message. Choosing a method of communication unsuited to the message, context, environment or channel also creates problems. Poor listening is one of the biggest barriers to effective communication, and not listening actively can create large gaps in meaning.

The chance for misunderstanding also increases substantially when the people involved in the communication are from different cultural backgrounds. In intercultural communication, the sender converts their thoughts into a message using his/her cultural filters, and the receiver converts the same message into thoughts using his/her different cultural filters. As culture is a major source of differences between people, this frequently creates problems and causes misunderstandings.

Barriers to effective communication are many and can include:

Physical barriers. These include: situations when space or distance physically separates people from others, obstacles such as furniture and closed doors, and distractions including noise.

Environmental barriers. These could include: too much humidity, inadequate or excess lighting, uncomfortable temperatures, or bad ventilation.

Organizational barriers. These include: poor organizational systems and processes, stringent rule and regulations, status, relationships, complexity, lack of recognition, and lack of opportunities for growth and improvement.

Chapter 10 Being an Effective Intercultural Communicator

Language barriers. Different languages, vocabularies, accents and dialects can also be barriers to effective communication. Language is vague in nature and its words are symbols which don't always represent only one meaning. The meanings of these symbols or words are understood by the sender and receiver in their own way, which can result in misinterpretation, badly expressed messages, and unqualified assumptions. If the communicator uses jargon, or difficult or inappropriate words, or if the message is not explained in a proper manner, then it can result in misinterpretation and confusion.

Cultural barriers. These can include: cultural backgrounds, age, education, gender, social status, economic positions, religions, political beliefs, ethics, values, motives, assumptions, aspirations, standards and priorities. These can all separate one person from another and create a barrier.

Emotional barriers. Emotional interferences including hostility, anger, resentfulness, jealousy and fear contribute to difficulty in listening to others or in understanding the message conveyed. These emotions can also lead to a lack of patience and sudden reactions, unfair assumptions and defensiveness.

Attitudinal barriers. Attitudes such as prejudice, distrust, skepticism, stubbornness, disinterest and unwillingness to cooperate all contribute to ineffective communication.

Stress. When a person is under immense stress, he/she may find it difficult to understand the message, leading to communication distortion. At the time of stress, our psychological frame of mind depends on our beliefs, experiences, goals and values. Thus, we may fail to realize the essence of the communication.

Lack of subject knowledge. If the person who sends or receives a message lacks subject knowledge, then they may not be able to convey the message clearly or understand it.

Inappropriate channel. This occurs when the channel (medium) used to communicate is not the most suitable for the circumstances or for the nature of the message, e. g. conveying complex and detailed instructions over the phone.

Inappropriate timing. Communicating information at the wrong time also creates a barrier to effective communication, e. g. passing on information that requires the listener to concentrate intently at the end of a tiring and stressful day.

Limited communication elements present. The communication process often combines the use of a number of communication elements, e. g. speech, tone and volume of voice, facial expressions, body language, etc. These all combine and contribute to the understanding of the message. If several of these elements are missing or are conflicting then the message is more likely to be distorted.

Poor listening skills. The inability to listen attentively and concentrate on the message is a common barrier to effective communication.

Removing barriers

To deliver messages effectively, and to ensure we fully understand the message transmitted, we need to commit to breaking down the barriers that exist within each of the stages of the communication process. If the message is too lengthy, disorganized or contains errors, we can expect the message to be misunderstood and misinterpreted. The use of poor verbal and body language can also confuse the message. Offering too much information too fast also creates problems and does not allow the receiver enough time to analyze and digest what has been transmitted.

Many attempts to communicate are nullified by saying too much.

Robert Greenleaf

In a situation where there are cultural barriers, overcoming the problem can involve learning more about acceptable forms of communicating and listening in the other party's culture. We need to work to understand our audience's culture, making sure we can converse and deliver our message to people of different backgrounds and cultures both within and outside of our own country.

It is also important to remember that, even within the same culture, there are significant differences between individuals and thus there will be differences in communication styles. A forceful message may motivate one person and overwhelm another. Understanding individual differences and adapting to those differences is an important way to keep our communication effective and barrier-free.

Other strategies that can be used to overcome communication barriers and increase the effectiveness of the message include:

- using empathy (i. e. putting yourself in the other person's shoes);
- being positive (i. e. using positive language/words);
- selecting an appropriate location (i. e. eliminating distractions and protecting privacy);

Chapter 10 Being an Effective Intercultural Communicator

- selecting an appropriate time (i. e. when the receiver is most receptive to the message);
- selecting the most appropriate medium for the type of information conveyed and the characteristics of the audience;
- maintaining eye contact;
- using active listening skills;
- asking for clarification or repetition where necessary;
- giving and receiving feedback;
- building effective relationships;
- being aware of your body language and ensuring it supports and reinforces the message;
- choosing words carefully and most appropriate for the audience;
- carefully planning the communication before delivering it;
- conveying information in small manageable and easily digestible chunks;
- checking for understanding;
- always being clear as to the objective of the communication;
- avoiding communication when strong emotions are likely to distort the message;
- ensuring the information to be conveyed is accurate before communicating it;
- ensuring the organization's structures systems and processes are designed to support effective communication;
- communicating in a non-threatening and relaxed environment (e. g. over a coffee rather than behind a desk).

Active listening

Listening skills are another very important element in communication. Barriers stemming from miscommunication can be prevented by listening more actively. Active listening is the process in which a listener actively participates in the communication interaction by attempting to grasp the facts and feelings being expressed by the speaker. Actively listening for both content and feelings is important to understand the message's total meaning.

When listening, remember that what isn't said is also part of the message.

We can improve active listening skills by:

- listening patiently to what the other person has to say, although we may believe it is wrong or irrelevant. Signaling simple acceptance (not necessarily agreement) of what is being said by nodding or injecting an occasional "I see".

- trying to understand the feelings the person is expressing as well as cognitive content. Most of us have difficulty talking clearly about our feelings, so careful attention is required.

- allowing time for discussion to continue without interruption.

- avoiding confrontational questions or assertions. This may entail not engaging in direct questions and arguments about facts at this stage and allowing the person to keep talking. The accuracy of the facts and the evidence can be reviewed later.

- encouraging exposition of topics of interest. If the person does touch on a point we want to know more about, simply repeating the statement as a question provides encouragement for them to expand on the statement.

- listening for omissions. What isn't said is also a part of the message.

- giving honest opinion only if it is solicited. In the listening stage, it is best to limit the expression of views, since these may condition or suppress what the other person says.

- Not making judgments until all information has been conveyed and has been fully understood.

Seek first to understand and then be understood.

Steven Covey (Habit No. 5 from the book
"The Seven Habits of Highly Effective People")

Most people listen with the intent to reply, not understand.

Steven Covey

Communication is an essential skill for successful business and personal relationships and can be used effectively to influence every interaction in a positive way. In order for this to occur we must be aware of the communication process and the barriers involved, and then focus on reducing those barriers. The main fundamental that everything else revolves around, and that we must therefore always focus on, is that we need to understand our audience and adapt to that audience.

(Adapted from Ioppolo, Sebastian, "Intercultural Communication-Connecting with Cultural Diversity", Chapter 1)

Chapter 10 Being an Effective Intercultural Communicator

Word list:

1. hindrance [ˈhɪndrəns]
   n. 障碍；妨碍；阻碍物
2. aspiration [æspəˈreɪʃən]
   n. 渴望；抱负；吸引术
3. scepticism [ˈskeptɪsɪzəm]
   n. 怀疑；怀疑主义
4. cognitive [ˈkɒgnɪtɪv]
   adj. 认知的；认识的
5. confrontational [ˌkɒnfrənˈteɪʃənəl]
   adj. 对抗的；对抗性的
6. assertion [əˈsɜːʃən]
   n. 断言；声明；主张
7. entail [ɪnˈteɪl]
   vt. 使需要，必需；承担
8. omission [əʊˈmɪʃən]
   n. 疏忽；遗漏；省略
9. solicit [səˈlɪsɪt]
   vt. 征求；请求；恳求

Task 1 Reading comprehension

Exercise One: Work with your partners, decide whether the following statements are true (T) or false (F) according to what you have learned in the passage.

1. _____ Problems with communication occur only at the early stage of communication process.
2. _____ In intercultural communication, the sender converts their thoughts into a message using his/her cultural filters, and the receiver converts the same message into thoughts using his/her different cultural filters.
3. _____ When a person is under immense stress, he/she may find it difficult to understand the message, leading to communication distortion.

4. _____ The more the sender of a message explains, the better the receiver understands.

5. _____ Physical barriers to communication refer to the physical conditions of the communicators.

6. _____ Language is vague in nature and its words are symbols which don't always represent only one meaning.

7. _____ Jargon or difficult words can't really affect communication because words explain themselves.

8. _____ When listening, focus on what is said because that's everything that matters.

9. _____ We need to work to understand our audience's culture, making sure we can converse and deliver our message to people of different backgrounds and cultures both within and outside of our own country.

10. _____ We should not make judgments until all information has been conveyed and has been fully understood.

Exercise Two: Fill in the blanks with the words given below and change the form when necessary.

skepticism   confrontational   cognitive   omission   frequency
distort   misinterpretation   aspiration   counterproductive   inadequate

1. The goal should be to lessen the _____ of problems at each stage of this process with clear, concise, accurate and well-planned communications.

2. Unclear language can create a hindrance in understanding, as can delivering in a tone or manner that is _____ to the meaning of the message.

3. The meanings of words are understood by the sender and receiver in their own way, which can result in _____.

4. Attitudes such as prejudice, distrust, _____, stubbornness, disinterest and unwillingness to cooperate all contribute to ineffective communication.

5. We can improve our listening skills by trying to understand the feelings the person is expressing as well as _____ content.

6. Assertions or _____ questions should be avoided while listening.

7. We should listen for _____ because what isn't said is also a part of the message.

8. Emotions can be barriers to effective communication since strong emotions are likely to _____ the message.

9. Environmental barriers include too much humidity, _____ or excess lighting, uncomfortable temperatures, or bad ventilation.

10. Cultural barriers include cultural backgrounds, religions, political beliefs, ethics, values, assumptions, _____, standards and priorities.

Task 2 Case study

Case 1

Cinderella. Billboard. Mo Money. Lady Gaga. What do they all have in common? They are a few of the unusual English names young Chinese have adopted over the years in hopes of mixing more easily with Westerners. Such offbeat names, though, sometimes have the opposite effect, generating puzzlement and the wrong kind of smiles.

Lindsay Jernigan, an American entrepreneur, has set up a new website, bestenglishname.com, to help Chinese choose more appropriate names.

Jernigan, 25, noticed a need for the service while working in her first job in Shanghai. She said some female colleagues were using English names that were inappropriate—and they didn't know it.

"These names that we would see (as) 'stripper' names for really smart young women," Jernigan recalls recently at her office in Shanghai. "So, I've heard a lot of people laughing about the 'Candy' and the 'Cherry' ... 'Sapphire', 'Twinkle'."

Instead of facilitating communication, Jernigan says, other names that the Chinese chose just sowed confusion. For instance, she had a co-worker named "Eleven".

"Scheduling meetings at 10:30 and then saying that 'Eleven' was coming was causing a lot of issues," Jernigan says. Foreign colleagues rolled their eyes and asked Eleven if they could just call her by her Chinese name.

Jernigan's website offers customers a quiz that uses an algorithm to generate five suitable names. Users are asked to choose their favorite sport, music and personal style: Are you more like Zac Efron or Justin Bieber? Users can put in their birthdays, professions and choose whether they want a name that's easy to pronounce. Jernigan says the service costs about $2.50 and has drawn more than 2,000 customers.

Questions for discussion:
1. Why do Chinese students often choose strange English names?
2. What are the differences in name picking between Chinese and Americans?
3. What do you think of Lind say Jernigan's website?

Case 2

Monica is Japanese American born and raised in Chicago, Illinois. Sayaka is an international student born and raised in Tokyo, Japan.

Monica: "When I came to university in a small town, I had so many people ask me, 'Where are you from?' When I say 'I'm from Chicago', they often respond, 'Well, where are you really from?' It's frustrating when people do not believe that I belong here. This is the only country I know. My grandparents immigrated to the United States from Japan, but I see myself as an American."

Sayaka: "When people ask me where I am from, I'm proud to say, 'I'm from Japan.' It's complicated though when they start asking me all kinds of questions about Japan. I feel like I have to represent all people in Japan. There are so many kinds of people in Japan. It makes me feel like they see me only as Japanese and nothing else."

Monica's avowed identity is American, yet many people ascribe a Japanese or foreign identity to her, which causes tension. An unexamined assumption that "American" means "White" underlies the response she gets. For Sayaka, congruence exists in terms of national culture between her avowed and ascribed identities, yet, in conversation, her cultural "differences" obscures her other identities and she is expected to speak for all Japanese people.

Questions for discussion:
1. What are the common views on "home" and identity?
2. How do each of their identities and positionalities impact what they can say and what others expect to hear?

III After-tasks

Task 1 Movie and cultural discussion *The Karate Kid*

Introduction to the movie *The Karate Kid* (2010)

12-year-old Dre Parker (Jaden Smith) and his mother, Sherry (Taraji P. Henson), arrive in Beijing from West Detroit to start a new life. Dre develops a crush on a young violinist, Mei Ying (Wenwen Han), who reciprocates his attention, but Cheng (Zhenwei Wang), a kung fu prodigy whose family is close to Mei Ying's, attempts to keep them apart by beating Dre, and later harassing and humiliating him in and around school. During a particularly brutal beating by Cheng and his friends, the enigmatic maintenance man of Dre's building, Mr. Han (Jackie Chan), comes to Dre's aid, revealing himself as a kung fu master who adeptly dispatches Dre's tormentors.

After Han mends Dre's injuries using fire cupping, they go to Cheng's teacher, Master Li (Rongguang Yu), to attempt to make peace, but the brutal Li, who teaches his students to show no mercy to their enemies, challenges Dre to a fight with Cheng. When Han declines, Li threatens him, saying that they will not be allowed to leave his school unless either Dre or Han himself fights. Han acquiesces, but insists the fight take place at an upcoming tournament, and that Li's students leave Dre alone until the tournament. The amused Li agrees.

Han begins training Dre, but Dre is frustrated that Han merely has Dre spend hours taking off his jacket, hanging it up, dropping it, and then putting it back on again. After days of this, Dre refuses to continue, until Han demonstrates to him that the repetitive arm movements in question were Han's method of teaching Dre defensive block and strike techniques, which Dre is now able to display instinctively when prompted by Han's mock attacks. Han emphasizes that the movements Dre is learning apply to life in general, and that serenity and maturity, not punches and power, are the true keys to mastering the martial arts. During one lesson in the Wudang Mountains, Dre notices a female kung fu practitioner (Michelle Yeoh, in anuncredited cameo) apparently copying the movements of a cobra before her, but Han informs him that it was the cobra that was imitating the woman, as in a mirror reflection. Dre wants Han to teach him this technique, which includes linking Han's hand and feet to Dre's via bamboo shafts while practicing their forms, but Dre's subsequent attempt to use this reflection technique on his mother is unsuccessful.

As Dre's friendship with Mei Ying continues, she agrees to attend Dre's tournament, as does Dre her upcoming recital. Dre persuades Mei Ying to cut school for a day of fun, but when she is nearly late for her violin recital, which has been rescheduled for that day, she tells him that her parents have deemed him a bad influence, and forbid her from spending any more time with him. Later, when Dre finds Mr. Han despondent, he learns that it is the anniversary of his wife and son's deaths, which occurred years ago when he lost control of his car while arguing with his wife. Dre reminds Han that one of his lessons was in perseverance, and that Han needs to heal from his loss, and tries to help him do so. Han then assists Dre in reading a note, in Chinese, of apology to Mei Ying's father, who, impressed, allows Mei to attend the tournament.

At the tournament, the under-confident Dre is slow to achieve parity with his opponents, but soon begins to beat them, and advances to the semifinals, as does Cheng, who violently finishes off his opponents. Dre eventually comes up against Liang, another of Master Li's students, who is instructed by Master Li to break Dre's leg. When Liang insists that he can beat Dre, Master Li sternly tells him that he doesn't want him beaten, but broken. During the match, Liang delivers a devastating kick to Dre's leg, along with a series of brutal follow-up punches. Although Liang is disqualified for his illegal strikes, Dre is incapacitated, which would allow Cheng to win by default.

Chapter 10 Being an Effective Intercultural Communicator

Despite Han's insistence that he has earned respect for his performance in the tournament, Dre convinces Han to use his fire cupping technique to mend his leg, in order to see the tournament to the end. Dre returns to the arena, where he confronts Cheng. Dre delivers impressive blows, but Cheng counters with a debilitating strike to Dre's already injured leg. Dre struggles to get up, and adopts the one-legged form he first learned from the woman on the mountain, attempting to use the reflection technique to manipulate Cheng's movements. Cheng charges Dre, but Dre flips, and catches Cheng with a kick to his head, winning the tournament, along with the respect of Cheng and his classmates, both for himself and Mr. Han.

Task 2 Extended reading

Cross Cultural Competence

Cross-cultural approaches, at least as I view them, strive to replace the rejection and dehumanization of "the other", including the type of demonization that ultimately leads to war, with active forms of understanding, communication, and respect. Cross-cultural management asks some very fundamental questions: How do I recognize, respect, and act with civility toward people who are different from me, and then, based on their very differences, build better teams, better organizations, better communities, better companies, and a better world?

—Nancy J. Adler

Walk into any organization today and you will see cultural differences, whether you are comparing and contrasting people according to age, gender, personality, ethnicity, nationality, or all of these and more. Increasingly, people are pursuing education in a variety of countries. They are learning foreign languages, traveling to foreign locations, and expatriating to gain career experiences. They live in culturally diverse neighborhoods, have friends from different cultural backgrounds, enter multiracial marriages, and enjoy the sports, art, music, and literature of other cultures. While doing something as simple as standing in the line at the local coffee shop, you can observe a tapestry of cultural backgrounds, hearthe music of different languages, and feel uniquely individual while also part of a wide-ranging, complex world of humanity.

The Increasing Demand for Intercultural Competence

Prompted by globalization, the evolution of technology, and migration, and moved by sheer opportunity, organizations are fast becoming complex, culturally mixed "salads". Everyone working in any type or size of firm—whether board members, senior leaders, middle managers, field employees, knowledge workers, line workers, support people, or entrepreneurs—must connect, communicate, collaborate, and compete with others who are culturally unlike themselves. This is true whether their associates are located in the next cubicle or on the other side of the world. The expression "the world is your oyster" has new meaning today as firms search the world for the best suppliers, employees, customers, and even societies in which to grow, contribute, and compete.

Furthermore, in our knowledge-based society, leaders know that people are their best resource. They must create the organizational cultures that invite culturally diverse people to fully contribute information, creativity, passion, and commitment to achieve innovation and competitive success. It has become imperative that they know how to leverage the benefits of their organizational smorgasbords of talent.

Unfortunately, many people, employees and managers alike, are unskilled in acting, speaking, and negotiating in environments of extensive cultural differences. Not recognizing the degree of cultural bias or prejudice that pervades their perceptions and judgments, they may react to new, culturally complex situations by applying whatever "worked" in the past. You can think of this pervasive situation as "unconscious incompetence" —poor performance caused by a fundamental lack of awareness—and it is extremely costly. If cultural differences remain under the radar, and the skills needed to mine those differences on behalf of the organization are not deliberately developed, the entire effort suffers. Unconscious incompetence reduces creativity, impedes communication and problems solving, and ultimately creates a drag on productivity and performance that can be detrimental—even fatal—to an organization.

Our Cross Cultural Competence Model

As difficult as cross cultural competence may be for both individuals and organizations to achieve, its learning and practice are not complicated. True cross cultural competence arises from gaining cross cultural experience while holding the intention to learn, grow, and change and the desire to meaningfully connect with others who are different. We've found that people obtain cross cultural experience by developing four areas of learning and practice: awareness, values, skills, and practice.

The first step is to develop cultural awareness, which plays a role in how we perceive, react to, and interact with other people. Research has shown that cultural awareness is interactive, selective, and co-creative through dialogue and requires us to continually ask ourselves questions—to be self-aware, in other words—so we avoid bringing biases into our work. Ask questions like, "What is culture?" "What's your own culture?" The goal here is to help each person understand his or her "inner cultural system". An inner cultural system develops over time, starting with when, where, and how a person is raised and progressing through many choices and life experiences. It includes the things that make up a cultural way of life and cultural way of coping in the world.

The second step for gaining cross cultural competence is to increase levels of cross cultural skills; attributes and behaviors that can be learned, practiced, and assessed. Research shows that three categories of skills are important to learn for success when experiencing a new or different culture: those that help a person maintain him- or herself in a new environment; those need to create relationships with people in the new or different culture; and the cognitive skills necessary to correctly perceive new or different cultures and their members.

The numerous desired cross cultural skills that will help participants function effectively in new environments and cross cultural differences include being flexible and able to function in a state of ambiguity, keeping an open mind, developing emotional intelligence, a having a healthy degree of cultural self-confidence, humility, and humor.

The third step for enhancing cross cultural experience is to understand and develop cultural values. This is enormously important for gaining cross cultural competence. When we think of values, we usually think of what is important to us. Values are beliefs that are grounded in emotion rather than fact. They motivate us all to reach for a higher purpose, the "goodness" of human life and action, something we strive for in our everyday decisions and actions. They guide how we evaluate people, events, things, and situations or even whole organizations or governments.

There is usually a hierarchy to our values; one thing is more important to us than something else. Some values are shared—drawing us together as human beings who are all experiencing the human condition—and some are unique, serving to differentiate us from others. Values also range from the esoteric and abstract (such as "justice", "harmony", or "equality") to those that are pragmatic in nature (including "industry", "generosity", or "curiosity"). What is even more interesting—and challenging—is that values can be detected or defined at personal, organizational, national, and even regional levels. And values themselves can change as people adapt according to life circumstances.

The last step in gaining cross cultural experience is to develop a personalized set of cultural practices. Remember: cross cultural competence can be learned. Learning in turn, best happens through practice, practice, practice, and by participating in a variety of learning experience that activate different parts of the brain.

We believe there are three kinds of experiences that give people the chance to actively practice cross cultural awareness, skills, and values:

1. Consciously developing relationships with people who are different

2. Traveling to culturally new or different places

3. Actively and deeply reflecting on one's own culture, that is, one's "place" in the world, along with one's purpose and meaning, dreams, desires, and wishes

All three experiences are holistic and comprehensive in nature, invoke a healthy degree of stress— which, perhaps counterintuitively, actually helps promote and provoke change—and positively inspire growth.

(Adapted from Dolan, Simon L. and Kawamura, Kristine Marin, "Cross Cultural Competence: A Field Guide for Developing Global Leaders and Managers", Chapter 1)

Critical thinking questions:

1. Give some examples to show the increasing demand for cross cultural competence.

2. What do you think of the English idiom "When in Rome, do as the Romans do"? Does it make sense in intercultural communication today?

3. What is your idea of cultural values? Do they change over time?

References

[1] ADLER, N. J. *International Dimensions of Oganizational Behavior* (2nd ed.) [M]. Boston, MA: PWS-KENT Publishing Company, 1991.

[2] ADLER, N. J. & GUNDERSON, A. *International Dimensions of Organizational* Behavior [M]. Canada: Thomson Learning, Inc. , 2008

[3] ADLER, P. *Beyond Cultural Identity: Reflections on Multiculturalism* [M]. Honolulu East-West Center Press, 2002.

[4] BENNETT, M. *Basic Concepts of Intercultural Communication: Paradigms, Principles, and Practices* [M]. London: Nicholas Brealey Publishing, 2013.

[5] BENNETT, M. *Basic Concepts of Intercultural Communication: Selected Readings* [M]. Yarmouth, ME: Intercultural Press, 1998.

[6] BOCHNER, S. *Cultures in Contact: Studies in Cross-Cultural Interaction* [M]. Oxford: Pergamon Press, 1983.

[7] BROWN, L. Worlds Apart: The Barrier Between East and West [J]. *Journal of International and Intercultural Communication*, 2009, 2 (3): 240—259.

[8] CARTER, K. M. Culture Shock: How to Speak Business Anywhere [EB/OL]. http://www.bbc.com/capital/story/20141006-talk-shock-youre-doing-it-wrong.

[9] CARTER, S. B. Are We Talking the Same Language? How Communication Styles can Affect Relationships [EB/OL]. [2016 - 03 - 18]. https://www.psychologytoday.com/blog/high-octane-women/201104/are-we-talking-the-same-language-how-communication-styles-can-affect.

[10] FURNHAM, A. & Bochner, S. Social difficulty in a foreign culture: an empirical analysis of culture shock [J]. *Cultures in Contact*, 1982, 3: 161—198.

[11] FURNHAM, A. Education and Culture Shock [J]. *The Psychologist*, 2004, 17 (1): 16—19.

[12] GAREIS, E. Communication and Culture, Interpersonal Communication [EB/OL]. [2016 - 01 - 23]. http://communication.oxfordre.comiew/10.1093/acrefore/9780190228613.001.0001/acrefore-9780190228613-e-161.

［13］ GAW, K. F. Reverse Culture Shock ［C］. Reverse Culture Shock in Students Returning from Overseas. 1995: 1—30.

［14］ GOMAN, C. K. The American Management Association ［EB/OL］. ［2016 – 02 – 12］. www. amanet. org.

［15］ GRATIS, B. Overcoming Interpersonal Barriers to Communication ［EB/OL］. ［2017 – 06 – 10］ https: //nulab-inc. com/blogpetalk/overcoming-interpersonal-barriers-communication/.

［16］ GUDYKUNST, W. B. & KIM, Y. Y. *Communicating with Strangers* ［M］. Boston: Mc Graw Hill, 2003.

［17］ JACKSON, J. *Introducing Language and Intercultural Communication* ［M］. London and New York: Routledge, 2014.

［18］ KIM, Y. Y. *Becoming Intercultural: An Integrative Theory of Communication and Cross-Cultural Adaptation* ［M］. London: Sage Publication Inc. , 2001.

［19］ KISS, G. A theoretical approach to intercultural communication ［J］. *Communication*, 2008, 7 (3): 435— 443.

［20］ MASGORET, A. M. & WARD, C. *The Cambridge Handbook of Acculturation Psychology* ［M］. Cambridge University Press, 2006.

［21］ O'NEIL, D. *Characteristics of Culture* ［M］. Hershey: IGI Global, 2012.

［22］ OXFORD, R. L. and Scarcella, R. C. *A Few Family Structures and Values Around the Globe* ［M］. McGraw-Hill Companies, Inc. , 2005.

［23］ POGOSYAN, M. Between Cultures: Understanding Transition Stress ［EB/OL］. ［2017 – 03 – 21］. https: //www. psychologytoday. com/blog/between-cultures.

［24］ ROBILA, M. *Handbook of Family Policies Across the Globe* ［M］. London, New York: Springer, 2013.

［25］ ROGERS, E. M. & Steinfatt, R. M. *Intercultural Communication* ［M］. Illinois: Waveland Press, Inc. , 2009.

［26］ VELLIARS, D. M. & Coleman, D *Handbook of Research on Study Abroad Programs and Outbound Mobility* ［M］. Hershey: IGI Global, 2012

［27］ 胡素芬，杨亚丽. 跨文化交际案例教程 ［M］. 北京：中国农业出版社，2014.

［28］ 马晶文. 影视作品中的跨文化交际 ［M］. 成都：西南交通大学出版社，2015.

［29］ 宋莉. 跨文化交际导论 ［M］. 哈尔滨：哈尔滨工业大学出版社，2004.

［30］ 许力生. 新编跨文化交际英语教程 ［M］. 上海：上海外语教育出版社，2013.

［31］ 严明. 跨文化交际理论研究 ［M］. 哈尔滨：黑龙江大学出版社，2009.

［32］ 13 benefits and challenges of cultural diversity in the workplace in 2017 ［EB/OL］. ［2017 – 02 – 12］. http: //www. hult. edu/news/benefits-challenges-cultural-diversity-workplace/.

［33］ What is Intercultural Communication? ［EB/OL］. ［2016 – 12 – 05］. https: //moniviestin. jyu. fijelmat/humiesti/en/ics/2.

[34] The Global Cultural Imperative [EB/OL]. [2016 – 12 – 05]. http: //globalbizleader. com/the-global-cultural-imperative/.

[35] KLUCKHOHN, F. R., STRODTBECK, F. L. & ROBERTS, J. M. *Variations in value orientations* [M]. Evanston, Illinois: Row, Peterson and Company, 1961.

[36] CONDON, J. C. & YOUSEF F. S. *An introduction to intercultural communication* [M]. New York: Free Press, 1975.

[37] SAMOVAR L. A., PORTER R. E. & MCDANIEL E. R. et al. *Communication Between Cultures* [M]. New York: Wadsworth, 2004.

[38] SPNCER-OATEY, H. 与英美人交往的习俗和语言（英文版）[M]. 上海：上海外语教育出版社，1990.

[39] SPNCER-OATEY, H. and XING, J., *Culturally speaking: Culture, Communication and Politeness Theory* [M]. London: Continuum, 2008.

[40] SPNCER-OATEY, H. and FRANKLIN P. *Intercultural interaction: A Multidisciplinary Approach to International Communication* [M]. 北京：外语教学研究出版社，2010.

[41] DALAN S L. KAWAMURA K M. *Cross Cultural Competence: A Field Guide for Developing Global Leaders and Managers* [M]. Emerald Group Publishing Limited, 2015.

[42] IOPPOLO S. *Intercultural Communication: Connecting with Cultural Diversity* [M]. Tilde Publishing and Distribution, 2015.

[43] SAMOVAR L A. PORTER R E. MCDANIEL E R. *Cross-cultural Communication* [M]. 北京：北京大学出版社，2015.

[44] SORRELLS K. *Intercultural Communication Globalization and Social Justice* 2nd ed. [M]. SAGE Publication Inc, 2016.

[45] 文旭，杜平，姚连兵. 跨文化交际教程 [M]. 北京：中国人民大学出版社，2015.

[46] GUDYKUNST W. & KIM Y. Y. *Communicating With Strangers: An Approach to Intercultural Communication* [M]. In Bridges Not Walls. New York: McGraw, 1995.

[47] WILLIAM A. Resolving Conflict in a Multicultural Environment [J]. *MCS Conciliation Quarterly*, Summer, 1994, pp. 2—6.

[48] Cross-Cultural Communication Strategies [EB/OL]. [2017 – 06 – 06]. http: //www. colorado. edu/conflict/peace/treatment/xcolcomm. htm.

[49] Exploring Emigration: Cultural Identity [EB/OL]. [2017 – 07 – 09]. https: //www. teaching-channel. orgideos/teaching-cultural-identity.

[50] Introduction to Intercultural Communication [EB/OL]. [2017 – 07 – 10]. https: //moniviestin. jyu. fijelmat/humiesti/en/ics/11.

[51] 胡超. 跨文化交际实用教程 [M]. 北京：外语教学与研究出版社，2006.

[52] Larry A. SAMOVAR, RICHARD E. PORTER, EDWIN R. MCDANIEL, *Cross-cultural Communication* [M]. Peking University Press, 2017.

[53] TIMOTHY R. LEVINE, KIM B. SEROTA, HILLARY C. SHULMAN, The Impact of Lie to Me on Viewers' Actual Ability to Detect Deception [J]. *Communication Research*, 2010, 37: 847 originally published online 17 June 2010, DOI: 10.1177/0093650210362686.

[54] WILLIAM B. GUDYKUST, YOUNG YUN KIM, *Communicating with Strangers: An approach to intercultural communication* [M]. McGraw Hill, 2003.

[55] Guide to reading micro-expressions [EB/OL]. [2017-09-08]. https://www.scienceofpeople.com/2013/09/guide-reading-microexpressionstp://www.arinanikitina.com/what-is-non-verbal-communication.html [2017-09-01].

[56] Cultural Differences in Daily Communication between China and the US [EB/OL]. [2017-08-24]. http://9512.net/read/b176c39ec6900596b8b88237.html.

[57] Intercultural communication [EB/OL]. [2017-07-23]. http://www.diplomacy.edu/language/intercultural-communication.

[58] Manage Verbal Intercultural Communication Effectively [EB/OL]. [2017-07-23]. http://www.ehow.com/how-5067247-manage-verbal-intercultural-communication-effectively.html.

[59] Communication [EB/OL]. [2017-01-08]. https://en.wikipedia.org/wiki/Communication.

[60] Gestures [EB/OL]. [2017-06-09]. https://en.wikipedia.org/wiki/List-of-gestures.

[61] Nonverbal Communication [EB/OL]. [2017-08-20]. http://nonverbalcommunication.wikispaces.com/.

[62] Nonverbal Communication in Business, [2017-08-09]. http://www.people-communicating.comnverbal-communication-in-business.html.

[63] Develop Good Communication Skills [EB/OL]. [2017-08-25]. http://www.wikihow.com/Develop-Good-Communication-Skills.

[64] Cultural Shock in a Foreign Country [EB/OL]. [2017-08-19]. http://www.wikihow.com/Overcome-Culture-Shock-in-a-Foreign-Country.

Keys

Chapter 1 Culture and Cultural Diversity

Section I
II While-tasks
Task 1 Reading comprehension
Exercise One
1. F 2. F 3. T 4. T 5. F 6. F 7. F 8. F 9. T 10. F
Exercise Two
1. integral 2. constitutes 3. perspectives 4. surroundings 5. subscribing
6. stagnant 7. enculturation 8. unconsciously 9. effectively 10. enduring

Section II
II While-tasks
Task 1 Reading comprehension
Exercise One
1. F 2. F 3. F 4. T 5. F 6. T 7. F 8. F 9. T 10. T
Exercise Two
1. extended nuclear 2. prohibited 3. family-oriented 4. framed
5. extensive 6. priority 7. sacrifice 8. commitment 9. cohesion
10. hierarchical

Chapter 2 Intercultural Communication

Section I
II While-tasks
Task 1 Reading comprehension

Exercise One

1. F 2. F 3. T 4. F 5. T 6. F 7. F 8. T 9. T 10. F

Exercise Two

1. exaggerated 2. categories 3. interpersonal 4. unintentionally
5. minimized 6. encounters 7. anticipating 8. distinct 9. explosion
10. clarification

Task 2 Case study

Case 1

Hints: In the process of encoding agreement (the meaning) into yeah (a word symbol) and decoding the "yeah" spoken by a new employee to the boss (a word, behavior, and context symbol), the boss received an entirely different message than the employeehad meant to send. Unfortunately, as is the case in most miscommunication, neither the sender nor the receiver was fully aware of what had gone wrong and why.

Section II

II While-tasks

Task 1 Reading comprehension

Exercise One

1. F 2. T 3. T 4. T 5. F 6. F 7. F 8. F 9. F 10. T

Exercise Two

1. subconsciously 2. guaranteed 3. nuanced 4. orientation 5. variables
6. dominate 7. cues 8. assumptions 9. volubility 10. succinct

Chapter 3 Verbal Intercultural Communication

Section I

II While-tasks

Task 1 Reading comprehension

Exercise One

1. T 2. T 3. F 4. T 5. F 6. T 7. F 8. T 9. T 10. F

Exercise Two B

Exercise Three

1. impact 2. interrupt 3. authority 4. engage 5. contributions
6. pitch 7. sensitive 8. aware 9. worthwhile 10. modify

Section II

II While-tasks

Task 1 Reading comprehension

Exercise One

1. T 2. T 3. F 4. T 5. T 6. T 7. F 8. T 9. F 10. T

Exercise Two D

Exercise Three

1. complex 2. expanding 3. compliment 4. gender 5. vital
6. eliminates 7. diverse 8. frequently 9. enhanced 10. attempt

Chapter 4 Non-verbal Intercultural Communication

Section I

II While-tasks

Task 1 Reading comprehension

Exercise One

1. T 2. T 3. T 4. T 5. F 6. F 7. F 8. T 9. T 10. T

Exercise Two B

Exercise Three

1. concentrating 2. identify 3. indicator 4. sarcasm 5. perception
6. emotional 7. signify 8. perceived 9. Chronemics 10. dominance

Section II

II While-tasks

Task 1 Reading comprehension

Exercise One

1. T 2. T 3. T 4. F 5. T 6. F 7. F 8. T 9. T 10. F

Exercise Two B

Exercise Three

1. melodramatic 2. affirmative 3. frustration 4. performances
5. exasperation 6. psychological 7. consequence 8. parallel
9. solidarity 10. connotation

Chapter 5 Daily Life Differences in Intercultural Communication

Section I

II While-tasks

Task 1 Reading comprehension

Exercise One

1. T 2. T 3. F 4. T 5. T 6. F 7. T 8. T 9. F 10. T

Exercise Two D

Exercise Three

1. gratitude 2. compliments 3. individualism 4. terminate 5. frequently
6. compliment 7. convey 8. uttered 9. misunderstandings 10. interpret

Section II

II While-tasks

Task 1 Reading comprehension

Exercise One

1. T 2. F 3. F 4. T 5. T 6. T 7. F 8. T 9. T 10. T

Exercise Two

1. mismatch 2. erupts 3. adapt 4. ultimately 5. amazed
6. misconceptions 7. exploration 8. accurak 9. unambiguars 10. filter

Chapter 6 Value Differences in Intercultural Communication

Section I

II While-tasks

Task 1 Reading comprehension

Exercise One

1. F 2. F 3. T 4. F 5. T 6. T 7. F 8. T 9. F 10. F

Exercise Two

1. mobility 2. interpretation 3. hypothetical 4. accelerate 5. recreations
6. encounter 7. orientation 8. horizons

Task 2 Case study

Case 1

Hints: If you are invited to a dinner at 6 p.m., it is appropriate to arrive close to that time or a few minutes later to give the hostess enough time to get prepared in America. While in China, it is advisable to arrive a few minutes earlier.

Case 2

Hints: People in Brazil enjoy a warm and friendly relationship at work. Socializing and personal conversation in office stimulate the stuff to be more concentrated on the tasks at job later.

Section II

II While-tasks

Task 1   Reading comprehension

Exercise One

1. F   2. F   3. T   4. F   5. T   6. F   7. T   8. F

Exercise Two

1. cognitively   2. categories   3. perception   4. sphere   5. paradoxical
6. irrational   7. primary   8. stimuli

Task 2   Case study

Case 1

Hints: In America, people attach great importance to punctuality. People always strictly adhere to the scheduled timetable no matter it is a meeting, a banquet, an appointment or other activities. While in China, if it is an event of great significance, such as a business meeting or a ceremony, people will be punctual. However, if it is not that important, people will stretch the schedule a little bit. They may even change the schedule to give way to things with greater priority.

Case 2

Hints: In America, child-parent relationship is different from that of China. Parents would like to be friends with their children in America. They provide physical and metal support for their children until they are 18 years old. Children will pay a visit to their parents occasionally or on special holidays. While in China, parents guide their children through governance and family rules. Young people are learning to be friends with their children. When Chinese parents get older, children will buy them jewels, holidays, even cars or houses for their parents out of gratitude and filiality to their parents.

Case 3

Hints: Americans are very direct people. When they want something they say "yes" and when they don't they say "no". If they want something different from what is given, they ask for it. While being modest is virtue in China and that modesty has left many a Chinese hungry at an American table, for Chinese politeness calls for three refusals before one accepts an offer, and the American hosts take a "no" to mean "no", whether it's the first, second, or third time. Thus in America, a host will offer more food usually only once. While it is customary in China and many other Asian countries for hosts to ask guests again and again to take more. Jack didn't have to eat extra food if he didn't want any more.

Chapter 7 Contextual Differences in Intercultural Communication

Section I

II While-tasks

Task 1   Reading comprehension

Exercise One

1. T   2. F   3. F   4. T   5. T   6. F   7. F   8. F

Exercise Three

1. 舒肤佳   2. 梅赛德斯·奔驰   3. 雪碧   4. 香奈尔

5. 万宝路   6. 佳洁士

Exercise Four

1. stipulate   2. prominent   3. egalitarian   4. protocol   5. hierarchical

6. philosophy   7. harmony   8. detrimental

Task 2   Case study

Case 1

Hints: The tea break is a sacred native island practice. If you're a visitor to the British Isles, ready yourself for offers of cups of tea. And this can happen at almost any time of day or night. Tea is expected. If you hire a plumber, give him a cup of tea. This way he will actually fix your problem rather than make it worse. When visitors arrive, offer them a cup of tea. Tea is the social lubricant. Tea break during work is a must for British workers.

Case 2

Hints: The US salesman in this case was acting according to ideas about dress that seemed appropriate to him in his culture. He may have considered the informality of his dress as signaling a willingness to put aside rigid rules of behaviors and be friendly. He may have been cold and enjoyed the warmth of a large sweater. He may have spent the previous 20 hours on plane and, without a chance to change his clothes, may have gone straight to the trade show, because, to him, being there was more important than being a certain way. But in the Japanese culture, this kind of dress is considered very inappropriate for such a formal business occasion.

Case 3

Hints: In a country where there are very strict cultural taboos on nudity, such packaging would be considered a form of obscenity. The US firm had to pay a high price for not understanding the culture of their customers. Religion usually plays an important role in influencing customs, people's attitudes toward life, what and how to buy and so on. More seriously, people may even refuse to buy certain products or services for religious reasons. So it's no wonder that a common and well-received product in one culture may meet its Waterloo in another culture. According to the Hofstede's analysis of Saudi Arabia, the Muslin faith plays a significant role in people's lives. For example, Saudi Arabia should never show bare shoulders, stomach, calves or thighs. Despite heat, most of the body must always remain covered. Men should wear long pants and a shirt, preferably long-sleeved, buttoned up to the collar. Women should always wear modest clothing in public. Therefore, how could it be possible for Saudi customs officials to accept a package like that? If the US knitwear firm had been aware of the Muslin faith before their packaging, they could not have suffered a loss of thousands of dollars. This case demonstrates that moral standards vary from country to country. Thus when doing international trade, one should never take his own religion and moral standards for granted but should always bear those differences in mind.

Section II

II While-tasks

Task 1   Reading comprehension

Exercise One

1. F 2. T 3. F 4. T 5. F 6. F 7. T 8. F

Exercise Two

1. initial 2. facilitate 3. essential 4. status 5. distributors

6. ancestors 7. Israel 8. inappropriate

Task 2 Case study

Case 1

Hints: The shipping agent is serving the customers in the way that is considered efficient in Venezuelan culture. To the Canadian, however, this is unfocused activity that is not nearly as efficient as it would be—particularly from her point of view—if the agent simply dealt exclusively with her scheduled appointment. In Canada, business people typically write appointments and activities into the day's agenda every day. They then work sequentially through the agenda until they have completed each task or the day is over. In other words, Canadians prefer to do one thing at a time, while the South Americans, including Venezuelans, tend to do a few things simultaneously.

Case 2

Hints: People begin to communicate with others by greetings. Westerns often employ the following expressions to greet each other: "Good morning/evening/afternoon." "Fine day, isn't it?" or "How is everything going?"

How do the Chinese greet each other? Informally, if we meet a friend in the street, we are used to say: "Hi, have you had your meal?" or "Where are you going?" That is a customary way of greetings in China between acquaintances. However, in the western countries, the above questions are just questions, not greetings at all. They may think you're inviting them to dinner if you ask about their meals.

Case 3

Hints: Egypt is a predominantly Muslim nation and alcoholic drinks are religiously forbidden.

Japanese people think the gift of clock is inappropriate because it kminds the redpient that time is running ont and you should study or work harder.

The use of leather products including belts or handbags may be considered offensive in India, especially in temples. Hindus revere cows and do not use leather products.

French wine is famous worldwide.

Chapter 8 Culture Barrier and Culture Shock

Section I
II While-tasks
Task 1 Reading comprehension
Exercise One
1. T 2. T 3. F 4. T 5. F 6. T 7. F 8. F 9. F 10. F
Exercise Two
1. mindsets 2. Ethnocentrism 3. stereotyped 4. perspectives
5. non-vertbal 6. norms 7. displays 8. complex 9. disrapts
10. dissimilar

Section II
II While-tasks
Task 1 Reading comprehension
Exercise One
1. T 2. F 3. F 4. T 5. T 6. F 7. F 8. F 9. T 10. F
Exercise Two
1. involuntary 2. dimensions 3. strain 4. deprivation 5. isolated
6. distortion 7. indignation 8. discontent 9. initiate 10. familiavity

Chapter 9 Cultural Identity in Intercultural Communication

Section I
II While-tasks
Task 1 Reading comprehension
Exercise One
1. T 2. T 3. F 4. T 5. F 6. T 7. T 8. F 9. F 10. F
Exercise Two
1. cornerstone 2. androgynous 3. over-generalize 4. internalize
5. superior 6. reinforced 7. construal 8. jeopardize 9. familial
10. contextual

Section II

II While-tasks

Task 1   Reading comprehension

Exercise One

1. T 2. F 3. T 4. F 5. T 6. F 7. T 8. T 9. F 10. T

Exercise Two

1. hurdle   2. synergy   3. upbringing   4. ethnocentric   5. perception

6. validity   7. exposure   8. visualizing   9. description   10. distorted

Task 2   Case study

Case 1

Hints: Human burial practices are the manifestation of the human desire to demonstrate "respect for the dead", and to prevent the possibilities of revenants [ghosts] harming the living. Cultures vary in their mode of respect.

Respect for the physical remains is a Chinese tradition, and burial can be seen as an attempt to bring closure, both physically and psychologically. In China, burial is sometimes believed to be a necessary step for an individual to reach the afterlife.

Chapter 10   Being an Effective Intercultural Communicator

Section I

II While-tasks

Task 1   Reading comprehension

Exercise One

1. T 2. F 3. F 4. F 5. T 6. F 7. F 8. T 9. T 10. T

Exercise Two

1. problematic   2. unfavorable   3. tolerant   4. appropriately   5. adverse

6. ethnocentric   7. normative   8. punctuality   9. essential   10. nonjudgmental

Section II

II While-tasks

Task 1   Reading comprehension

Exercise One

1. F 2. T 3. T 4. F 5. F 6. T 7. F 8. F 9. T 10. T

Exercise Two

Keys

1. frequency 2. counterproductive 3. misinterpretation 4. skepticism
5. cognitive 6. confrontational 7. omissions 8. distort 9. inadequate
10. aspirations

Task 2 Case study

Case 1

Hints: There is a certain amount of inter-cultural misunderstanding when it comes to names in China because the way that they are selected is different than in the West. In Chinese, character is a potential name, so when foreigner teachers laugh and grow irate over the creative and unusual English names their students choose, it should be kept in mind that this anarchic style of name picking is precisely how their official, Chinese names were selected.